THE HOSTESS
COOK BOOK

THE HOSTESS
COOK BOOK

ANNE AGER · PAMELA WESTLAND

Foreword by
PRUE LEITH

Exeter Books

NEW YORK

CONTENTS

Copyright © 1983 by Hennerwood Publications Limited

Published in USA 1984
by Exeter Books
Distributed by Bookthrift
Exeter is a trademark of Simon & Schuster
Bookthrift is a registered trademark of Simon & Schuster
New York, New York

ALL RIGHTS RESERVED

ISBN 0 671 06798 2

Reprinted 1984

Printed in Hong Kong

FOREWORD
BY
PRUE LEITH

The first cookery book I ever wrote, in 1969, was devoted to party entertaining. Like this one, it consisted of menus – everything from breakfast for a pair of honeymooners to a garden party for half the County. It was not on the market for very long and was not reprinted. But, fifteen years later, hardly a month goes by without someone ringing me up asking for a copy of that book, or for advice on where to find a "Hostess" book that tells you everything from the quantity of spinach needed for 12 people, to the shape the champagne glasses should be. Well, at last there is such a book, and my pleasure in it is only fractionally marred by the knowledge that it is a much better book than mine ever was.

The authors have sensibly devoted most of the book to dinner menus for four and six people, but should you want to, say, give four people a gastronomic long week-end they'll never forget, you could follow instructions for all meals from Friday night supper to Monday morning brunch. At first sight such an undertaking looks daunting – it includes a fresh fish soup, little parcels of turkey breast stuffed with mushrooms and kidneys and a raspberry meringue cheesecake, plus a host of other recipes. But it is so skilfully planned that a good half of the work is done before anyone arrives at all, and many of the recipes are five-minute affairs. However, for all the careful planning and nutritional balance my bet is that the lucky week-enders are going to go home considerably fatter than they arrived. But I think a little excess is forgivable, even commendable in a book like this. It is for the special occasion that justifies a bit of special effort, a bit of extra expenditure, and a bit of diet-breaking.

There are, of course, many, many cookery books on the market but a good number of these are written by enthusiastic amateurs who do not always write recipes that work. So what makes a good cookery writer? First, I'd say, he or she must be not just a keen cook, but fairly greedy – so that enthusiasm remains undimmed when writing about meringues after a whole morning of testing and tasting meringue-based dishes. Second, the author must be painstakingly careful – checking, and checking and checking again: a process to which these recipes were subjected both before and after composition.

I was sent a copy of *The Hostess Book* when it was still in the loose-leaf 'galley proof' stage. Fairly soon the kitchen, and a good bit of the house, were littered with pages I had extracted because I could not wait to have a go. The test of a good book is how it gets you out of your chair and into the kitchen.

This book may be a good bedside read, but it carries the danger that you'll have to get up at midnight to have a go at Cheese Soufflé Courgettes or Buckwheat Blinis.

NOTE

1. All recipes serve four unless otherwise stated.

2. All spoon measurements are level.

3. All eggs sizes are 3, 4, 5 unless otherwise stated.

4. Preparation times given are an average calculated during recipe testing.

5. Metric and imperial measurements have been calculated separately. Use one set of measurements only as they are not exact equivalents.

6. Cooking times may vary slightly depending on the individual oven. Dishes should be placed in the centre of the oven unless otherwise specified.

7. Always preheat the oven or grill to the specified temperature.

8. All sugar is granulated unless otherwise stated.

9. In some menus the symbol "†" is used to indicate a serving suggestion only. No recipe is provided.

10. The asterisk "*" in some recipes is used to indicate the point to which a dish can be prepared in advance. The dish is then chilled or left to stand accordingly and finished just before cooking and/or serving.

ENTERTAINING
KNOW-HOW

We are entertaining at home more frequently than ever before, and enjoying it more. Entertaining is far less formal than it used to be; gone are the days of lengthy menus with everything done to etiquette-book standards. The modern hostess simply sticks to the one cardinal rule of entertaining – the comfort and enjoyment of her guests. If you have a liking for people and a desire to please them, you are well on the way to being a good hostess.

The secret of successful entertaining is individuality – in other words, your own style. Only you can entertain with the special feeling for colour and design, food, drink and atmosphere, that is *your* personal style. Good food and good conversation are virtually inseparable, and, if you provide the former in convivial surroundings, the latter will almost surely follow.

There are many different occasions for entertaining but the skills and techniques that a hostess employs are the same for each, irrespective of whether it is a sit-down dinner party or a large fork buffet. The following four points will act as a helpful general guide when you are planning to entertain:

- Invite guests in numbers you know you can cope with, bearing in mind the space that you have, number of plates, knives and forks, etc.

- Plan menus carefully, so that not all the dishes are new to you – try out anything that is really experimental on the family, before you try it out on guests.
- Do as much preparation in advance as possible, leaving yourself free to enjoy your guests, and allowing time for your guests to enjoy your company.
- Deal with as much washing-up as you can before guests arrive, so that you have a clean kitchen in which to finish off and serve food.

PLANNING THE OCCASION

Once you have decided on the type of party you wish to give, start planning whom you are going to invite. When you have worked this out, organize the invitations and keep a clear record of the replies or you may lose track of those who have accepted and those who haven't been able to come and for whom replacements may be needed. For something larger than a dinner party, it is very easy to get carried away by over-enthusiasm, and that is when you find that the party you planned for 20 people has

Left: A formal setting for a dinner party. A relaxed atmosphere with a special feeling for colour and design contribute to stylish and successful entertaining.

Right: A less formal dinner party setting with the accent still on style and atmosphere.

suddenly snowballed into a gathering of 40. The occasion and space that you have at your disposal will dictate to a certain extent the number of guests you decide to invite. Few people have a table that will seat more than 6 to 8 guests for a sit-down dinner party, whereas most homes can accommodate about 20 people for a buffet party.

There are no hard and fast rules when it comes to sending invitations. Generally speaking, invitations by telephone suffice for most adult occasions, especially those that are fairly casual. For formal parties it is more usual to send a written or printed invitation – not only is it more polite, but it is much easier to keep a check on who is coming if people have to reply by post. Children love invitations and are fairly insistent on sending them out, as they are regarded as being very much 'part of the party'. Most department stores and stationers have a wide selection of invitations, ranging from simple fun ones to printed formal ones.

For children's parties it is quite a good idea to make your own invitations, and it gives you the chance to be more original. You can be more adventurous than just sticking to paper, cards and envelopes. For a Christmas party you can attach the written invitation to a small Christmas stocking, which will fit inside a medium-sized envelope. Encourage the children to make their own party invitations, cutting out appropriate shapes from cardboard and decorating them with crayons, gummed shapes, etc., for example, a figure '4' for a fourth birthday party. Alternatively, try a balloon invitation – blow balloons up, write the message on each balloon, and then let the balloons down again before putting into envelopes.

People lead busy lives these days, so give as much advance warning of the planned date as possible – 3 to 4 weeks if possible, especially if the party is to be at a weekend. Tick off replies as they come in so that you have a firm idea of numbers.

For some entertaining occasions, particularly large functions, such as wedding receptions, you may not have all the items that you need. Glasses can usually be borrowed or hired from your local wine shop, and there are several companies up and down the country that will hire out cutlery and china, tressle tables and chairs, wedding cake stands, or even a butler! Entertainers, such as conjurers and puppeteers, are a good idea for children's parties. (Check in Yellow Pages or your local directories for useful contact addresses and telephone numbers.)

On the left is a table laid for an outdoor buffet. For these special occasions stands, tablecloths and glasses can be hired. Even a marquise can be hired for convenience.

Right: Entertainers, conjurers and puppeteers, go down a treat at children's parties. Check Yellow Page local directories for contacts.

Below: For children, invitations are very much 'part of the party'. Buy them or be adventurous and make your own.

PLANNING YOUR MENU

There is a certain art in planning a menu, but it is something that anyone can master. If you plan your menu carefully and imaginatively, and arrange to prepare some of the food ahead of time, then you will find yourself a more relaxed and charming hostess when guests arrive. Panic tends to have a chain reaction in the kitchen, and once one thing 'goes wrong', then a succession of untimely incidents tend to occur. The more planned and organized you are, the calmer you will be.

You will find a wide selection of menus in this book, all of which have been put together so that one course blends well with the next. You can, of course, team dishes from different menus, just as long as they complement one another. If you work slowly or are easily confused by interruptions, it is advisable to plan a menu with just a few courses, and to avoid temperamental dishes such as soufflés. Think each course through carefully, making sure that the dishes you finally decide upon blend well together as far as colour, texture and flavour are concerned. At the same time it is important to bear in mind the dishes that you are going to need for serving your chosen menu, and to check that you have the necessary cutlery.

An organized storecupboard is invaluable to the hostess who wants to be prepared for any occasion.

The fewer last-minute tricks that you have to employ, the better; if at all possible, avoid sauces that might curdle, piping potato rosettes around a prepared dish, or the preparation of complicated garnishes. The more you can get done 'behind the scenes', the more relaxed you will feel about the whole affair.

SHOPPING LIST AND SHOPPING

Your shopping list is every bit as important as your guest list; check through it once, twice and three times if necessary – it will not be time wasted. The danger is not in forgetting the essentials, such as sole fillets for a special fish dish, or the principal vegetable, but of overlooking the more minor but important items, such as sufficient butter to put on the table, brown sugar to serve with coffee, or for that matter the coffee itself.

You will find the whole business of entertaining far less complicated if you can do as much advance shopping as possible. Highly perishable items can only be purchased the day before or on the day, but if these last-minute things can be kept to a minimum, you will feel much more relaxed and have time to spend on the advance preparation of the food.

STORECUPBOARD STANDBYS

The hostess who wants to feel really organized, as well as being prepared for any unexpected occasion, will find the following list of items invaluable to have in her storecupboard and/or freezer at all times:

> brown and white sugar, including sugar crystals
> ground and instant coffee
> a selection of mustards
> creamed and grated horseradish
> Worcestershire sauce
> Tabasco sauce
> tomato purée
> canned tomatoes
> vinegar – preferably a red and a white wine variety
> olive oil and cooking oil
> ground pepper and peppercorns (black and white)
> a selection of dried herbs and spices
> general pudding decorations (such as orange and lemon segments, chocolate vermicelli, nuts, etc)
> plain chocolate
> grated Parmesan cheese
> black and green olives
> savoury biscuits for cheese
> powdered milk (invaluable for sauces if you have run out of fresh milk)
> dried breadcrumbs
> rice
> a selection of dried pasta
> frozen pastry (puff and shortcrust)
> a selection of frozen vegetables (useful for making into purées)
> frozen fruit juice
> frozen cream

PREPARATION IN ADVANCE

However ambitious the menu choice that you make, there are always things that can be prepared, or partly prepared, in advance. Throughout the book, an advance preparation symbol, an asterisk "*", is used to indicate the point to which a dish can be prepared. The dish is then chilled or left to stand accordingly and finished just before cooking and/or serving. Where possible it is worth planning your menu so that at least one dish can be completely prepared in advance, usually either the starter or dessert. The fewer dishes that you have to cook on the day, the better the end result will be. Pâtés and terrines, soups, fruit mousses, and a wide variety of chilled desserts all lend themselves to being prepared one if not two days in advance.

Electric mixers and food processors are invaluable pieces of equipment when it comes to advance preparation. They save you a great deal of time and often do a better job than you can do by hand. You can make your pastry and other doughs in a mixer or processor. The liquidizer and processor are both excellent for blending soups, fruit and vegetable purées and sauces. They also take the chore out of jobs like whisking egg whites, shredding carrot and cabbage and preparing breadcrumbs.

Most of the side dishes and garnishes that go to make a complete meal can be prepared ahead of time, such as vinaigrette dressing for salads, mayonnaise, melba toast and croûtons (page 52), garlic bread (wrapped and ready to put into the oven), frozen lemon slices ready for drinks, frozen chopped parsley and herbs for garnishing and adding to sauces, and a good basic stock which can either be chilled or frozen.

To be really organized, prepare as many dishes and garnishes in advance as possible.

DRESSING YOUR TABLE

The way you arrange your table is as much a reflection of your individual taste as the food you like to serve. For special parties, where you really want to impress, use the best that you possess. Entertaining is the perfect excuse to show off your most treasured china, cutlery, glass and table linen. Your table sets the mood for the occasion, and it is the first impression that guests receive of the forth-coming meal.

However informal or formal the occasion, a lot of thought and care should go into making sure that the table looks exactly right. The colours that you choose should tone or contrast, without clashing, remembering that the overall style of the table should be in keeping with the occasion, for instance a damask cloth and shining silver would be quite out of place for an informal supper.

Most people only have one dining table in their home, but there are ways of 'spreading a meal'. Use a small table, such as a coffee table, or a trolley for extra side plates, the salad bowl, replacement cut-lery, etc. This will ensure that you have the maxi-mum amount of space on the actual dining table; covered with a matching or toning cloth it will not look at all out of place.

Seating requires more than a little consideration: not only who should sit next to whom, but making sure that you allow sufficient space for comfort between each place setting. If you plan on entertain-ing more than 8 to 10 people for a sit-down meal, it is well worth considering using several small tables (such as card tables), each one seating 4 people. You can then put one person 'in charge' on each table, to be responsible for making sure that wine glasses are kept topped up, thus relieving you, the hostess.

Separate tables can also be a good idea for children's parties. If you seat children around a coffee table (or tables), they can sit on the floor on cushions, and there is less likelihood of spillage and chairs being tipped over.

Right: The way you arrange your table is as much a reflection of your individual taste as the food you like to serve.

Below: If your dining table is not large enough use extra tables on which you can stand drinks, side dishes and desserts.

CUTLERY

Most people have one standard set of cutlery. If they are lucky, they may have a set of 'everyday' cutlery as well as one for more special occasions. However, the way you present the cutlery is more important than the type or style that you use. If you want to set a classic place setting, arrange the cutlery in the order in which it is to be used, starting from the outside and working inwards to the plate. This can prove to be space consuming, but it looks most effective.

For buffet parties and most large functions 'cutlery parcels' are a perfect solution; wrap all the cutlery that is likely to be needed by each person in a napkin. For children's parties and outdoor eating, plastic cutlery or a set that will not get damaged is the most sensible.

DISHES

It is the dream of every hostess to have all dishes matching, of the same pattern or design, but this is not always possible. You can at least aim for harmony by choosing colours and/or designs that tone in with one another. Certain foods do, however, look better on certain colours of china, and it is often worth chatting up a friend or neighbour to see if you can borrow a few items, in order to achieve 'the complete look' for your table. Paper or plastic plates are a good idea for children's functions and outdoor eating such as picnics, to avoid unnecessary breakages and they are light to carry.

One way of 'setting off' dishes at each place setting is to use an under-plate beneath the main plate or bowl. If you do not have colours that tone in particularly well with one another then cover each under-plate with a doily. This can look attractive at Christmas time if you use silver doilys.

TABLECLOTHS

The effect of a laid table looks more striking if the tablecloth tones in with everything that is to be put on it. What you use to cover your table will depend very much on the size of the table (or tables), and on the type of function. A damask cloth or subtle plain coloured cloth is the best choice for a formal occasion. You can achieve a delicate look for a small dinner party by laying a lace or openwork cloth over the top of a plain coloured cloth – cream lace on top of a pastel green or pink cloth gives a pretty, soft effect. If you have a large table to cover, or more than one table put together, then you can use a white or pastel coloured sheet, pleating the corners decoratively. For a large formal occasion, such as a wedding reception, pin flowers to the edge of the cloth, matching the colours to the flower arrangements. Ribbons are in vogue at the moment, and a series of bows and trailing ribbons can be fixed to the corners and edges of a plain tablecloth. You can always hire large damask cloths for formal occasions, at a reasonable price, and you can even send them back unlaundered!

Left: For picnics, use paper or plastic plates to avoid unnecessary breakages. They are also light to transport.

Below: For a delicate look, place a lace or openwork cloth over a plain coloured cloth.

For less formal occasions it can be fun to choose a bold coloured cloth, as long as it tones in with all the other bits and pieces that you are going to use. Keep a look out in department stores for suitably-sized remnants; you can often find a piece large enough to cover an average size table, and they can usually be bought quite cheaply. All that you need to do is hem the edges or bind them with a contrasting colour. Such tablecloths make an inexpensive choice for children's parties, and you can stick on cut-out shapes from gummed paper – moons, stars, etc. Paper cloths will suffice for toddlers' parties where the guests tend to be more messy than their elder brothers and sisters. Alternatively, investigate the range of PVC patterned tablecloths now available, which are ideal for young children's parties.

TABLEMATS

Tablemats often look just as effective as a table-cloth, and they now come in just as many styles and colours, from crisp pure linen to brightly coloured PVC. They can either be used on their own, or in conjunction with a contrasting or toning cloth.

Highly polished tables can easily be ruined if the surface is not adequately protected; when using mats on such a table top, it is advisable to make sure that there are sufficient protective (i.e. heatproof) mats to take hot vegetable dishes and the like. If you really want to play safe, slide a heatproof mat under the centre of each table setting place mat. These tips also apply if a glass-topped table is to be used, even though many of them have been specially treated to withstand a certain level of heat.

Pine-topped tables can look rather cold. By using brightly coloured tablemats, the table immediately comes to life.

For less formal occasions, choose bold colours and tone in the cutlery, service and napkins. Look out for material remnants to cut down on cost.

Pine-topped tables can look rather cold, especially when they are being used for entertaining; if you add some brightly coloured tablemats, such as a textured hessian or bold check, the table immediately comes to life. If you are laying a table for 4 people, then an alternative choice could be 'table runners' (rather like long narrow tablecloths). Place two matching table runners at right angles across the table, so that they cross at the centre of the table and give a 'covered area' in front of each seat.

NAPKINS

A table is made by the way it is 'dressed' with napkins and tablecloth. One of the simplest and most fundamental arts of dressing a table is with attractively displayed napkins. Naturally they should tone in with the chosen cloth (or cloths), but the way of folding and presenting them depends very much on the occasion, whether formal or informal.

The following suggestions are for fairly formal place settings, but can be adapted to suit almost any table or occasion.

Napkins à deux: Perfect when laying a table for two. Using lace edged or delicately patterned napkins, pull each napkin casually through a napkin ring. Tuck a rosebud on a stem (or similar bloom) between the ring and the napkin.

Napkin flutes: Choose two voile (or similar light-weight fabric) napkins, in harmonizing colours but preferably different patterns. Lay them flat, placing one napkin on top of the other, and gather the napkins together at the centre, shaking them so that they fall in gentle folds. Pull the centre part of the napkins through a napkin ring, so that the edges of the napkins splay out forming a flute shape.

Chinese napkin: Roll a plain coloured napkin into a thin neat cylinder shape. Tuck it through a napkin ring, together with two chopsticks. Instead of using a napkin ring, you can tie the rolled napkin and chopsticks together with coloured raffia.

The cone:

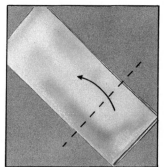

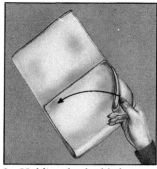

1. Use a crisp damask napkin. Lay the napkin flat and fold the bottom and top thirds over the centre third. Fold the righthand edge one third in towards the centre.

2. Holding the doubled section between the thumb and forefinger, turn the hand inwards to form a half cone around it, with a point appearing at the bottom.

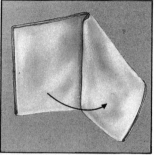

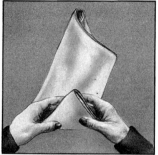

3. With the other hand, bring the lefthand corner of the remaining third across to meet the point of the cone at the right. Allow the remaining fabric to fall over the cone.

4. Holding the corners firmly in place, turn up a cuff and the free corner will fall open like a sail. Stand in its cone shape.

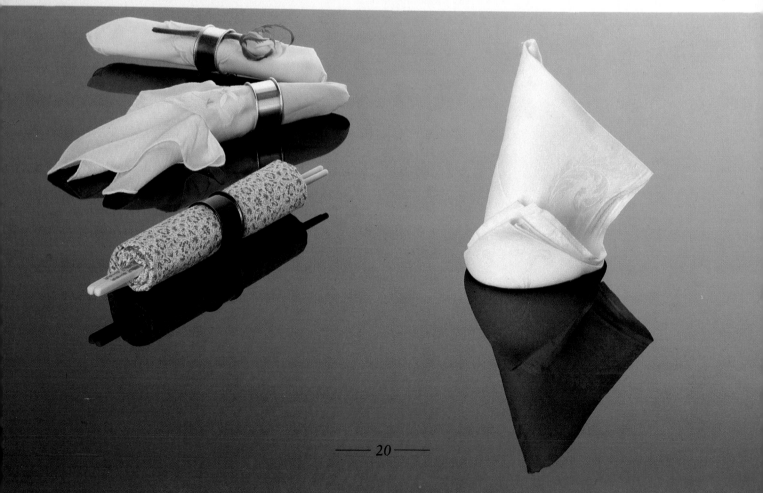

The bishop's mitre:

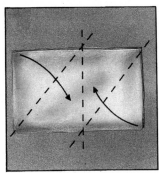

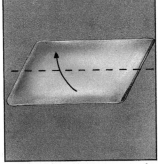

1. Fold the napkin in half, then a quarter to establish the centre point. Open out, then fold the corners into the centre. Repeat, bringing the new corners into the centre.

2. Turn the napkin over and repeat the corners-to-centre exercise for the third time, bringing the 4 new corners into the centre and pressing down the folds well.

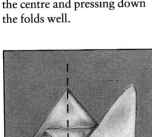

3. Take the righthand point and fold it in and under the diagonal fold of the lefthand section of the 'W'.

4. Turn the napkin over, and slip the righthand point up and under the diagonally placed fold on the other side. Stand the napkin into its mitre shape.

The lily:

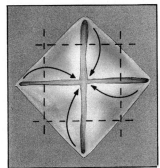

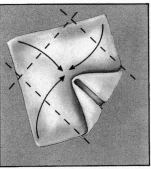

1. Lay the napkin flat and fold in half away from you. Fold the bottom righthand corner to the centre and the top lefthand corner down to the bottom centre.

2. Turn the folded napkin over carefully. With a long side in front of you, fold in half upwards, forming a 'W' by releasing the tip under the lefthand fold.

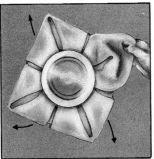

3. To finish, place a small dish in the centre of the napkin and press it down to hold the centre. Reach under the folded corners and pull the free section forward.

4. Once the first 4 petals are formed, reach between them and pull forward the intermediate leaves towards the centre. Keep pressing on the dish until complete.

GLASSES

You may not have a large selection of glassware, but it is worth having one set of rather special glasses, especially for more formal occasions. They can look elegant without being unduly expensive – the glass departments in most large stores stock glassware from several countries that actually looks like crystal, but is not the real thing. For very informal large gatherings, you might well prefer to use plastic 'glasses'; they come in many different shapes and designs and are perfectly adequate.

The thing that confuses most people when planning a fairly formal occasion is which glass to use for a particular drink, and how to arrange the glasses on the table. The answer to the second is simple: glasses are arranged in the same way as cutlery: in the order in which they will be used, working from the outside (on the knife side) inwards to the centre above the plate. As to the first question, common sense can be your guide. Nothing would tempt you to serve hock in a tumbler, because the heat of your skin would warm it too much; for the opposite reason, you would not serve brandy in a long-stemmed glass, when it could not benefit from your body heat.

Here is a brief guide to what glass to use for which drink:

Tall tumbler: Ideal for long drinks such as Campari soda and Pimms, allowing plenty of room for ice and diluting with a 'mixer'. It is also used for some cocktails, such as 'highballs'.

Small stubby tumbler: For short drinks, such as whisky 'on the rocks', Bloody Marys, and of course for fruit juices.

Champagne flute: A cleverly designed shape which helps to retain the bubbles in the wine, unlike the saucer-shaped glass that is so often used.

White wine glass: Generally speaking, the glass should be tall and slender, on a fairly long stem – this prevents the warmth of the hand taking the necessary chill off the wine. Some hock and moselle glasses have a bulbous bowl on a coloured thick stem, generally green – the idea being that the colour of the stem is reflected in the pale golden hue of the wine.

Red wine glasses: The 'Paris goblet' is one of the most popular shapes to use for nearly all red wines, apart from the few that are served chilled. The glass has a wide deep bowl, on a medium length stem which adds grace to the shape; the wide bowl allows

Tall Tumbler

Small Stubby Tumbler

Champagne Flute

White Wine Glass

Red Wine Glass

Sherry Glass

you to appreciate the bouquet or 'nose' of the wine, and you can nestle it in your hand to keep it at the best temperature. Remember that a red wine glass should only be filled to between a third and a half of its depth; you will not be considered mean by your guests! If you are using a flute shaped glass for red wine you need to fill it to between two-thirds and three-quarters full, as the bowl of this style of glass is not as large.

Sherry glass: There are two basic shapes usually used for sherry, the small flute-shaped glass or schooner on a stubby stem, or the more traditional 'copita' – the Spaniards and sherry purists always choose the latter, more delicately shaped glass.

Liqueur glass: The shape of glass used for serving a liqueur is very similar to that used for sherry, but smaller. You can in fact use any small attractive glass, preferably on a short stem. For liqueurs 'on the rocks' use a slightly larger glass.

Port glass: Port is normally served in a larger measure than a liqueur, so the best glass will be a sherry glass.

Cocktail glass: Cocktails are as popular now, if not more so, than they were in the '30s. There is a tremendous range of glasses to choose from as far as colour and decorative finish is concerned, but they are mostly the same classic shape – a tall stem, topped with a cone-shaped bowl.

Brandy glass: The classic brandy glass or 'balloon' has a short stem with a bowl that is wide at the bottom and gradually tapering in at the top. The shape fits neatly into the palms of the hands, so that you can warm the brandy, and the narrow neck prevents all the delicious aroma from escaping into the air.

Decanters: If you have a decanter, use it; a cheap red wine looks much more special if it is decanted, and psychologically it tastes better.

Liqueur Glass

Brandy Glass

Cocktail Glasses

Wine Decanter

Liqueur Decanter

CANDLES

There is an art in lighting effectively, and the keynote is that it should be subtle. No one likes sitting 'under floodlights' when eating a meal, and harsh light does little to enhance the enjoyment of a good meal. If you want to have lighting directly over a table, then the lower the level the better, e.g. one of the electric light fittings that can be lowered to the desired level on a cord.

Candles are without doubt the most successful way of lighting a dinner table in the evening. This does not mean that the rest of the room has to be in complete darkness, but that the immediate area in which you are actually eating is bathed in soft candlelight. Choose the shape and height of candles carefully. For an evening buffet, where people are stretching across to serve themselves, the candles should either be put at one end of the table, a short distance away from the food, or towards the back of the table, if it is against a wall. At a sitdown dinner, guests should be able to see over or round the candles, without having to dodge from side to side to talk to one another. However you arrange your candles, do make sure that they are firmly fixed, and that they are of the non-drip variety; many a tablecloth has been ruined by trickling hot wax.

If you do not have any special candle holders you can make the appropriate number and size of holes in a decorative piece of wood; fix the candles firmly into position and nestle clusters of leaves and/or flowers around the base of the candles. You can buy candle lights which give quite a good level of light to a dining table; a stubby candle or night light fixes into the holder, and a glass dome fits neatly over the top. A candle surrounded by flowers in a small glass container makes an attractive centrepiece.

-FLOWERS AND TABLE DECORATIONS-

Flowers, like candles, need to be decorative without being too obtrusive – no one wants to feel that they are sitting in Kew Gardens! Beware also of strongly-scented flowers, which may well interfere with the aromas of the food. The type of arrangement that you choose depends very much on the size and shape of the table, and on the occasion. A long narrow table, looks very effective with a 'trailing arrangement' running almost the full length of the centre of the table. A round or square dining table looks better with a centre cluster arrangement of flowers, so that guests can see over the top to talk to one another. When planning flowers, always bear in mind the size of the table, and everything else that has to go on it. For a formal dining table, a small individual arrangement of flowers can be placed adjacent to each place setting.

Do not feel that you have to use fresh flowers; silk, paper or dried flowers make an equally effective alternative, and you need have no worries hunting for blooms that are in season. Flowers can also help to add a seasonal touch or special theme to your table. For the centre of a Christmas table, pine cones that have been sprayed silver, nestling in a bed of holly, look particularly festive, and this sort of arrangement could also form a base for your

Above: When entertaining, subtle lighting is essential. If you want to have lighting directly over the table, the lower the level the better. An electric light fitting that can be lowered by a cord is effective, as shown in the picture.

Left: Candles are undoubtedly the most successful way of lighting a dinner table. If you want to use taller candles, position them so they are not placed directly in front of the guests but so that each guest can see through and between them as shown in the picture.

Right: Flowers need to be decorative without being obtrusive. The type of arrangement depends on the size and shape of the table. A long central arrangement with trailing greenery looks particularly effective on a long narrow table.

candles. At Easter time, try sitting an avocado dish in a cardboard half egg; add water to the dish and then fill with small seasonal flowers. If the meal that you are preparing has a distinct foreign flavour, then decorate the table accordingly, e.g. for a Chinese meal, try a single bloom arrangement with a decorative piece of driftwood (sanded if necessary).

TABLE EXTRAS

Many things contribute to a perfectly laid table – not just the china, glass and cutlery, but items that play their own part in the total enjoyment of a meal.

Finger bowls: If you are serving foods that need to be eaten wholly or partially with fingers, such as whole unpeeled prawns, globe artichokes or fresh asparagus, then finger bowls are essential. When serving guests with a Chinese meal, it is also customary to provide each place setting with a finger bowl. The water should be slightly warm, with a slice of lemon, a few flower petals or a sprig of mint floating in each individual bowl. Alternatively, use warm jasmine tea instead.

Ash trays: Although public smoking is more frowned on now than ever before, there are likely to be guests who wish to smoke at any gathering. At a set table it causes less conflict if each place setting is provided with an individual ash tray. As the hostess, you have every right to signal an appropriate time

for smoking at your own table. Smoking between courses is very off-putting for non-smokers, whilst the flavour of food is still being savoured, but a certain amount of flexibility can be allowed, especially when it comes to coffee and liqueurs.

Additional napkins: It is a wise hostess who has a supply of extra napkins. If one course is particularly messy to eat, the napkins placed on the table at the beginning of the meal may not be sufficient. There is always the likelihood of spillages, even at the most formal of meals; this is not the time to produce the kitchen cloth, but an extra napkin or two will help to mop up spilt wine or gravy.

SEATING ARRANGEMENTS

A plan for seating is not necessary, apart from on particularly formal occasions. However, the hostess usually knows the people that she is inviting quite well, and if there is likely to be a clash of personalities, she will seat people diplomatically, even at the smallest and most informal of parties.

A well-planned formal dinner always separates husband and wife, and this procedure is often worth following at a less formal meal; it usually helps conversation to spread around the table more successfully. At a sizeable dinner party or function, place cards can be used, so that no one is in any doubt as to where they sit; they can of course be used at less formal occasions, and there are some very pretty holders available.

Finger bowls are essential when serving foods that need to be eaten wholly or partially with the fingers. For a Chinese meal, it is customary to provide each place setting with a finger bowl. A few flower petals, slice of lemon or a sprig of mint adds a delicate touch.

SERVING THE FOOD

Many people think that once the food has been cooked and/or prepared in advance, all the entertaining problems are over. One of the greatest problems, however, is how to keep the food hot effectively. Nothing is more off-putting than tepid food, and it is something that every hostess wants to avoid. Where appropriate, the recipes in this book give a clear guideline as to how far each dish can be prepared in advance, together with the appropriate tips for finishing off or reheating.

Hostess trolleys: These specially heated trolleys, with separate compartments for different foods, are becoming increasingly popular. Most of them have the space for keeping a main course and three vegetables for six people at a freshly cooked temperature. The basic idea is that you can put the ready-cooked food into the preheated trolley an hour or so before you plan to eat, giving you the chance to have a relaxed drink with your guests. Remember that foods kept warm in this way dry out slightly, so add a little extra moisture, such as melted butter, to cooked vegetables.

Wrapping food in foil: Breads, such as garlic bread and pitta bread, can be wrapped in foil and kept warm in a moderately hot oven, as can jacket potatoes and many firm-textured vegetables. If

Hostess trolleys are a boon to entertaining. The food can be kept warm and transported conveniently to the dining area, giving time for a relaxed drink before eating.

cooked joints and poultry are wrapped securely in foil once they come out of the oven, they will keep hot enough for 15 to 20 minutes; this 'relaxing period' also makes the meat much easier to carve.

Electric hot trays: These are heated trays which can either be placed on the table, or on an adjacent sideboard; the cooked food can be put into the appropriate serving dishes and then placed on the hot tray (do check that the serving dishes are suitable to withstand the heat). They are particularly useful when you are 'keeping back' food for second portions.

Bains maries (double saucepans): This is an excellent way of keeping sauces and soups warm. The top saucepan is covered and placed over a saucepan filled with water. Make sure that the water in the bottom saucepan is kept just at simmering point.

Microwave cookers: These are a great boon to the busy hostess. Not only will they cook items such as jacket potatoes in a matter of minutes, but they can also be used for thawing and reheating prepared frozen foods.

Pressure cookers: These can cut cooking times by a third to a quarter of the normal cooking time and will cook foods that use a moist method of cooking, eg steaming, boiling, braising, pot roasting.

WINES AND OTHER DRINKS TO SERVE

The drinks that you decide to serve when entertaining depend very much on the occasion, and on your pocket. Remember the more varied and numerous the drinks that you offer, the more it will cost you.

As an aperitif for a lunch or dinner party, it is a sensible suggestion to stick to two varieties of sherry, one dry and one medium, or to serve a made-up drink. For example you could make a 'poorman's Buck's Fizz', using sparkling white wine instead of Champagne, and orange juice, or in summer a refreshing Pimm's cup.

Cocktails are very much the 'in' thing, and they need not be that expensive to prepare. The more unusual ingredients can be bought in half bottles or even in miniatures, and the cocktails can be decorated very attractively with fruit, paper cocktail parasols and straws. (For suitable glasses see pages 22 and 23.) To frost the rims of the glasses attractively, rub a wedge of lemon, lime or orange around the rim of each glass and dip it into a saucer of caster sugar. Stand upright and leave to dry.

If you are serving a large number of people, a punch or fruit cup could be the perfect answer. All that you need is a reasonable quality wine, still or sparkling, pepped up with the addition of a little spirit, and a garnish of fruit. When the weather is cold, try a mulled wine; a cheaper red wine will do, and you can either mull it with your own selected spices, or you can use one of the ready-prepared mulled wine sachets.

Left to right: Snowball; Pink gin; Screwdriver

OLD-FASHIONED

1 sugar lump	1–2 ice cubes
1–2 drops Angostura bitters	1 measure whisky
	½ slice orange

Preparation time: 5 minutes

1. Put the sugar into a tumbler, shake in the bitters and stir until the sugar has dissolved.
2. Add the ice cubes and stir to coat with the liquid.
3. Add the whisky, stir then float the orange slice on top.

PIMMS

ice cubes	sprig of mint or borage
50 ml/2 fl oz Pimms	strip of cucumber rind
175 ml/6 fl oz lemonade, chilled	slice of apple, orange and lemon

Preparation time: 5 minutes

1. Put some ice into a tall glass. Stir in the Pimms.
2. Top up with lemonade.
3. Float the herb, cucumber and fruit on top.

PINA COLADA

cracked ice	TO DECORATE:
1 measure white rum	1 slice orange
2 measures cream of coconut milk	1 cocktail cherry
2 measures fresh pineapple juice	slice of canned or fresh pineapple

Preparation time: 5 minutes

1. Place some ice, the rum, the coconut milk and pineapple in a cocktail shaker. Shake lightly to mix.
2. Strain into a large glass and decorate with the fruit.

PINK GIN

1–4 drops Angostura bitters	1 measure gin
	iced water

Preparation time: 5 minutes

1. Shake the bitters into a cocktail glass and roll it around until the sides are well coated.
2. Add the gin, then iced water to taste.

SCREWDRIVER

2–3 ice cubes	juice of 1 orange
1 measure vodka	

Preparation time: 5 minutes

1. Put the ice cubes into a tumbler.
2. Add the vodka and orange juice, and stir lightly.

SNOWBALL

lightly beaten egg white	lemonade
caster sugar	TO DECORATE:
cracked ice	1 cocktail cherry
1 measure advocaat	1 slice orange
dash of lime juice	

Preparation time: 5 minutes

1. Dip the rim of a glass in the egg white then sugar.
2. Put some cracked ice into the glass. Add the advocaat and lime juice, and stir to mix.
3. Top up with lemonade to taste. Decorate with the cherry and orange slice.

Left to right: Pimms; Old-fashioned; Pina colada

MANHATTAN

cracked ice
2 measures rye whisky
1 measure sweet vermouth
dash of Angostura bitters

TO DECORATE:
1 cocktail cherry
strip of lemon peel

Preparation time: 5 minutes

1. Put some cracked ice in a glass
2. Mix together the whisky, vermouth and bitters, then pour over the ice.
3. Stir once. Add the cherry and lemon peel on a cocktail stick, to decorate.

Variation: A dry version can be made by using dry vermouth instead of sweet.

MARTINI

FOR A DRY MARTINI:
cracked ice
1 measure gin
2 measures dry vermouth

TO DECORATE:
strip of lemon peel
1 green olive

Preparation time: 5 minutes

1. Put some cracked ice in a glass.
2. Pour the gin and vermouth over and stir. Hang the strip of lemon peel over the rim of the glass so that one end is in the cocktail or place it in the glass.
3. Add the olive.

Left to right: Manhattan;
Dry Martini; Sweet
Martini; Negroni

FOR A SWEET MARTINI:
few drops of orange
  bitters (optional)
2 measures gin
1 measure sweet vermouth
1 cocktail cherry, to
  decorate

1. Shake a few drops of bitters into a glass and swirl it round to coat the sides.
2. Add the gin and vermouth, and stir to mix, Decorate with the cherry.

NEGRONI

1 measure dry gin
1 measure sweet vermouth
1 measure Campari
cracked ice
½ slice orange
soda water (optional)

Preparation time: 5 minutes

1. Place the gin, vermouth and Campari in a tumbler. Stir to mix.
2. Add some cracked ice, the orange slice and soda water to taste, if using.

WINE KNOW-HOW

The subject of wine is an enormous one, so the following advice on the buying, caring for and serving of wine is intended only as a broad, practical guide. Thankfully, the snobbery once associated with wine is disappearing, and it is no longer the prerogative of the specialist and the rich; everyone can now enjoy wine at a reasonable price. Wine 'know-how' comes from sampling and tasting a variety of wines; the more different wines that you drink, the more you will enjoy them and know about them. A glass of wine is not only a pleasure to drink, but it also greatly enhances the food which it has been chosen to complement.

BUYING WINE

The most important factors to consider when buying wine are what food the wine has to go with and the numbers you have to cater for (see chart opposite). The occasion also has a certain bearing on the wine that you decide to buy – a smart dinner party deserves a good quality, carefully chosen wine; whereas for a stand-up informal buffet, you can easily serve one of the lower priced wines, which often come in the larger size bottles.

Excellent wines, covering a wide price range, can be bought from supermarkets and off-licences, as well as from specialist wine merchants. Wine is bottled in a number of different sizes – 35 cl (½ bottle), 70 cl and 75 cl (a standard wine bottle), 1 litre, 1½ litre and 2 litre bottles.

Many new methods of 'packaging' wine have now been introduced. Small quantities of wine can be bought in foil sachets or cans, and larger quantities of wine are sold 'boxed'. Wine boxes are extremely convenient to have in the house, and you literally have 'wine on tap'. The wine is first sealed in a strong polythene bag, fitted with a special dispenser tap, and the complete unit is enclosed in an outer cardboard container. The wine keeps in such a box for up to 3–6 months after opening depending on the type of wine, and it is an excellent way of buying wine for those who only drink the odd glass. Screw top bottles offer the same facility.

If you are one of the people who regard wine as somewhat of a hobby, it is worth keeping an eye open for good wine buys; wine merchants often offer specially chosen wines at an advantageous price per case, so do ensure that you have both the facilities and sufficient space for storing the wine you plan to buy.

STORING WINE

There are several advantages in keeping wine in stock rather than buying it for immediate consumption. Good wines invariably improve if they are correctly 'aged'; wines can be bought when they are

A vineyard in the Veneto region of Italy which produces famous wines such as red Valpolicella and Bardolino, and the white Soave.

available at an advantageous price, and you need never be caught out without wine, on an impromptu occasion. A cellar is not essential for storing wine. Any cupboard which is dark, draught and vibration free will do, and there should also be room to lay the bottles on their side, either in wine racks, or wooden wine crates laid on their sides. Wines are traditionally stored 'flat' so that the cork is always in contact with the wine; otherwise the cork dries and shrinks and the wine deteriorates. The ideal temperature for long term storage of all wines is 7°C–10°C, 45°F–50°F.

SERVING WINE

The appropriate glasses to serve different types of wine are discussed on page 22. Although the shape and size of the glass is important, the temperature at which you serve the wine is even more so. White and rosé wines are chilled before serving, as are some light red burgundies. Most red wines are served 'chambré', at room temperature – about 20°C, 68°F.

White wines should be chilled for 2–3 hours in the refrigerator before serving (slightly longer on a hot day). Never be tempted to put them in the freezer for 'a quick chill', otherwise the bottles are likely to explode. In summer keep the wine well chilled during a meal by standing the bottle in an ice bucket: for a picnic wrap each bottle in cold wet newspaper.

Red wines are best left in the dining room or other warm room for 24 hours before serving. Uncork the bottle 1 hour or more before you intend to serve the wine, to allow it to 'breathe'. Red wine should be served at room temperature, but not 'mulled'; do not be tempted to stand the bottle at the edge of a hot stove or radiator, as this does not 'warm' the wine evenly, and can ruin it. If you are really pushed for time, and your red wine feels cool, the best way of raising it to a drinking temperature is to stand the bottle of wine in a bucket of warm (not hot) water – the level of the water should be equal to that of the wine. Do check the temperature from time to time.

MATCHING THE WINE WITH THE FOOD

Certain wines do without doubt go best with certain types of food, due to the delicacy and/or depth of flavour. Some bad choices of food and wine combinations are very obvious, for instance, a heavy claret with sole fillets, or a sweet white wine with a cheese soufflé.

The following chart should not be regarded as 'wine law'; something that cannot be broken. It is intended as a guide when planning your menu and the appropriate wine or wines to serve, at the same time allowing for personal preferences.

The most convenient way of storing wine is in a rack, as shown, or in a wine crate laid on its side, in a dark room or cupboard. It is essential that the wine is in contact with the cork so the cork does not dry out or shrink on storage.

	Crisp Dry White	Medium Dry White	Sweet White	Champagne	Light Red	Medium Red	Claret	Rosé
Cold hors d'oeuvres	○			○				○
Hot hors d'oeuvres	○	○			○			
Soups (depending on type)	○				○			○
Hot fish dishes	○	○						○
Cold fish dishes	○			○				○
Chicken/turkey	○				○	○		
Duck						○	○	
Game						○	○	
Beef						○	○	
Veal	○				○			○
Lamb/Pork					○	○		○
Cheese						○	○	
Desserts		○	○	○				

CHOOSING CHEESE

Left to right: Brie, Stilton, Cheddar, Wensleydale

Many hostesses devote a lot of thought to putting a cheeseboard together, and some of this effort can be wasted. If you are providing a four-course meal, you may well find that only one or two guests have any room left for cheese. For a sit-down dinner party it is best to offer just three or four different textured and flavoured cheeses, rather than a greater number. A good selection would be a blue cheese, such as Stilton or Danish blue, a soft textured French cheese, such as Brie or Camembert, and a typical British cheese, such as Double Gloucester or Wens-

leydale. Garnish the cheeseboard with grapes or watercress, and serve sticks of celery as a crisp accompaniment, as well as a selection of biscuits.

For a larger gathering, such as a buffet party, it is quite a good idea to serve one or two whole or half cheeses; bought in this way they can prove to be quite economical, and they dry out less quickly than small wedges. A fun idea for an adult birthday celebration is a 'birthday brie': fix the appropriate number of candles with holders into a whole cheese.

COFFEE

It is worth giving a certain amount of consideration to the coffee at the end of the meal. There are so many different methods of making fresh coffee – and it must be fresh, not instant – and it really depends on the coffee-making equipment that you have at your disposal. If you do not have a percolator, filter machine, cona machine or cafetière, you can make fresh coffee in the 'old fashioned' way, using a jug. Warm the jug thoroughly in advance; add the appropriate amount of fairly finely ground coffee, and top up with freshly boiled water. Cover with a lid or saucer, and leave to infuse for about 4 minutes. Strain the prepared coffee into small cups.

Brown sugar gives a much 'rounder' flavour to fresh coffee than the white varieties, and cream is more luxurious than milk. Do remember that some people do not drink coffee; it is polite to offer tea as an alternative. If you are catering for a large number of people, it may be advisable to hire a coffee urn.

TO THE RESCUE

However organized and proficient you are, there is always the possibility a dish will not turn out quite as expected. Here's what to do!

Curdled sauces: Most sauces that curdle unexpectedly can be rectified by a quick whisking, or a few minutes in the blender. If you are preparing an egg-based sauce such as hollandaise, start off again with another egg yolk and add the prepared sauce gradually.

Collapsed meringue: Meringue does not always turn out as planned; it can break, or it can be too soft or 'marshmallowy' in texture. Crush the meringue and mix it with lightly whipped cream and a little chopped fresh or well drained canned fruit; few people will know that anything went wrong behind the scenes.

Foods that are too salty: It is very easy to over season soups and sauces. If you have the chance, taste well ahead of time. The addition of milk or cream will usually solve the problem with an over-salty sauce, provided you make sure that you do not alter the consistency drastically. With a soup you mash in a boiled potato, or add a tablespoon or two of breadcrumbs, remembering to add a little extra liquid to counteract the resulting thickening.

Over-cooked vegetables: This can be easily rectified. Return the cooked vegetables, well drained, to a clean pan, and leave over a fairly low heat to evaporate as much excess moisture as possible. Mash the vegetables, or blend in a mixer, with butter, salt and pepper to taste, and a little cream, to give a smooth vegetable purée. Heat through.

1. Meringue does not always turn out as planned. It can break or can be too soft.

2. Crushed meringue combined with whipped cream and sliced strawberries.

SPECIAL SKILLS AND TECHNIQUES

Certain foods need to be prepared and/or cooked in a way that is peculiar to that particular food. Other foods are either messy or difficult to tackle, such as boning meat, and there are helpful hints in this section to cope with such tasks.

PREPARING AND DRESSING A CRAB

1. Lay the cooked crab on its back and remove the claws by twisting them clockwise and pulling them free from the body.

2. Tilt the crab so it is sitting up and twist the legs off in the same way.

3. Having put pressure on the back with the palm of the hand, pull out the pointed flap or 'apron'.

4. Pull the centre body of the crab out, discarding the 'dead men's fingers' – the poisonous spongy sacs and the stomach sac lying behind the head.

5. Remove any white meat from the body shell of the crab and put it into a bowl.

6. Crack the legs and claws, removing as much white meat as possible. Scoop the dark meat from the main shell into a second bowl.

7. Having wiped out the crab shell with a damp cloth, and brushed with oil, arrange the white meat on either side of the prepared shell.

8. Mix the dark meat with mayonnaise and place in the centre. Decorate with hard-boiled chopped egg white and sieved egg yolk, parsley.

PREPARING AND DRESSING A LOBSTER

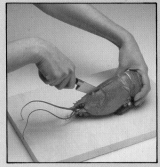

1. Make a small cut between the eyes of the cooked lobster and shake out any residue liquid.

2. Lift the head end and remove the claws by twisting them clockwise and pulling them free from the body.

3. Lay the lobster down then twist the legs off in the same way.

4. Using a sharp knife, cut into the body where it joins the tail, and cut along the central line towards the head.

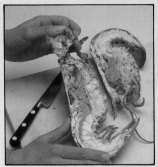

5. Stretch the lobster out and following the line on the shell cut down the centre of the tail. Split completely in half.

6. Remove the fine dark intestinal vein that runs towards the outer edge of the shell.

7. Remove the stomach sac and gills which lie in the head portion of the lobster. The green creamy liver in the head is a delicacy and the spawn should also be kept.

8. If you are serving the lobster as it is, with mayonnaise, it is not necessary to remove the meat but you should ease up the first layer of shell and remove the 'dead men's fingers'. Serve with lobster crackers for the claws, and lobster picks for the more fiddly pieces of flesh.

GUTTING FISH

SKINNING FISH

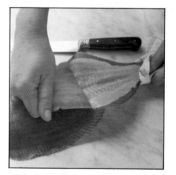

Round Fish: With a sharp knife, slit the belly from the gills to just above the tail. Scrape out the entrails on to paper towels and discard. Wash the cavity and the whole fish thoroughly. Pat dry with paper towels.

Flat fish: With a sharp knife, cut a slit on the dark skin side just below the head and scrape out the entrails on to paper towels and discard. Wash cavity and the whole fish thoroughly. Pat dry with paper towels.

Whole flat fish: With the dark skin uppermost and tail towards you, make a slit above the tail and raise the skin with the tip of the knife. Hold the tail and pull off the skin towards the head with the free hand. Dip fingers in salt for a better grip.

Large fillets: Lay the fish on a board skin side down. Raise the flesh slightly at the tail end with the tip of the knife. Hold the tail skin firmly and run the knife blade towards the thicker end of the fish to detach the skin completely.

SCALING FISH

TO BONE OILY FISH SUCH AS MACKEREL OR HERRING

Hold the fish firmly by the tail under cold running water. Scrape the length of the fish with the blunt edge of a knife or fish scaler from the tail to head. Cut off the fins.

1. With a sharp knife, split the scaled fish the full length of the belly and open it out. Spread the fish out flat on a board, skin side uppermost.

2. Press down firmly along the length of the backbone to loosen the flesh from the bone. Then run the fingers firmly along the backbone several times.

3. Turn the fish over, flesh side uppermost, and release the bone with the tip of a knife. Remove any small loose bones.

FILLETING ROUND FISH

1. Cut the head off the cleaned and gutted fish, then cut along the backbone. Working towards the tail, run the knife blade at an angle to the bone and with slicing movements, ease the flesh from the bone.

2. Continue cutting in line with the backbone until the fillet is freed, then open out the fish and cut the fillet off at the tail. With the tip of the knife, free the backbone along the length of the fish to produce the second fillet.

FILLETING FLAT FISH

1. With tail towards you, cut down the centre of the backbone. Insert the knife between the flesh and bone to the left of the backbone at the head end. Run the blade down, easing the fillet away. Turn the fish round and repeat.

2. Turn the fish over and fillet the second side in a similar way to the first side.

Smaller flat fish are sometimes divided into two fillets only, one from each side of the fish. Ease the fillet away from the bone starting at the head end.

EATING A WHOLE COOKED FLAT FISH

1 & 2. Run the blade along one side of the backbone and lift the fish flesh towards you. Repeat in the same way with the flesh the other side of the bone.

3. Cut through the exposed bone at the head and tail end of the fish and carefully lift out the whole bone.

PREPARING, COOKING AND EATING ASPARAGUS

1. Trim any tough stalk from the base of each asparagus stem. Discard the tough base.

2. Tie the asparagus stems together in serving portions in a bundle with fine string.

3. Stand the bundle of asparagus upright in a deep narrow pan. Add boiling water to come half way up the asparagus and add a squeeze of lemon juice.

4. Cover and cook until tender. Drain thoroughly. Serve hot with melted butter or hollandaise sauce, or cold with vinaigrette.

Fingers are always used for eating asparagus, so a finger bowl is essential. Dip each spear into the chosen sauce or dressing, holding it by its base, and bite off the edible part.

PREPARING, COOKING AND EATING GLOBE ARTICHOKES

1. Break or cut off the stem from each artichoke and trim the base quite flat with a very sharp knife.

2. Cut a thin slice from the pointed end of each artichoke with a very sharp knife to make a level top.

3. With kitchen scissors, cut off a small amount of the tip from each leaf on the globe artichoke.

4. Rub all the cut surfaces with the juice from half a lemon. This ensures that the cut surfaces do not become dry and browned.

5. Drop the artichokes into a large pan of boiling water. Cook until tender, about 30–40 minutes. Test for tenderness by inserting a skewer into the base of each artichoke.

6. Lift the artichokes out of the pan with a slotted draining spoon and turn upside down to drain thoroughly. Serve hot with hollandaise sauce, melted butter, or cold with vinaigrette.

7. To eat, pull off each leaf in turn with the fingers, dip the base of the leaf into the chosen sauce or dressing and pull the base of the leaf between the teeth to remove the edible part.

8. Once all the leaves have been removed, cut off the centre hairy choke to expose the much prized artichoke heart. Use a knife and fork to eat the heart with any remaining sauce or dressing.

TRUSSING A CHICKEN

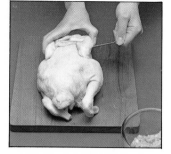

1. Stuff the chicken if the recipe specifies. Draw back the neck flap and pack some of the stuffing firmly over the breast. Replace the flap and neatly reshape the breast.

2. Turn the chicken over with its back uppermost. Press the wings against the body and fold the wing tips over the flap. Pass a skewer through the right wing, through the end of the flap and left wing.

3. Turn the chicken over onto its back and spoon the remaining stuffing through the rear vent into the body cavity of the chicken.

4. Press the thighs against the side of the body, and insert a skewer into the bird from one leg to the other. Secure the ends of the legs and the parson's nose together with fine, cotton string.

JOINTING A CHICKEN

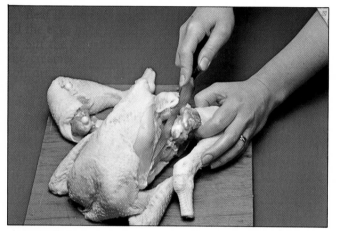

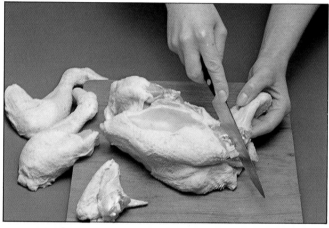

1. With the legs of the bird facing you, cut the skin between the right thigh and body without piercing the flesh. Pull the thigh and body apart until the joint is dislocated. With the point of the knife, cut between the ball and socket joint. Repeat the jointing process with the other thigh.

2. Cut down to the joint where the right wing joins the body, working as close to the joint as possible. Insert the knife between the ball and socket and cut off the wing. Remove the wing tips. Repeat with the other wing.

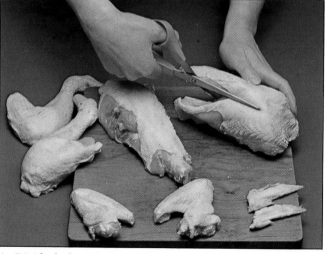

3. If jointing a 1½ kg (3½ lb) bird or smaller leave the breast intact. If larger, slice off part of the breast behind the wishbone. With kitchen scissors or a large, sharp knife, cut along the bottom of the rib cage on each side to separate the breast from the back. Dislocate the front bones.

4. Divide the breast into two by cutting along one side of the breast bone with a knife or scissors. If liked, the breast can be filleted off each side of the breastbone.

BONING A CHICKEN

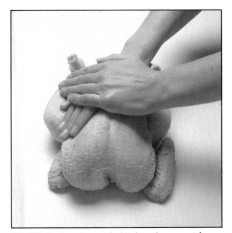

1. With the cleaned chicken breast side uppermost, press down quite firmly on the breast bone to flatten the bird.

2. Dislocate the legs by levering them up and inwards. Work the legs in this circular movement until the ball and socket joints eventually loosen.

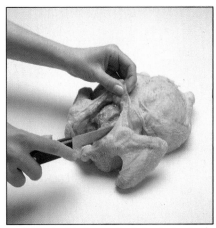

3. Turn the bird over. Push back the flesh at the neck, and cut through the wing joints as soon as they become exposed.

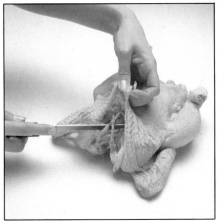

4. Turn the bird breast side up again. Work the flesh from the breastbone by easing it away with your fingers. Remove the wishbone.

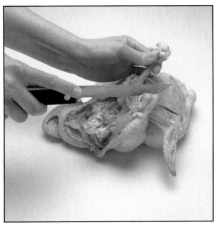

5. Turn the bird over once again and loosen the flesh from the backbone with a small sharp knife, levering the shoulder blades free once they are exposed.

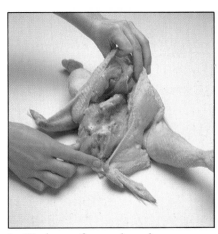

6. Work your fingers along the carcass to loosen the breast meat, and continue cutting the flesh away from the backbone.

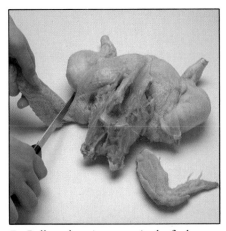

7. Pull on the wings to strip the flesh back from the carcass, and then cut through the wings to free them.

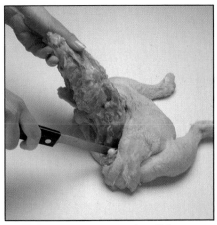

8. Ease the flesh completely off the carcass, cutting it free at the tail end.

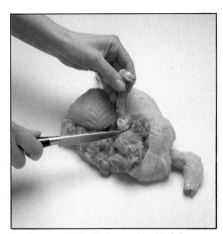

9. Scrape the flesh down the thigh bones until you reach the joints. Sever the tendons and remove the thigh bones, leaving the drumsticks in place.

BONING A LEG OF LAMB

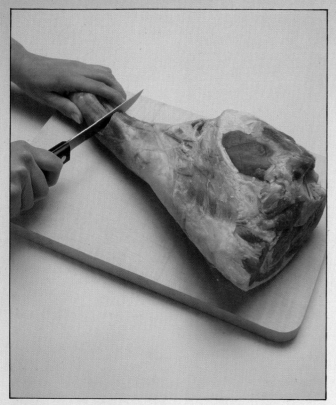

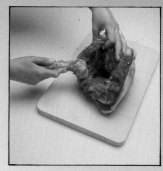

2. Using a sharp boning knife, loosen the meat around the ball on top of the thigh bone, then ease the meat away.

3. Cut carefully round the knee, leaving the kneecap in place, and scrape down the thigh bone, twisting it free.

1. Lay the leg on its outer side on a board, and with the thick end away from you cut off the aitchbone with a very sharp knife or meat cleaver. The aitchbone can be used to flavour stocks, soups or casseroles.

4. Cut down the shin bone, easing the meat away with the knife blade. Work carefully so the knife does not cut the skin.

5. Pull the shin bone out carefully. The boned leg is now ready for stuffing and tying as desired.

PREPARING A CROWN ROAST OF LAMB

1. Take two best ends of lamb. Using a boning knife, cut each best end a third of the way down from the bone tips.

2. Cut away all the surface fat and small amount of meat from the top third of each bone. Use to flavour gravy.

3. Carefully cut between each exposed bone, removing the meat and fat.

4. Scrape each bone so that it is completely clean.

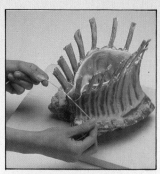

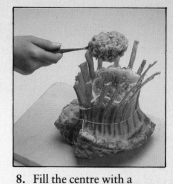

5. Make a small cut in the meat at the base of each rib bone, so that each rack of lamb is quite flexible.

6. Curve each rack of lamb into a semi-circle.

7. Standing the two together to form a circle, with the 'meat' side innermost, tie together with fine string.

8. Fill the centre with a stuffing and any trimmings of meat. After cooking, dress the bone tops with cutlet frills.
Preparing a guard of honour
Lamb for a guard of honour is prepared in the same way as above up to and including step 4. Stand the two racks side by side with the meat on the inside and interlocking the exposed bones. After cooking, dress the bone ends with cutlet frills.

CARVING A SHOULDER OF LAMB

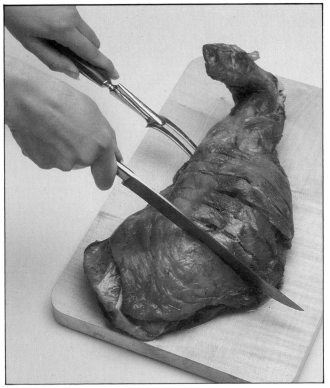

2. Pass the knife along the length of the bone so as to free the cut slices.

3. Then cut neat slices from the other side of the central bone.

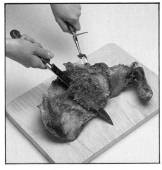

1. Leave the meat to stand for 10–15 minutes to make carving easier. Hold the shoulder firmly on the edge with the carving fork and make parallel cuts down to the centre bone, starting at the elbow and ending at the shoulder blade.

4. Turn the shoulder of lamb over and cut large flat slices from the underside, until you reach the bone.

5. Cut down on to the shoulder blade on both sides of the natural ridge. Cut any remaining meat away.

CARVING A LEG OF LAMB

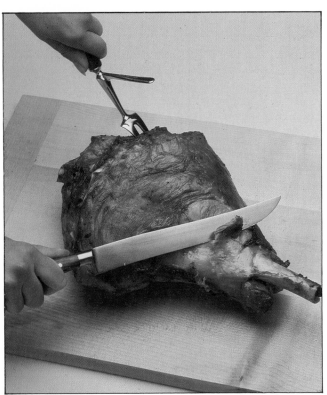

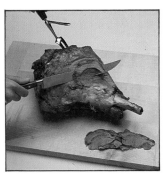

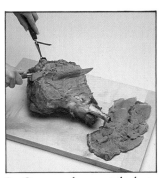

2. Carve thin, even slices at an angle, working towards the top of the leg.

3. Once you have cut the last possible slice from the top, turn the joint over.

1. Leave the meat to stand for 10–15 minutes after cooking. This makes carving easier. With the outer side of the leg facing down on a board or carving dish, steady the joint with a carving fork. Begin carving from the narrow end of the leg.

4. Carve in horizontal slices, starting at the top of the leg and working towards the shank end.

5. Cut any remaining meat as neatly as possible away from the bone.

CARVING A RIB OF BEEF

2. Cut across the joint in even fairly thick slices, until the blade of the knife reaches the rib bone; cut down close to the bone to loosen each slice. Then cut the slices away completely.

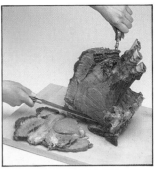

3. Continue cutting slices along the joint, removing the ribs as you go.

1. Stand the joint on its wide end and hold securely with a carving fork. If the butcher has left the chine bone (portion of back bone) on, remove it before carving by severing the ribs close to the chine bone and cutting it free.

CARVING A HAM ON THE BONE

1. Stand the ham with its rounded side uppermost. Score along the centre to mark two distinct sides to the ham.

2. Hold the joint on one side then work along the bone, carving slices at an angle, taking a slice from one side.

3. Then carve a slice from the other side cutting the meat neatly away from the bone.

4. Continue carving slices from each side. Cut any remaining meat away from the bone. Use the bone for flavouring soup.

UNMOULDING JELLIES AND OTHER 'MOULDED' FOODS

For mousses, jellies, and other cold foods that are set with gelatine, make sure that the mould or container is well oiled before the mixture is put in; this will ensure that it will turn out more evenly. Use a light oil, such as ground nut oil, so that it does not flavour the food. If the set food is somewhat stubborn when you try to unmould it, wrap a cloth, that has been wrung out in hot water, around the outside of the mould for a minute or two; the warmth will help to loosen the set mixture.

For pâtés and terrines, which are turned out for serving, make sure that you line the mould well with greased greaseproof paper before adding the mixture. You cannot, of course, do this with a curved mould, so just make sure that you grease it really well, and turn the food out of the mould as soon as it is firm enough to do so.

GARNISHES AND DECORATIONS

The presentation and 'decoration' of food is every bit as important as the actual preparation of the food itself. Carefully chosen decorations and garnishes frequently add that special finishing touch to a dish, making it more pleasing both to the eye and to the appetite. A delicate curl of chocolate or a cluster of sugared grapes quickly transforms the simplest of sweet dishes; and a radish rose or spring onion water lily adds a professional flair to many fish and meat dishes.

Most garnishes and decorations are relatively simple to prepare, and many of them can be prepared in advance and frozen, such as shaped croûtons and chocolate leaves. If any special technique is involved, this is fully explained under the appropriate garnish or food decoration.

BUTTER

Butter can be shaped and moulded in many different ways. A whole block of butter can be pressed with a special butter mould, or 'scored' with the prongs of a fork; or you can shape individual portions of butter.

Butter curls: Special gadgets are available for forming curls of butter, either with a flat or curled ridged blade. Put a block of well-chilled butter on a chopping board, with one of the short sides facing you. Dip the butter curler into a bowl of iced water, place the blade on the opposite edge of the butter, and pull it firmly towards you along the length of the block, so that it forms a neat curl. Put the butter curls into a bowl of iced water as you prepare them.

Butter balls: You need two ridged butter pats to make butter balls. Cut firm butter into small cubes, about 2 cm (¾ inch) square. Run the butter pats under the cold tap, then place a cube of butter on the ridged side of one pat, and position the other pat, ridged side down, on the butter. Using a circular motion, roll the butter between the pats until it forms a ridged ball. Place in a bowl of iced water.

Flavoured butters: These are not only a decorative way of presenting butter, but they are also a tasty addition to the food with which they are served. The flavoured and/or coloured butter is shaped into a sausage and chilled until firm. Slices of the chilled butter can then be served on top of grilled fish, steaks, chops, etc.

Mix softened butter with one or more of the following: chopped fresh tarragon, parsley or another herb; anchovy essence; finely chopped walnuts or hazelnuts; finely grated lemon or orange rind; crushed garlic; paprika. Shape the flavoured butter into a sausage shape on a piece of greaseproof paper and roll up securely, twisting the ends of the paper like a cracker, so as to condense the butter and seal it tightly — ideally the sausage of butter should be about 2 cm (¾ inch) in diameter. Chill in the refrigerator until firm.

PASTRY

Most pastry decorations are extremely simple to make and yet look particularly effective – pastry leaves on top of a pie are just one example.

Pastry leaves: These can be made from diamond shapes of pastry, but they look much more professional if they are a true leaf shape. If you are worried about cutting the leaf shapes 'freehand', cut a template out of cardboard by tracing round a well-shaped bay leaf. Roll out the pastry, shortcrust or puff, fairly thinly. Place the card template on the pastry and cut round carefully with a sharp knife, repeating for as many leaves as you need. With the back of a knife mark 'veins' down the centre of each leaf, and shorter veins on either side. Arrange them on top of a glazed pie crust, twisting each leaf gently as you put it on, so that it has a natural kink.

Pastry flower: This usually goes right in the centre of a pie crust. Roll out a thin strip of pastry, about 4 cm (1½ inches) wide and 13 cm (5 inches) long. Cut evenly spaced slits, three-quarters of the way across the strip, to form a 'fringe'. Roll the pastry strip around a skewer, with the fringed edge towards the top of the skewer. Place the point of the skewer into the top of the pie crust (into the pie funnel, if you are using one), and press the base of the pastry fringe firmly into place on top of the pie. Remove the skewer and open out the 'petals' of the pastry flower. All pastry decorations have a better finished appearance if they are chilled prior to baking.

Pastry fleurons: These little crescent shapes of pastry are used for garnishing many poached fish dishes, and for floating on fish soups. You can buy crescent-shaped cutters for cutting fleurons; alternatively you can use a 5 cm (2 inch) pastry cutter. Use puff pastry and roll it out quite thinly. Press out a round in the lower right hand corner of the pastry, then working from right to left, cut out a series of crescent shapes by pressing only a section of the cutter over the pastry. Make a criss-cross pattern on each crescent with a sharp knife. Place on a greased baking sheet and bake in a preheated hot oven for 5 minutes or until puffed and golden. The baked fleurons can be kept in an airtight tin for a week or two, or they can be frozen.

CHOCOLATE

Grated chocolate is the simplest form of chocolate decoration, but there are many other ways of cutting and shaping chocolate decoratively. Handle chocolate decorations as little as possible.

Chocolate scrolls: You can make neat chocolate scrolls either with a potato peeler or with a sharp, straight-bladed knife. Hold a chilled bar of plain chocolate, flat side uppermost, firmly on a chopping board. Holding the blade of the potato peeler or knife at a 30° angle to the chocolate, pull the blade the length of the chocolate, forming a neat curl. Keep in a cool place once made.

Chocolate leaves: Melt plain chocolate in a basin over a pan of hot water. Lightly oil pliable bay leaves or clean rose leaves on one side, and spread an even, thin layer of chocolate over the oiled side of each leaf. Leave on an oiled work surface or tray until the chocolate has set completely. Carefully peel off the chocolate leaves from the real leaves. Store the prepared leaves in a box, interleaved with tissue.

NUTS

Many different varieties of nuts can be bought to use in cooking and for decoration: whole, flaked, nibbed, and stripped almonds; chopped and halved walnuts; whole and flaked hazelnuts; and desiccated coconut. One of the prettiest ways of using shelled nuts as a decoration is to colour them.

Rainbow almonds: Make up a light sugar syrup and tint the syrup with a pastel food colouring of your choice — green or pink looks particularly effective. Add blanched almonds to the coloured sugar syrup and leave to stand in the syrup for at least 3 to 4 hours. Drain and allow to dry, spread out on a sheet of greaseproof paper. If you keep the nuts in a screw-top jar in a cool place they will keep for 2 to 3 weeks. The rainbow almonds look extremely pretty on ice creams and sorbets, and on poached fruits.

VEGETABLES

Radish roses: Choose good coloured, unblemished radishes. Remove the stem and excess stalk. Using a small sharp knife, make vertical cuts through each radish at regular spaced intervals, without cutting through the base of the radish. Plunge the prepared radishes into a bowl of iced water and chill for about 30 minutes or until the radish roses 'open up'.

Turned button mushrooms: Make sure that the mushrooms that you use are firm and a good colour. Using the scooped end of a potato peeler, or a small sharp knife, cut curved ridges in each mushroom, so that they look like petals. Gently sauté the mushrooms in melted butter, with a little lemon juice added to keep their colour. These make a good garnish for steaks, chops, etc.

Cucumber twists: Using a potato peeler or very sharp small knife, cut paper thin strips of cucumber peel, about 15 cm (6 inches) long. Plunge them into a bowl of iced water and chill for about 30 minutes or until they curl into spirals. They are particularly attractive for garnishing fish dishes and starters. Sliced cucumber is a traditional garnish for cold terrines, pâtés and mousses. It makes an attractive garnish when ridged with a fork or cannelle knife. Wipe the cucumber but do not peel. Score it along its length with the fork or cannelle knife so that it has a serrated edge when cut into slices.

Spring onion water lilies: This is one of the simplest of vegetable garnishes to prepare, but it looks most effective. Use spring onions that are a good colour and shape. Cut off the top green end from each spring onion, leaving a bulb end approximately 8 cm (3 inches) long. Using kitchen scissors or a small sharp knife, cut through the length of the spring onion bulb at regular intervals, without cutting right through the base of the onion. Plunge the cut spring onion bulbs into a bowl of iced water and chill until the 'lilies' open up. Spring onion water lilies can be made with the lilies opening at both ends. Prepare the lilies as above, cutting through the length of the onion from both ends but leaving a small bar about 2.5 cm (1 inch) uncut in the centre of the onion.

Straw potatoes: This is a classic garnish for many grilled dishes, such as steak, as well as being used for a garnish for poultry and game. Peel old potatoes and cut into thin slices. Trim the slices to neat oblongs and cut into matchstick strips. Pat the potato strips dry on paper towels. Deep fry in hot oil until crisp and golden, then drain on paper towels and serve hot. Game chips can be prepared and cooked as above, but are sliced very thinly.

Carrot roses: Use firm, brightly coloured carrots. Peel the carrots thinly. Using a potato peeler or a small sharp knife, cut long spirals from the carrot. Twist each carrot spiral around your finger, to form a 'rose' shape, securing each one with a cocktail stick or stainless steel pin if necessary. Plunge them into a bowl of iced water and chill for 30 minutes to 1 hour. Remove the sticks or pins before using as a garnish.

Sugared fruits and leaves: These look spectacular for decorating a wide variety of desserts and sweet dishes, as well as some fruit-based starters, such as melon. Use small clusters of grapes, cherries on their stems, perfect mint leaves or rose leaves, or orange segments that have been patted dry on paper towels. Dip the prepared fruits or leaves into lightly beaten egg white and then dust with an even coating of caster sugar. Leave to dry for 4 to 6 hours.

BREAD

Melba toast: This is often served as an accompaniment to meat and fish pâtés, mousses, etc. Using ready-sliced bread, toast the bread to a medium golden colour on both sides. Trim off the crusts evenly. Using a very sharp knife, carefully split each slice in half through the middle. Toast the cut side of each halved slice gently until it curls and turns quite crisp, without burning. Once the Melba Toast has cooled, store it in an airtight tin.

Croûtons: Croûtons come in many different shapes and sizes, according to how they are going to be used. Croûtes are cut from fairly thick slices of bread, to fit the size of the meat or fish portion that is to sit on top of them. The croûte should be about 2 cm (¾ inch) thick. Shallow fry in butter on both sides until crisp and golden.

Cubed croûtons are usually served as an accompaniment to soups. Cut slices of crustless bread into small even-sized cubes, and deep fry in hot oil until crisp and golden. Drain on paper towels and serve while still hot.

Bread sippets are another traditional soup accompaniment. Toast thin slices of bread on both sides and then cut into small triangles.

For triangular and heart-shaped croûtons, use thin slices of bread with the crusts removed and cut into triangles or into small heart shapes (using a special cutter). Shallow fry on both sides in melted butter until crisp and golden. The tips of the croûtons can be dipped into finely chopped parsley if liked.

Whipped and piped cream: It is worth remembering that some 'double' creams are particularly rich, and over-whip very easily. If you want to ensure that your cream will not curdle on whipping, use a standard double cream or whipping cream and make sure that it is really cold. A balloon whisk gives greater control than electric beaters. Whip slowly to start with, watching the texture of the cream carefully as it thickens. Cream for swirling does not need to be as thick as for piping. To fill a piping bag, connect or drop the appropriate nozzle into the piping bag so that it protrudes beyond the opening. Place the bag nozzle down into an empty jar and fold the top edge over the rim of the jar. Spoon the cream into the bag until half full and push down well towards the nozzle. Gather the sides of the bag upwards, lift out and twist the loose bag.

For piping rosettes, use a large star nozzle: the small nozzles squeeze the cream through under too great a pressure, so that it loses its shape and texture. To pipe neat rosettes, hold the piping bag at right angles to the surface that you are decorating. Squeeze the cream out gently, pressing down and then lifting the nozzle fairly swiftly so that each rosette of cream forms a peak. The same technique applies when piping meringue.

To pipe a succession of cream shells, use the same star-shaped nozzle. First, press the nozzle down on to the surface that you are decorating. Force the cream away from you, then pull it back towards you, forming a shell shape. Continue in this manner until you have formed a complete border of cream shells.

To make a rope of cream, you can use a piping bag made from greaseproof paper. Fill the bag with whipped cream, and cut off a section from the end of the bag about 1 cm (½ inch) wide. Using an up and down motion, pipe the cream diagonally, 'rope fashion'. This is a particularly useful decoration for bordering unmoulded desserts such as mousses and charlottes.

SOME MORE IDEAS

There are many other fun ways of presenting food decoratively. Here are a few ideas used in the menus. Look through the book for many more.

- Instead of a traditional simple parsley garnish, try celery leaves, the very small centre leaves of chicory, or feathery pieces of endive.
- Serve vegetables tied into 'bundles', e.g. small French beans or thin asparagus tips 'tied' with strips of pepper, or spring onion.
- For a garnish/accompaniment to meat or fish dishes, fill small hollowed-out tomatoes with a vegetable purée — peas, carrots, spinach, etc.
- Serve accompanying sauces in small 'baskets' cut from citrus fruits — cranberry sauce or redcurrant jelly in an orange 'basket', and tartare or mint sauce in a lemon 'basket'.
- For fish starters, cut a thick slice of cucumber, about 2.5 cm (1 inch) thick, hollow it out slightly and fill with black or red lumpfish roe.

For orange or lemon butterflies, thinly slice the lemon crossways. Divide each slice into small triangular sections by cutting along the natural membranes. To decorate, position the points of the triangles together in the shape of butterfly wings, so the brightly coloured skin of the fruit shows clearly.

QUANTITY GUIDE

PASTRY

Many of the recipes in this book refer to a pastry quantity in the ingredients e.g. 225 g (8 oz) short-crust pastry. This is a prepared weight, so if you are making your own pastry, then the combined weights of the flour and fat should equal this quantity.

All the recipes in this book are specific as to how many people they serve. However, there are occasions when you may need a more general guide for portion sizes and quantities to buy. This particularly applies when you are catering for a large function, such as a buffet or reception.

The following quantities will help as a portion guide when planning the occasion and working out your shopping lists. All quantities are given per person.

SOUP	200 ml (⅓ pint)
PÂTÉ	75 g (3 oz)
FISH (raw weight)	about 225 g (8 oz)
MEAT (raw weight)	about 175 g (6 oz)
COOKED MEATS, such as ham, etc	100 g (4 oz)
VEGETABLES (raw weight)	about 150 g (5 oz)
ACCOMPANYING SAUCES, such as hollandaise	100 ml (3 fl oz)
WINE (for dinner parties and buffet parties)	½ bottle
PRE-DINNER DRINKS	2 glasses/measures
CHEESE (for a wine and cheese party)	100 g (4 oz)

MENUS
FOR
TWO

HEARTY BREAKFAST
—FOR TWO—

Breakfast time may not be the most popular of times to entertain, but it can prove to be quite a talking point. Choose a fairly leisurely time, such as 11 to 11.30 am, so that the meal becomes more of a brunch.

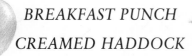

BREAKFAST PUNCH

CREAMED HADDOCK

HOME-MADE SODA BREAD
QUICK FRUIT JAM

BREAKFAST PUNCH

1 ripe peach, peeled,
  halved and stoned
1 ripe pear, peeled, cored
  and chopped

juice of ½ lemon
300 ml (½ pint) apple
  juice

Preparation time: 10 minutes, plus chilling

1. Put the peach and pear into a blender or food processor with the lemon juice and apple juice. Purée until smooth. The punch is fairly thick, and can be diluted to taste with water.
2. Chill thoroughly.*

CREAMED HADDOCK

225 g (8 oz) smoked
  haddock fillet, cut into
  cubes or strips
plain flour
salt
freshly ground black
  pepper
50 g (2 oz) butter
1 lean back bacon rasher,
  rind removed, finely
  chopped

75 g (3 oz) button
  mushrooms, sliced
150 ml (¼ pint) single
  cream
finely chopped fresh
  parsley
triangular croûtons (page
  52)

Preparation time: 10 minutes
Cooking time: about 5 minutes

1. Coat the haddock lightly in flour, seasoned with salt and pepper. Heat half the butter in a shallow frying pan. Add the pieces of fish and cook gently for about 2 minutes, turning the fish once.
2. Meanwhile, heat the remaining butter in another pan. Add the bacon and mushrooms and fry until the mushrooms are just tender. Drain.
3. Stir the cream into the fish and simmer gently for 2 minutes. Stir the bacon and mushrooms into the fish mixture. Taste and adjust the seasoning.
4. Spoon into a warmed serving dish, sprinkle with chopped parsley and garnish with croûtons.

HOME-MADE SODA BREAD

110 g (4 oz) plain flour
generous pinch of salt
15 g (½ oz) margarine
½ teaspoon bicarbonate
  of soda

5 tablespoons buttermilk,
  or fresh milk mixed
  with a squeeze of lemon
  juice

Preparation time: 15–20 minutes
Cooking time: 20–25 minutes
Oven: 230°C, 450°F, Gas Mark 8;
*   190°C, 375°F, Gas Mark 5*

The metric amount of flour is slightly higher than usual in order to give the right texture to the dough.

1. Sift the flour and salt into a bowl and rub in the margarine. Dissolve the bicarbonate of soda in the milk. Make a well in the centre of the flour mixture and add the milk. Mix to a dough.
2. Knead the dough lightly and form into a small, deep round-shaped loaf. Place on a greased baking sheet. Brush with milk and make 3 parallel cuts in the top.
3. Bake in a preheated oven for 10 minutes, then reduce the oven temperature and bake for a further 10–15 minutes.* Serve hot with butter. If baking ahead of time, reheat before serving.

QUICK FRUIT JAM

375 g (12 oz) prepared
  ripe fruit, e.g. peeled,
  halved and stoned
  peaches or apricots,
  hulled strawberries,
  topped and tailed
  dessert gooseberries

75 g (3 oz) caster sugar
juice of 1 orange
1 teaspoon powdered
  gelatine

Preparation time: 10 minutes, plus setting

The fruit must be of perfect quality or the jam will not keep.

1. Put the prepared fruit into an electric blender with the sugar and process until smooth.
2. Place the orange juice in a small cup and sprinkle over the gelatine. Stand the cup in a pan of hot water and stir to dissolve the gelatine. Stir the gelatine mixture into the fruit purée.
3. Pour into a jam jar or suitable pot and cool. Cover and store in the refrigerator.* It will keep for 2 days. Makes about 375 g (12 oz).

DINNER TO IMPRESS
—FOR TWO—

The food may be impressive but none of the courses are that difficult to prepare. Make sure that the soup is really smooth, by blending it thoroughly; that the duck is not over-cooked; and that the chocolate mousse is served really well chilled.

ARTICHOKE AND HAZELNUT SOUP

DUCK WITH BLACKCURRANT SAUCE

FRENCH BEAN BUNDLES

CHOCOLATE MOUSSE

ARTICHOKE AND HAZELNUT SOUP

75 g (3 oz) shelled hazelnuts, lightly toasted
1 × 400 g (14 oz) can globe artichoke hearts
1 small onion, peeled and chopped
450 ml (3/4 pint) chicken stock
15 g (1/2 oz) butter

1 tablespoon plain flour
150 ml (1/4 pint) single cream
salt
freshly ground black pepper
TO GARNISH:
1 tablespoon hazelnuts, lightly toasted and chopped
watercress sprigs

Preparation time: 15 minutes, plus cooling
Cooking time: 45 minutes

1. Put the hazelnuts into a blender or food processor and crush them coarsely. Transfer to a saucepan.
2. Drain the liquid from the artichoke hearts and add to the pan. Roughly chop 3 of the artichoke hearts and add with the onion and chicken stock. Bring to the boil and simmer for 20 minutes.
3. Allow to cool thoroughly, then strain the flavoured stock.
4. Melt the butter in a saucepan. Stir in the flour and cook for 1 minute. Gradually stir in the flavoured stock. Finely chop the remaining artichoke hearts and add. Simmer gently for 20 minutes.
5. Purée the soup in the blender or food processor until smooth.* Pour the soup into a clean saucepan. Stir in the cream and heat through gently. Add salt and pepper to taste. Serve in soup cups, garnished with the chopped hazelnuts and watercress.

DUCK WITH BLACKCURRANT SAUCE

1 oven-ready duck 1.5 kg (3 1/2 lb), halved
salt
freshly ground black pepper
1 tablespoon chopped fresh rosemary
4 tablespoons brandy
olive oil

SAUCE:
25 g (1 oz) butter
1 small onion, peeled and finely chopped
1 × 300 g (11 oz) can blackcurrants in syrup
2 tablespoons red wine vinegar
fresh rosemary, to garnish

Preparation time: 20 minutes, plus marinating
Cooking time: 1 hour 10 minutes
Oven: 200°C, 400°F, Gas Mark 6

1. Put the halved duck into a large shallow dish. Pierce in a few places with a fine skewer. Add salt and pepper to taste, the chopped rosemary, brandy and a sprinkling of olive oil. Cover and marinate in the refrigerator for at least 6 hours or overnight.*
2. Remove the duck, reserving any marinade. Place the duck halves on a rack in a roasting tin, skin side uppermost. Rub a little olive oil into the duck skin. Roast in a preheated oven for 1 hour or until the duck is tender.
3. Meanwhile, prepare the sauce. Melt the butter in a saucepan, add the onion and fry gently for 3 minutes. Add the blackcurrants, syrup, wine vinegar and reserved duck marinade. Bring to the boil and simmer gently for 5 minutes.
4. Purée the sauce in a blender or food processor until smooth. Return to the saucepan and heat through. Taste and adjust the seasoning.
5. Place the duck halves on a serving dish, spoon the sauce over the top and garnish with rosemary. Serve accompanied by French bean bundles (see next page).

FRENCH BEAN BUNDLES

175 g (6 oz) French beans,
   topped and tailed
25 g (1 oz) butter
salt

freshly ground black
   pepper
1 canned red pimento, cut
   into 4 long thin strips

Preparation time: 10 minutes
Cooking time: 6–8 minutes

---

1. Cook the beans in sufficient boiling salted water to
half cover the beans, until just tender. Drain the beans
thoroughly and return to the pan.
2. Add the butter, salt and pepper to taste and toss well.
3. Divide the beans into 4 bundles, and lay a strip of
pimento over each, overlapping the ends. Serve hot.

CHOCOLATE MOUSSE

75 g (3 oz) bitter dark
   chocolate, broken into
   pieces
25 g (1 oz) plain chocolate,
   broken into pieces
25 g (1 oz) butter
2 eggs, separated

1 tablespoon ginger wine
150 ml (¼ pint) double
   cream
50 g (2 oz) caster sugar
little chopped crystallized
   ginger, to decorate

Preparation time: 20–25 minutes, plus chilling

---

1. Place the chocolate in a heatproof bowl with the
butter. Stand over a pan of hot water and stir until the
chocolate has melted. Allow to cool slightly.
2. Whisk the egg yolks with the ginger wine until creamy.
Whip the cream until thick.
3. Stir the whisked egg yolk mixture into the melted
chocolate, then fold in the whipped cream. Whisk the egg
whites until thick and foamy. Add half the sugar and
whisk until stiff. Finally whisk in the remaining sugar.
Fold into the chocolate mixture lightly but thoroughly.
Spoon into stemmed sundae dishes and chill.*
4. Serve decorated with a little chopped crystallized
ginger. Alternatively decorate each mousse with a chocolate leaf (page 50).

SPECIAL PICNIC
—— FOR TWO ——

GAZPACHO

COLD JELLIED CHICKEN
INDIVIDUAL AVOCADO AND SHRIMP QUICHES

REDCURRANT CHEESE PIE

GAZPACHO

1 small onion, peeled and chopped
½ green pepper, cored, seeded and chopped
½ red pepper, cored, seeded and chopped
1 tomato, skinned, halved and seeded
300 ml (½ pint) tomato juice

1 garlic clove, peeled
2 tablespoons olive oil
salt
freshly ground black pepper
TO SERVE:
2 tablespoons fresh breadcrumbs
25 g (1 oz) butter

Preparation time: 20 minutes, plus chilling
Cooking time: 2–3 minutes

For easy transportation, carry the soup in a vacuum flask.

1. Put the onion, green and red peppers and tomato into a blender or food processor with the tomato juice, garlic, olive oil and salt and pepper to taste. Blend until smooth. Chill for 3–4 hours.
2. Fry the breadcrumbs in the butter until crisp. Drain on paper towels.*
3. Serve the fried crumbs sprinkled over the chilled soup.

COLD JELLIED CHICKEN

175 g (6 oz) freshly cooked chicken meat, chopped
1 tablespoon chopped fresh parsley
1½–2 tablespoons chopped fresh tarragon or chives

salt
freshly ground black pepper
300 ml (½ pint) liquid aspic jelly
1 hard-boiled egg, sliced

Preparation time: 20 minutes, plus chilling

---

1. Mix the chicken with the parsley, tarragon or chives and salt and pepper to taste. Dampen a 600 ml (1 pt) soufflé dish or mould. Pour in a very thin layer of aspic jelly and arrange the sliced egg on top. Chill until set.
2. Mix the remaining liquid aspic jelly with the chicken mixture and pour into the mould. Chill until set.*
3. To serve, turn out, or leave in the dish or mould, depending on where the picnic is to be held.

INDIVIDUAL AVOCADO AND SHRIMP QUICHES

100 g (4 oz) shortcrust pastry
1 small avocado, peeled, stoned and chopped
3 tablespoons peeled shrimps
150 ml (¼ pint) single cream

2 eggs
salt
freshly ground black pepper
grated Parmesan cheese, for sprinkling

Preparation time: 20 minutes
Cooking time: 25–30 minutes
Oven: 190°C, 375°F, Gas Mark 5

---

1. Roll out the pastry dough and use to line two 10 cm (4 inch) individual loose-bottomed flan tins. Pinch up the edges of the pastry well. Prick the bottom. Bake 'blind' in a preheated oven for 5 minutes.
2. Divide the chopped avocado and shrimps between the pastry cases. Beat the cream with the eggs and salt and pepper to taste. Pour into the pastry cases and sprinkle with grated Parmesan cheese.
3. Return to the oven and bake for 20–25 minutes or until the filling has set. Leave to cool in the tins.*

REDCURRANT CHEESE PIE

100 g (4 oz) shortcrust pastry
4–5 tablespoons redcurrant jelly
75 g (3 oz) full-fat soft cheese, softened
1 egg, separated
50 g (2 oz) caster sugar

3 tablespoons double cream
2 tablespoons orange juice
1 teaspoon powdered gelatine
fresh redcurrants (when in season), or small crystallized orange segments, to decorate

---

Preparation time: 25 minutes, plus chilling
Cooking time: 15 minutes
Oven: 190°C, 375°F, Gas Mark 5

---

1. Roll out the pastry dough approximately 3 mm (⅛ inch) thick and use to line a 15 cm (6 inch) loose-bottomed flan tin. Pinch up the pastry edges well and prick the base. Bake 'blind' in a preheated oven for about 15 minutes. Cool slightly.
2. Spread 2 tablespoons of the redcurrant jelly over the bottom of the pastry case.
3. Beat the cheese with the egg yolk, half the caster sugar and the double cream. Put the orange juice into a small cup, sprinkle over the gelatine and stand the cup in a pan of hot water. Stir to dissolve the gelatine, then add to the cheese mixture, stirring until well mixed. Whisk the egg white with the remaining sugar until stiff. Fold lightly but thoroughly into the cheese mixture.
4. Pour into the pastry case and chill until set.
5. Melt the remaining redcurrant jelly and allow to cool.* To serve, spoon the jelly evenly over the top of the cheese filling and decorate with small bunches of redcurrants or crystallized orange segments.

INFORMAL SUPPER
—FOR TWO—

TABBOULEH SALAD

SPINACH WITH MINT AND YOGURT DRESSING

SOFT CHEESE AND ASPARAGUS PATTIES

ICED RASPBERRY FOOL

TABBOULEH SALAD

100 g (4 oz) fine bulgar (cracked wheat)	2 tablespoons finely chopped fresh mint
4 spring onions, peeled and finely chopped	2–3 tablespoons olive oil juice of ½ lemon
salt	
freshly ground black pepper	black olives, to garnish warm pitta bread, to serve
4 tablespoons finely chopped fresh parsley	

Preparation time: 40 minutes

1. Soak the bulgar in cold water for about 30 minutes. Cover with plenty of water as the bulgar expands a great deal in soaking. Drain the bulgar first in a sieve, then squeeze out in a piece of clean muslin to remove as much moisture as possible.
2. Mix the prepared bulgar with the spring onions, salt and pepper to taste, parsley, mint, olive oil and lemon juice. You may like to add a little extra olive oil and lemon juice according to personal taste.
3. Pile the tabbouleh into mounds on 2 small individual plates.* Garnish with black olives and serve with hot pitta bread.

SPINACH WITH MINT AND YOGURT DRESSING

12–14 young spinach leaves, well washed and dried	salt freshly ground black pepper
2 tablespoons plain unsweetened yogurt	2 teaspoons chopped fresh mint or tarragon
squeeze of lemon juice	

Preparation time: 5 minutes

If you feel that the mint is too over-powering in this menu, as it is also used in the tabbouleh, then use another fresh herb such as tarragon in this salad.

1. Tear the spinach into pieces and put into a bowl.
2. Mix the yogurt with the lemon juice (adding a little extra if liked), salt and pepper to taste, and the chopped fresh herb.* Trickle the yogurt dressing over the salad just before serving.

SOFT CHEESE AND ASPARAGUS PATTIES

225 g (8 oz) puff pastry
beaten egg, to glaze
2 hard-boiled eggs,
    chopped
100 g (4 oz) full-fat soft
    cheese, softened

8 cooked fresh or canned
    asparagus tips, halved
    crossways
salt
freshly ground black
    pepper

Preparation time: 25 minutes
Cooking time: 20–25 minutes
Oven: 200°C, 400°F, Gas Mark 6

1. Roll out the pastry dough thinly. Using a saucer as a guide, cut out 4 rounds about 13 cm (5 inches) in diameter. Brush the edges of the rounds with beaten egg.
2. Mix the chopped hard-boiled egg with the cheese. Spread one-quarter of the egg and cheese mixture over the centre of each dough round.
3. Arrange 4 pieces of asparagus on each round. Season to taste with salt and pepper.
4. Pull the edges of the rounds up and over the filling and pinch the edges together to seal.*
5. Place the patties on a lightly greased baking sheet and glaze evenly with beaten egg. Bake in a preheated oven for 20–25 minutes or until golden and risen. Serve hot accompanied by Spinach with mint and yogurt dressing (see previous page).

ICED RASPBERRY FOOL

225 g (8 oz) fresh
    raspberries
50 g (2 oz) caster sugar

grated rind and juice of ½
    orange
250 ml (8 fl oz) double
    cream

Preparation time: 20 minutes, plus chilling

Try adding a tablespoon of Grand Marnier or orange curaçao when you whip the cream, to give an interesting extra flavour.

1. Reserve 4 of the raspberries and put the remainder with the sugar, orange rind and juice into a blender or food processor and purée until smooth. Sieve the raspberry purée to remove the pips.
2. Whip the cream until it is thick. Fold the raspberry purée lightly but thoroughly into the cream.
3. Spoon into stemmed glass dishes and chill for 3–4 hours.* Decorate with the reserved raspberries just before serving.

CHINESE DINNER
—FOR TWO—

Chinese food is now so popular that a home-cooked meal is greatly appreciated. Although some of the actual preparation is rather fiddly, the cooking time involved is minimal.

WHITE FISH AND SPRING GREEN SOUP

QUICK FRIED LEEK AND PEPPER WITH BEEF

VEGETABLE FRIED RICE

ALMOND CURD WITH LYCHEES

WHITE FISH AND SPRING GREEN SOUP

1 egg white, (sizes 5, 6)
1 tablespoon cornflour
salt
freshly ground black
   pepper
4 spinach leaves, well
   washed and dried
12 slices of peeled
   cucumber

450 ml (¾ pint) chicken
   stock
4 spring onions, peeled
   and roughly chopped
2 small plaice fillets,
   skinned and cut into
   fine strips
squeeze of lemon juice
1 tablespoon dry sherry

Preparation time: 20 minutes
Cooking time: about 6 minutes

1. Beat the egg white and cornflour to a smooth batter with salt and pepper to taste.
2. Cut the spinach leaves into 2.5 cm (1 inch) squares. Stamp or cut the centre seeds out of the slices of cucumber.*
3. Bring the stock to the boil in a saucepan. Add the spinach, cucumber and spring onions and simmer for 2 minutes.
4. Dip the fish strips into the prepared batter. Drop into the hot stock. Add the lemon juice and sherry and simmer for 3–4 minutes or until the fish is just tender. Taste and adjust the seasoning. Serve hot.

QUICK FRIED LEEK AND PEPPER WITH BEEF

1 teaspoon cornflour
generous pinch of caster
   sugar
1 tablespoon soy sauce
freshly ground black
   pepper
225 g (8 oz) lean steak, cut
   into thin strips or slivers
2 tablespoons oil

1 medium leek, washed
   and cut into matchstick
   strips
1 small green pepper,
   cored, seeded and cut
   into matchstick strips
2 tablespoons beef stock
2 tablespoons dry sherry

Preparation time: 15 minutes
Cooking time: 7–8 minutes

1. Sprinkle the cornflour, sugar, soy sauce and pepper to taste over the beef.*
2. Heat half the oil in a large shallow frying pan or wok. Add the leek and green pepper strips and stir-fry for 3 minutes. Remove the vegetables with a slotted spoon and keep warm.
3. Add the remaining oil to the pan or wok and heat briskly. Add the strips of beef and stir-fry for 2 minutes. Return the leek and pepper to the pan and add the stock and sherry. Stir-fry together for 1 minute. Serve immediately with Vegetable fried rice (see below).

VEGETABLE FRIED RICE

2 eggs
salt
2 tablespoons oil
1 small onion, peeled and
   finely chopped

100 g (4 oz) cooked rice
1 tablespoon soy sauce
4 button mushrooms, very
   thinly sliced
2 tablespoons cooked peas

Preparation time: 3 minutes
Cooking time: about 8 minutes

1. Beat the eggs with a generous pinch of salt. Heat the oil in a large shallow pan. Add the onion and stir-fry for 1 minute. Pour in the beaten egg, tilting the pan so that the egg completely covers the bottom. Cook over a very low heat, stirring, allowing the egg to scramble lightly.
2. Add the rice with more salt to taste and cook gently, stirring for 1–2 minutes. Add the soy sauce, mushrooms and peas and continue stir-frying until the mixture is very hot. Serve immediately.

ALMOND CURD WITH LYCHEES

1½ teaspoons powdered
   gelatine
150 ml (¼ pint) water
150 ml (¼ pint) milk

1 teaspoon almond
   essence
8–10 canned lychees in
   syrup

Preparation time: 25 minutes, plus chilling

1. Put 2 tablespoons of the water into a cup and sprinkle over the gelatine. Stand in a saucepan of hot water and stir until the gelatine has dissolved. Stir the gelatine mixture into the remaining water, with the milk and almond essence. Pour into a small lightly oiled dish to make a layer about 2 cm (¾ inch) deep. Chill until set.*
2. Carefully unmould the almond curd and cut it into small squares or triangles. Mix the curd shapes gently with the lychees and their syrup. Spoon into shallow glass dishes to serve.

COOK-AHEAD SUPPER
FOR TWO

BABY ONIONS
IN HERBED TOMATO SAUCE

VEAL AND ORANGE CASSEROLE

CHEESY POTATO AND
MUSHROOMS

DIPLOMAT PUDDING

BABY ONIONS IN HERBED TOMATO SAUCE

2 tablespoons oil
1 small onion, peeled and
 finely chopped
1 garlic clove, peeled and
 crushed
300 ml (½ pint) red wine
2 tablespoons vinegar
2 tablespoons tomato
 purée

2 teaspoons brown sugar
salt
freshly ground black
 pepper
1 tablespoon chopped
 fresh herbs
225 g (8 oz) small button
 onions, peeled

Preparation time: 10 minutes, plus chilling
Cooking time: 15–20 minutes

---

1. Heat the oil in a saucepan, add the chopped onion and fry gently for 3 minutes. Add the garlic, red wine, vinegar, tomato purée, sugar, salt and pepper to taste, and the herbs. Bring to the boil and simmer gently for 5 minutes.
2. Add the button onions. Cover and cook gently until the onions are just tender.
3. Cool, cover and chill.* Serve with hot crusty bread.

VEAL AND ORANGE CASSEROLE

25 g (1 oz) butter
2 tablespoons oil
1 medium onion, peeled
 and finely chopped
finely grated rind and juice
 of 1 orange
3–4 fresh sage leaves,
 finely chopped
275 g (10 oz) lean boneless
 veal, cubed

plain flour
salt
freshly ground black
 pepper
150 ml (¼ pint) chicken
 stock
150 ml (¼ pint) dry
 vermouth

Preparation time: 4–5 minutes
Cooking time: 1 hour 10 minutes
Oven: 190°C, 375°F, Gas Mark 5

---

1. Heat the butter and oil in a heavy saucepan or flameproof casserole. Add the onion and fry gently for 3 minutes. Add the orange rind and sage leaves and cook gently for 1 minute.
2. Dust the cubed veal in flour, seasoned with salt and pepper, and add to the pan. Fry steadily until the veal is sealed on all sides. Gradually stir in the stock, vermouth and orange juice. Cover and simmer gently for about 1 hour or until the veal is tender. Allow to cool*.
3. To reheat, transfer to a casserole (if necessary) and place in a preheated oven. Heat for 25–30 minutes. Taste and adjust the seasoning before serving. Garnish with more chopped fresh sage or grated orange rind, if liked. Serve with Cheesy potato and mushrooms.

CHEESY POTATO AND MUSHROOMS

50 g (2 oz) butter
1 small onion, peeled and
  thinly sliced
75 g (3 oz) button
  mushrooms, thinly
  sliced
1 garlic clove, peeled and
  crushed
2 medium potatoes, peeled
  and thinly sliced

4 tablespoons milk
2 tablespoons double
  cream
salt
freshly ground black
  pepper
25 g (1 oz) cheddar cheese,
  grated

Preparation time: 10 minutes
Cooking time: 40–45 minutes
Oven: 180°C, 350°F, Gas Mark 4

1. Melt half the butter in a small frying pan, add the onion and fry gently for 3 minutes. Add the mushrooms and garlic and fry gently for a further 3 minutes.
2. Put half the sliced potato into a small greased oven-proof dish. Top with the onion and mushroom mixture. Cover with the remaining sliced potato.
3. Mix the milk and cream with salt and pepper to taste and spoon over the top. Dot with the remaining butter and sprinkle with the grated cheese.
4. Bake in a preheated oven for 30–35 minutes, or until the potatoes are tender.* (If you are preparing this dish in advance bake in the oven for only 20 minutes. Once cool, overwrap the dish and chill overnight. Heat through in a preheated oven at 190°C, 375°F, Gas Mark 5 for about 20 minutes.)

DIPLOMAT PUDDING

12 sponge finger biscuits
3 egg yolks
200 ml (⅓ pint) single
  cream
25 g (1 oz) caster sugar
1 teaspoon powdered
  gelatine

2 tablespoons water
2 tablespoons Kirsch
grated rind of 1 lemon
2 tablespoons chopped
  crystallized fruits
whipped cream, to
  decorate (optional)

Preparation time: 30 minutes, plus chilling
Cooking time: 6–8 minutes

1. Trim a small piece off one end of each sponge finger biscuit so that they will stand upright. Reserve the trimmings. Stand the sponge finger biscuits around the inside of a small greased soufflé dish so that they are touching and there are no gaps. Chop any remaining biscuits roughly.
2. Put the egg yolks, cream and sugar into a heatproof bowl and beat until smooth. Stand the bowl over a pan of gently simmering water and stir until the custard thickens sufficiently to coat the back of a wooden spoon. Allow the custard to cool slightly.
3. Put the water into a cup, sprinkle over the gelatine and place the cup in a pan of hot water. Stir until the gelatine has dissolved. Stir the gelatine mixture into the cooled custard. Chill until the mixture is on the point of setting, then stir in the kirsch, lemon rind, chopped fruits, and the chopped sponge finger biscuits and trimmings.
4. Pour the mixture into the sponge finger-lined dish. Chill until set.*
5. Carefully turn the set pudding out of its mould. The pudding can be decorated with whipped cream, if liked.

PASTA SPECIAL
—FOR TWO—

Pasta is quite a fun food to choose for informal entertaining. The menu below is based on a simple starter, a pudding that can be prepared a few hours in advance, and three different pastas with complementary sauces.

TARAMACADO

SPECIAL PASTA TRIO

CARAMEL OEUFS À LA NEIGE

TARAMACADO

1 small ripe avocado, peeled, stoned and chopped	juice of ½ lemon
1 garlic clove, peeled	1 tablespoon olive oil
1 × 90 g (3½ oz) can or jar smoked cod's roe, drained	salt
	freshly ground black pepper

Preparation time: 10 minutes

1. Put all the ingredients, with salt and pepper to taste, into a blender or food processor and purée until smooth. Cover and chill before serving.*
2. Serve with Melba toast (page 52) or hot crusty bread.

SPECIAL PASTA TRIO

SAUCE 1	salt
1 tablespoon oil	freshly ground black pepper
1 small onion, peeled and finely chopped	SAUCE 3:
4 tomatoes, skinned, seeded and chopped	15 g (½ oz) butter
1 tablespoon tomato purée	2 teaspoons plain flour
150 ml (¼ pint) red wine	150 ml (¼ pint) dry white wine
little chopped fresh basil	1 garlic clove, peeled and crushed
salt	2 tablespoons single cream
freshly ground black pepper	2 tablespoons cooked peeled prawns
SAUCE 2:	8 cooked shelled mussels
150 ml (¼ pint) single cream	juice of ½ lemon
1 tablespoon chopped fresh parsley	50 g (2 oz) spaghetti
2 tablespoons finely chopped cooked ham	50 g (2 oz) green noodles
	50 g (2 oz) white noodles
	melted butter
	grated Parmesan cheese, to serve

Preparation time: 5 minutes
Cooking time: 20 minutes

1. First make the sauces. To make sauce 1, heat the oil in a small saucepan, add the onion and fry gently for 3 minutes. Add the remaining ingredients, with salt and pepper to taste, and simmer gently for 5 minutes. Add a little stock or water if the sauce becomes too thick.
2. To make sauce 2, put all the ingredients, with salt and pepper to taste, into a small saucepan and heat through gently.
3. To make sauce 3, melt the butter in a small saucepan and stir in the flour. Cook for 1 minute. Gradually stir in the white wine, and bring to the boil, stirring constantly. Add the garlic, cream, prawns, mussels and lemon and simmer for 3 minutes.
4. Bring 3 pans of salted water to the boil. Drop 1 variety of pasta into each pan and cook steadily until the pasta is 'al dente' (tender but still firm to the bite) – about 8 minutes. Drain each variety of pasta separately, and toss lightly in melted butter.
5. Toss the spaghetti into sauce 1, the green noodles into sauce 2, and the white noodles into sauce 3.
6. Serve in sectioned dishes, with a bowl of grated Parmesan cheese.

CARAMEL OEUFS À LA NEIGE

2 eggs, separated	2 tablespoons water
100 g (4 oz) caster sugar	finely chopped walnuts, to decorate
300 ml (½ pint) milk	

Preparation time: 20 minutes, plus cooling
Cooking time: 15–20 minutes

1. Whisk the egg whites until stiff. Add half the caster sugar and whisk until very stiff.
2. Put the milk into a shallow pan and bring just to the boil. Drop in spoonfuls of the meringue mixture and poach gently until the meringues become fluffy and set on the underside. Flip them over and poach for a further 2 minutes. Drain the meringues in a large sieve or on paper towels. Reserve the milk.
3. Put the remaining sugar into a saucepan with the water. Stir over the heat until the sugar has dissolved, then boil steadily until the syrup turns caramel in colour.
4. Stir in the strained milk (from poaching the meringues) and cook gently, stirring, until the caramel has dissolved.
5. Beat the egg yolks in a heatproof bowl. Stir in the flavoured milk then return to the pan. Heat gently, without boiling and stir until the custard will coat the back of a wooden spoon. Pour into a shallow dish and allow to cool*.
6. Top with the poached meringues, and sprinkle with walnuts.

WINTER DINNER
—FOR TWO—

Even though the starter and dessert are both served cold to help with the preparation, one is served with warm fingers of toast and the other is topped with hot rum sauce.

CHOPPED LIVER PÂTÉ

PORK NOISETTES WITH RICH ONION SAUCE

CHICORY AND BEETROOT SALAD

RATAFIA ICE CREAM WITH HOT RUM SAUCE

CHOPPED LIVER PÂTÉ

50 g (2 oz) butter	1 garlic clove, peeled and
1 small onion, peeled and	crushed
finely chopped	salt
175 g (6 oz) chicken livers,	freshly ground black
trimmed and chopped	pepper
	2 hard-boiled eggs

Preparation time: 10–15 minutes, plus chilling
Cooking time: 4–5 minutes

1. Heat the butter in a frying pan. Add the onion and fry gently until soft. Add the chicken livers, garlic and salt and pepper to taste and cook until the livers are sealed on the outside but still pink in the centre.
2. Tip the liver mixture into a bowl and finely chop using 2 sharp knives with a criss-cross motion
3. Separate the hard-boiled egg whites from the yolks. Chop the egg white finely and stir into the liver. Push the egg yolks through a sieve and reserve. (For a smoother texture, the liver mixture and egg white can be puréed in a blender or food processor.)
4. Chill the pâté for 1–2 hours.* Pile in mounds on small plates garnished with the sieved egg yolk and serve with triangles of hot toast.

PORK NOISETTES WITH RICH ONION SAUCE

2 lean pork chops, boned	5 tablespoons water or
25 g (1 oz) butter	stock
1 large onion, peeled and	2 tablespoons medium
thinly sliced	sherry
2 tablespoons red wine	salt
vinegar	freshly ground black
1 tablespoon dark brown	pepper
sugar	

Preparation time: 20 minutes
Cooking time: 25 minutes

1. Curl each pork chop round in the shape of a noisette and tie quite securely with fine string.*
2. Heat the butter in a frying pan. Add the onion and fry gently for 3 minutes. Add the pork noisettes and fry gently for 6–8 minutes on each side. Remove the pork noisettes and keep warm.
3. Add the wine vinegar, brown sugar, water or stock, sherry and salt and pepper to taste to the pan. Bring to the boil and simmer gently for 4 minutes, stirring frequently.
4. Pour the onion mixture into a blender or food processor and purée until smooth.
5. Return the sauce to the pan, add the noisettes and heat through gently. Serve hot with Chicory and beetroot salad (page 72).

CHICORY AND BEETROOT SALAD

1 large beetroot, cooked,
   peeled and thinly sliced
1 small head of chicory,
   finely shredded
grated rind and juice of ½
   orange

4 tablespoons olive oil
salt
freshly ground black
   pepper

Preparation time: 15 minutes

Do not leave the salad standing too long before serving otherwise the colour will leach from the beetroot into the chicory.

1. Arrange the beetroot slices in a shallow serving dish. Sprinkle over the chicory.
2. Mix the orange rind and juice with the olive oil, and add salt and pepper to taste. Spoon the dressing evenly over the salad.

RATAFIA ICE CREAM WITH HOT RUM SAUCE

150 ml (¼ pint) double
   cream
2 teaspoons instant coffee
   powder
1 tablespoon hot water
150 ml (¼ pint) custard,
   pouring consistency

2 tablespoons crushed
   ratafia biscuits or
   macaroons
SAUCE:
3 tablespoons apricot jam
2 tablespoons rum
1 tablespoon raisins

Preparation time: 15–20 minutes, plus freezing
Cooking time: 2–3 minutes

1. Whip the cream until thick. Dissolve the coffee powder in the hot water. Fold into the whipped cream with the custard. Put into a freezer tray and freeze until the mixture starts to harden at the edges.
2. Tip into a bowl and beat until slushy. Stir in the ratafias. Return the mixture to the tray then to the freezer and freeze until firm.*
3. To make the sauce, sieve the apricot jam into a saucepan. Add the rum and raisins and heat through gently, stirring frequently.
4. Scoop the ice cream into serving dishes and spoon the hot sauce over the top.
Serve immediately.

MENUS
FOR
FOUR

SLIMMER'S SPECIAL
FOR FOUR

GREEN GARDEN SOUP

FISH DIABLE

SPINACH RAMEKINS

RED WINE JELLY

GREEN GARDEN SOUP

4 celery sticks, chopped
2 leeks, washed and
  shredded
1 bunch of watercress,
  stalks trimmed
3 courgettes, thinly sliced
600 ml (1 pint) chicken
  stock
salt

freshly ground black
  pepper
1 garlic clove, peeled and
  crushed
small bunch of parsley
150 ml (¼ pint) plain
  unsweetened yogurt
chopped fresh chives, to
  garnish

Preparation time: 10 minutes, plus chilling
Cooking time: about 15 minutes
Calories per portion: 40 (to nearest 10)

As an alternative this soup can be served hot. After blending, reheat then stir in all the yogurt. Serve immediately.

1. Put the celery, leeks, watercress and courgettes into a saucepan together with the chicken stock, salt and pepper to taste, garlic and parsley. Simmer gently until the vegetables are just tender – about 15 minutes.
2. Purée in a blender or food processor until smooth. Cool, then stir in half the yogurt. Chill.*
3. Serve in soup bowls with a little of the remaining yogurt swirled on top. Garnish with chopped chives.

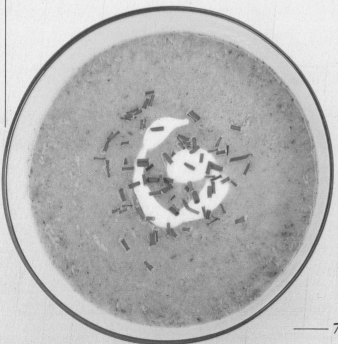

FISH DIABLE

2 large carrots, peeled and
  cut into matchstick
  strips
3 celery sticks, cut into
  matchstick strips
100 g (4 oz) button
  mushrooms, sliced
150 ml (¼ pint) chicken
  stock
salt
freshly ground black
  pepper
150 ml (¼ pint) plain
  unsweetened yogurt
1 tablespoon French
  mustard

4 large white fish fillets,
  about 225 g (8 oz) each
  (plaice, sole, etc.)
melted butter
SAUCE:
150 ml (¼ pint) milk
pinch of grated nutmeg
1 teaspoon cornflour
1 small red pepper, cored,
  seeded and finely
  chopped
TO GARNISH:
small lemon wedges
fresh dill sprigs (optional)

Preparation time: 25 minutes
Cooking time: about 45 minutes
Oven: 190°C, 375°F, Gas Mark 5
Calories per portion: 230 (to nearest 10)

---

1. Place the carrots, celery, mushrooms, chicken stock and salt and pepper to taste in a saucepan and poach for 15 minutes. Drain the vegetables thoroughly.
2. Mix the yogurt with the mustard. Spread a little of the yogurt mixture on each fish fillet, season with salt and pepper, top with strips of the poached vegetables and roll up. Place the rolled fish fillets in a shallow greased ovenproof dish and brush the fish with melted butter.*
3. Bake in a preheated oven for 20–25 minutes or until tender.
4. Meanwhile, make the sauce. Heat the milk with the nutmeg in a small saucepan. Blend the remaining yogurt and mustard mixture with the cornflour, and stir in the hot milk. Return the sauce to the saucepan and stir over a gentle heat until the sauce has thickened slightly.
5. Remove the cooked fish to a serving dish. Stir the chopped red pepper into the hot sauce and spoon over the fish. Garnish with lemon and fresh dill, if available.

SPINACH RAMEKINS

1 × 225 g (8 oz) packet
  frozen chopped spinach,
  thawed
½ teaspoon grated
  nutmeg

salt
freshly ground black
  pepper
2 eggs, beaten
5 tablespoons single cream

Preparation time: 10 minutes
Cooking time: 40 minutes
Oven: 190°C, 375°F, Gas Mark 5
Calories per portion: 80 (to nearest 10)

---

1. Drain the spinach thoroughly.* Mix the spinach with the nutmeg, salt and pepper, the eggs and cream.
2. Spoon the spinach mixture into 4 individual ovenproof dishes or ramekins, greased with oil or melted butter. Stand the dishes in a roasting tin and add sufficient hot water to come halfway up the sides.
3. Bake in a preheated oven for about 40 minutes.
4. Remove from the oven. Carefully run a small knife around the edge of each dish and unmould the ramekins.

RED WINE JELLY

300 ml (½ pint) plus 2
  tablespoons water
2 tablespoons redcurrant
  jelly
300 ml (½ pint) red wine
15 g (½ oz) powdered
  gelatine

artificial sweetener
  (optional)
cluster of red or black
  grapes, to decorate
  (optional)

Preparation time: 20 minutes, plus chilling
Cooking time: 3 minutes
Calories per portion: 80 (to nearest 10)

1. Put 300 ml (½ pint) of the water and the redcurrant jelly into a saucepan. Stir over a gentle heat until the jelly has melted. Bring to the boil and simmer gently for 2 minutes. Stir in the red wine and allow to cool.
2. Put the remaining water in a small cup and sprinkle over the gelatine. Stand the cup in a pan of hot water and stir until the gelatine has dissolved. Add the gelatine mixture to the wine liquid. Taste, and add a little artificial sweetener if liked.
3. Pour the jelly into a dampened 600 ml (1 pint) jelly mould or four 150 ml (¼ pint) moulds and chill until set.* Unmould the set jelly on to a serving dish and garnish with the grapes, if using.

LUNCH-OUT-OF-DOORS
FOR FOUR

TOMATO SALMON FLAN

LENTIL SALAD WITH WALNUTS

GARLIC AND CHEESE BREAD

POACHED PEACHES WITH
DAMSON SAUCE

TOMATO SALMON FLAN

175 g (6 oz) shortcrust
  pastry
75 g (3 oz) cooked rice
2 tablespoons chopped
  fresh parsley
2 spring onions, peeled
  and finely chopped
salt
freshly ground black
  pepper
4 tablespoons mayonnaise
1 × 200 g (7 oz) can red
  salmon, drained and
  flaked
4 gherkins, finely chopped
85 ml (3 fl oz) tomato juice
2 tablespoons dry sherry
1 tablespoon water
1 teaspoon powdered
  gelatine
TO GARNISH:
black olives
sprigs of watercress

Preparation time: 25 minutes, plus chilling
Cooking time: 25–30 minutes
Oven: 190°C, 375°F, Gas Mark 5

1. Roll out the pastry dough and use to line a 20 cm (8 inch) loose-bottomed flan tin. Pinch up the edges well. Line with greaseproof paper and baking beans. Bake 'blind' in a preheated oven for 10 minutes. Remove the paper and beans and continue baking the pastry case for a further 15–20 minutes or until golden brown. Allow the flan case to cool.
2. Mix the cooked rice with the parsley, spring onions, plenty of salt and pepper and half the mayonnaise. Spread evenly over the bottom of the pastry case.
3. Mix the canned salmon with the gherkins and remaining mayonnaise and salt and pepper to taste. Press the salmon mixture on top of the rice mixture. Chill the flan while you make the tomato glaze.
4. Mix the tomato juice with the dry sherry. Put the water into a small cup and sprinkle over the gelatine. Place the cup in a pan of hot water and stir to dissolve the gelatine. Stir the gelatine mixture into the tomato and sherry mixture. Chill until the mixture turns syrupy, then spoon it evenly over the salmon.
5. Chill the flan until the glaze has set.* Garnish with black olives and sprigs of watercress. Serve with Lentil salad with walnuts and Garlic and cheese bread.

LENTIL SALAD WITH WALNUTS

225 g (8 oz) dried lentils
3 spring onions, peeled
  and very finely chopped
2 tablespoons finely
  chopped fresh parsley
1 garlic clove, peeled and
  crushed
salt
freshly ground black
  pepper
1 tablespoon white wine
  vinegar
4 tablespoons olive oil
2 tablespoons double
  cream
2 bacon rashers, rind
  removed, grilled until
  crisp and chopped
2 tablespoons finely
  chopped walnuts

Preparation time: 10 minutes
Cooking time: 1–1½ hours

1. Cook the lentils in boiling water for 1–1½ hours or until tender but not 'mushy'. Drain the lentils thoroughly.
2. Mix together the spring onions, chopped parsley, garlic, salt and pepper to taste, vinegar, olive oil and cream.
3. Mix in the cooked lentils, bacon and half the walnuts. Spoon into a serving dish and sprinkle with the remaining walnuts. This salad is delicious served while still warm.

GARLIC AND CHEESE BREAD

1 small French stick loaf
25 g (1 oz) butter, softened
75 g (3 oz) full fat soft
  cheese, softened
2 garlic cloves, peeled and
  crushed
salt
freshly ground black
  pepper

Preparation time: 10 minutes
Cooking time: 10 minutes
Oven: 190°C, 375°F, Gas Mark 5

If you are having a barbecue in the garden, the bread can be wrapped in foil and kept warm on one side of the fire.

1. Split the French stick in half lengthways. Spread the cut surfaces on both halves with butter.
2. Beat the cheese with the garlic and salt and pepper to taste. Spread one half of the French stick with the cheese mixture and sandwich together with the other half. Wrap in foil.
3. Bake the French stick in a preheated oven for 10 minutes. Serve piping hot.

POACHED PEACHES WITH DAMSON SAUCE

225 g (8 oz) sugar
300 ml (½ pint) dry white wine
thinly pared rind of 1 lemon

8 small peaches, peeled
juice of 1 lemon
6 tablespoons damson jam
2 tablespoons brandy

Preparation time: 10–15 minutes, plus chilling
Cooking time: 25 minutes

To peel peaches easily, plunge them into boiling water for 30 seconds. Peel immediately then plunge them into ice cold water to prevent further cooking.

1. Put the sugar and wine into a saucepan. Stir over a gentle heat until the sugar has dissolved. Add the lemon rind, bring to the boil and boil steadily for 3 minutes.
2. Meanwhile, peel the peaches and put them into a bowl of cold water, with the lemon juice, to prevent them discolouring.
3. Drain the peaches and put them into the syrup. Poach gently for 15–20 minutes. Allow the peaches to cool in the syrup, then cover and chill.
4. Put the damson jam into a saucepan with 3 tablespoons of the cooking syrup from the peaches and stir until melted. Stir in the brandy. Chill the damson sauce.*
5. To serve, place 2 peaches on each serving dish and spoon over a little of the damson sauce.

Variation: Use fully ripe nectarines in place of peaches. Replace the damson jam with 6 tablespoons of seedless raspberry jelly.

LAST-MINUTE SUPPER
—FOR FOUR—

A quickly prepared main dish, such as Liver Stroganoff, *is a perfect choice for any last-minute occasion, together with a starter that only takes minutes to cook and a pudding prepared well in advance.*

ANCHOVY FRITTERS

LIVER STROGANOFF

BUTTERED NOODLES†
WATERCRESS AND ONION SALAD

LEMON HONEYCOMB MOULD

ANCHOVY FRITTERS

28 white anchovy fillets,
  drained
milk, for soaking
plain flour, for dusting
freshly ground black
  pepper
coating batter (made with
  100 g (4 oz) plain flour,
  1 egg and 150 ml (¼
  pint) milk)

oil for deep frying
TO GARNISH:
lemon wedges
parsley sprigs

Preparation time: 10 minutes, plus soaking
Cooking time: 3–4 minutes

White anchovy fillets can be bought in jars. If unavailable use canned fillets instead.

1. Soak the anchovy fillets in milk for 30 minutes.
2. Drain thoroughly, then dust the anchovy fillets in flour, seasoned with pepper. Dip each anchovy fillet into the batter to give a thin even coating.
3. Lower into a pan of hot oil and deep fry until crisp and golden – about 3–4 minutes. Drain thoroughly on paper towels.
4. Serve piping hot, garnished with lemon and parsley.

LIVER STROGANOFF

25 g (1 oz) butter
1 tablespoon oil
1 medium onion, peeled
  and finely chopped
450 g (1 lb) calves' liver,
  cut into thin strips
plain flour, for dusting
salt

freshly ground black
  pepper
6 tablespoons dry sherry
100 g (4 oz) button
  mushrooms, sliced
150 ml (¼ pint) soured
  cream

Preparation time: 5 minutes
Cooking time: 12 minutes

1. Heat the butter and oil in a large frying pan. Add the onion and fry gently for 3–4 minutes
2. Dust the strips of liver in flour seasoned with salt and pepper and add to the pan. Fry gently for 2–3 minutes, turning the strips of liver. Stir in the sherry and sliced mushrooms. Bring to the boil and simmer for a further 3 minutes.
3. Stir in the soured cream and heat through without boiling. Taste and adjust the seasoning. Serve hot with buttered noodles and Watercress and onion salad.

WATERCRESS AND ONION SALAD

2 large bunches of
  watercress, stalks
  trimmed
1/2 small onion, peeled and
  quartered
2 tablespoons chopped
  fresh parsley

1 garlic clove, peeled
grated rind and juice of 1/2
  lemon
4 tablespoons olive oil
salt
freshly ground black
  pepper

Preparation time: 15 minutes

1. Put the watercress sprigs into a salad bowl.
2. Put the remaining ingredients, with salt and pepper to taste, into a blender or food processor and purée until smooth. If the dressing is too thick, thin it down with a little cold water.*
3. Spoon the dressing over the watercress just before serving.

LEMON HONEYCOMB MOULD

4 eggs yolks
50 g (2 oz) caster sugar
finely grated rind of 1
  lemon
600 ml (1 pint) warm milk
4 teaspoons powdered
  gelatine

4 tablespoons water
2 egg whites
TO DECORATE:
1 lemon
fine strips of candied
  angelica

Preparation time: 20–25 minutes, plus chilling
Cooking time: 10 minutes

1. Whisk the egg yolks with the caster sugar and lemon rind in a heatproof bowl until thick. Whisk the milk into the egg yolk mixture. Place over a pan of simmering water and stir over a gentle heat until the custard will coat the back of a wooden spoon. Remove the custard from the heat.
2. Place the water in a small cup and sprinkle over the gelatine. Stand the cup in a pan of hot water and stir to dissolve the gelatine. Stir the gelatine mixture into the custard. Cool slightly.
3. Whisk the egg whites stiffly and fold lightly but thoroughly into the custard. Pour the custard into a dampened 900 ml–1.2 litre (1¾–2 pint) mould. Chill until set.*
4. Unmould the pudding on to a serving dish and decorate with leaf shapes cut out of the lemon rind and strips of angelica.

ELEGANT DINNER
—FOR FOUR—

Marinated raw smoked salmon; plump steaks with a tangy soured cream sauce; and a deliciously refreshing melon tart are the elegant components of this menu.

CEVICHE OF SALMON

FILLET STEAK PIQUANT

ALMANDINE POTATOES†
STUFFED TOMATOES

MELON TART

CEVICHE OF SALMON

1 × 375 g (12 oz) piece of
   salmon fillet
lemon juice, for sprinkling
olive oil, for sprinkling
salt

freshly ground black
   pepper
fresh dill or fennel sprigs,
   to garnish

Preparation time: 20 minutes

It is important that the salmon is fresh for this recipe. If prepared in advance (this should not be more than 2 hours before serving) sprinkle quite generously with olive oil only and cover with cling film. Lemon juice will cause the fish to turn opaque and spoil the appearance.

1. Using a sharp knife, cut down through the fillet of salmon into very thin slices – about the same thickness as sliced smoked salmon. Arrange the raw salmon on 4 plates in a single layer.
2. Sprinkle the salmon with lemon juice and olive oil, and season to taste with salt and pepper.*
3. Garnish with sprigs of fresh dill or fennel. Serve with brown bread and butter.

FILLET STEAK PIQUANT

4 fillet steaks, cut about
   2.5 cm (1 inch) thick
salt
freshly ground black
   pepper
50 g (2 oz) butter
1 garlic clove, peeled and
   crushed
1 tablespoon
   Worcestershire sauce

2 teaspoons grated fresh
   horse-radish
150 ml (¼ pint) soured
   cream
1 small red pepper, cored,
   seeded and finely
   chopped, to garnish

Preparation time: 3 minutes
Cooking time: 10 minutes

---

1. Season the steaks with salt and pepper. Heat the butter in a large frying pan. Add the garlic and the steaks and fry gently for 3 minutes on each side. Remove the steaks and keep warm. (If you like meat well done, cook the steaks for slightly longer.)
2. Add the Worcestershire sauce to the cooking juices in the pan and bring to the boil. Remove the pan from the heat and whisk in the horseradish and soured cream.
3. Return the steaks to the sauce in the pan and heat through gently without boiling. Garnish with the red pepper, and serve with almandine potatoes (creamed potatoes formed into small balls and rolled in chopped almonds, then baked or fried) together with Stuffed tomatoes (see below).

STUFFED TOMATOES

8 medium tomatoes
225 g (8 oz) frozen peas
25 g (1 oz) butter
generous pinch of ground
   mace
salt
freshly ground black
   pepper

1 tablespoon double
   cream
small parsley sprigs, to
   garnish

Preparation time: 15 minutes
Cooking time: about 18 minutes
Oven: 190°C, 375°F, Gas Mark 5

---

1. Cut a thin slice from the non-stalk end of each tomato and carefully hollow out the centre. (Reserve the centres for use in soups, sauces, etc.) Dry the inside of each tomato with paper towels. Once dried, these will stand for 5–6 hours.
2. Arrange the tomatoes in an oven-proof dish. Place in a preheated oven and heat through for 5 minutes.
3. Meanwhile, put the peas into a saucepan with the butter, mace, and salt and pepper to taste. Cover and simmer gently until the peas are tender. Mash the peas to a smooth purée and beat in the cream.
3. Fill the hollowed tomatoes with the creamy pea purée,* cover with foil and return to the oven. Heat for a further 3–4 minutes. Serve hot, garnished with parsley.

MELON TART

175 g (6 oz) rich shortcrust
    pastry
1 medium Ogen melon,
    halved and seeded
juice of ½ lemon
50 g (2 oz) caster sugar

2 tablespoons water
15 g (½ oz) powdered
    gelatine
fresh mint sprigs, to
    decorate

Preparation time: 30–35 minutes, plus chilling
Cooking time: 25–30 minutes
Oven: 190°C, 375°F, Gas Mark 5

---

1. Roll out the pastry dough thinly and use to line a 20 cm (8 inch) loose-bottomed flan tin. Pinch up the edges well. Line with greaseproof paper and baking beans. Bake 'blind' in a preheated oven for 10 minutes. Remove the paper and beans and bake for a further 15–20 minutes or until golden brown. Allow the pastry case to cool.
2. Scoop 12–14 balls from one-half of the melon using a melon baller. Cover with cling film and chill.

3. Scoop the remaining melon flesh from the 2 halves and either sieve or purée in a blender or food processor. Stir the lemon juice and sugar into the melon purée and measure it – you should have about 450 ml (¾ pint). If it is less than this, make up the quantity with medium dry white wine or apple juice.
4. Put the water into a small cup and sprinkle over the gelatine. Stand the cup in a pan of hot water and stir to dissolve the gelatine. Stir the gelatine into the melon purée. Chill until on the point of setting, then pour into the pastry case. Chill until set.*
5. Decorate the top of the tart with the prepared melon balls and sprigs of mint. Serve as soon as possible once the tart filling has set.

WINTER LUNCH
FOR FOUR

STILTON SOUP

SPICED MEATBALLS

SAFFRON RISOTTO

PUMPKIN PUDDING

STILTON SOUP

25 g (1 oz) butter
1 medium onion, peeled
   and finely chopped
2 tablespoons plain flour
300 ml (½ pint) chicken
   stock
150 ml (¼ pint) dry cider
150 ml (¼ pint) milk

1 teaspoon French
   mustard
175 g (6 oz) Stilton cheese
   (trimmed of outer
   crust), crumbled
salt
freshly ground black
   pepper

Preparation time: 10 minutes
Cooking time: 8–10 minutes

1. Heat the butter in a saucepan, add the onion and fry for 3 minutes. Stir in the flour and cook for 1 minute.
2. Gradually stir in the stock, cider and milk. Bring to the boil, stirring until thickened.
3. Add the mustard, crumbled Stilton and salt and pepper to taste. Stir until the cheese has melted and the soup is piping hot. Serve with hot crusty bread.

SAFFRON RISOTTO

½ teaspoon saffron
   powder
3 tablespoons hot water
2 tablespoons oil
75 g (3 oz) butter
1 small onion, peeled and
   finely chopped
350 g (12 oz) short-grain
   rice

1.2 litres (2 pints) chicken
   stock
salt
freshly ground black
   pepper
grated Parmesan cheese

Preparation time: 15 minutes
Cooking time: 25 minutes

1. Soak the saffron in the hot water for 15 minutes.
2. Meanwhile, heat the oil and half the butter in a saucepan. Add the onion and fry gently for 3 minutes.
3. Add the rice and stir over a gentle heat for about 5 minutes, making sure that the rice does not colour.
4. Add one-quarter of the stock to the rice, bring to the boil and simmer until the stock has been absorbed.
5. Add another quarter of the stock and cook until that has been absorbed. Add the saffron liquid.
6. Continue adding the remaining stock, gradually, until all the stock has been absorbed and the rice is tender.
7. Season the risotto to taste with salt and pepper and stir in the remaining butter.
Sprinkle with the cheese.

SPICED MEATBALLS

500 g (1¼ lb) minced veal
1 medium onion, peeled
   and grated
1 tablespoon chopped
   fresh sage
½ teaspoon ground
   cinnamon
generous pinch of
   turmeric
2 egg yolks
6 cm (2½ inch) piece of
   root ginger, scraped and
   finely chopped
salt
freshly ground black
   pepper

oil for frying
SAUCE:
2 tablespoons oil
1 medium onion, peeled
   and finely chopped
1 × 400 g (14 oz) can
   tomatoes
2 tablespoons tomato
   purée
150 ml (¼ pint) red wine
1 garlic clove, peeled and
   crushed
salt
freshly ground black
   pepper

Preparation time: 20 minutes, plus chilling
Cooking time: 40 minutes

1. Mix the veal with the onion, sage, cinnamon, turmeric, egg yolks, ginger, and salt and pepper to taste. Form the veal mixture into small balls, about the size of a walnut. Chill for 30 minutes.
2. Meanwhile, make the sauce. Heat the oil in a saucepan, add the onion and fry gently for 4 minutes. Stir in the undrained tomatoes, tomato purée, red wine, garlic and salt and pepper to taste. Simmer gently for 20 minutes or until reduced slightly.
3. Heat a little oil in a frying pan, add the meatballs (in batches if necessary) and fry gently until browned on all sides. Drain on paper towels.
4. Add the meatballs to the sauce and continue cooking for a further 10–15 minutes or until the meatballs are tender. Serve hot with Saffron risotto.

PUMPKIN PUDDING

450 g (1 lb) pumpkin,
   peeled, seeded and
   cubed
150 ml (¼ pint) cider
50 g (2 oz) soft brown
   sugar
¼ teaspoon mixed spice
50 g (2 oz) butter

2 eggs, separated
50 g (2 oz) caster sugar
2 tablespoons flaked
   almonds
icing sugar

Preparation time: 20 minutes
Cooking time: 50–55 minutes
Oven: 190°C, 375°F, Gas Mark 5

1. Put the pumpkin into a saucepan with the cider, brown sugar and spice. Cover the pan and simmer gently until the pumpkin is tender.
2. Beat the cooked pumpkin to a purée, then beat in the butter and egg yolks. Allow to cool.
3. Whisk the egg whites until stiff. Whisk in the caster sugar. Fold the meringue lightly but thoroughly into the pumpkin mixture.
4. Spoon the pumpkin mixture into a greased shallow ovenproof dish. Sprinkle with the flaked almonds. Bake in a preheated oven for 30–35 minutes.
Serve hot, with cream.

SEAFOOD SPECIAL
—FOR FOUR—

SMOKED TROUT PÂTÉ

TURBAN OF BROCCOLI AND FISH

CUCUMBER IN CREAM

RHUBARB CHARTREUSE

SMOKED TROUT PÂTÉ

175 g (6 oz) smoked trout
  fillet
75 g (3 oz) butter
2 tablespoons double
  cream
grated rind and juice of ½
  lemon

½ teaspoon anchovy
  essence
salt
freshly ground black
  pepper

Preparation time: 15 minutes, plus chilling

If you want to present this pâté in a particularly attractive manner, spoon it into hollowed-out large tomatoes.

1. Remove any skin and bones from the trout, then flake the flesh.
2. Beat the butter until softened, then mix in the lemon rind and juice, cream, anchovy essence, and salt and pepper to taste.
3. Stir in the flaked smoked trout.
4. Chill the pâté for at least 2 hours.* Serve with toast.

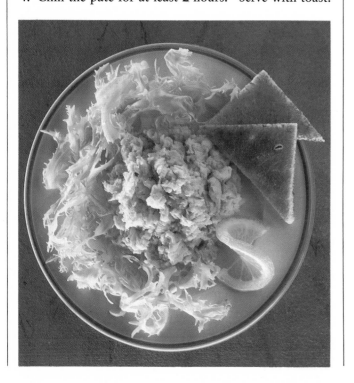

TURBAN OF BROCCOLI AND FISH

225 g (8 oz) broccoli
salt
2 eggs
3 tablespoons soured
  cream
2 tablespoons grated
  Parmesan cheese
sprig of fresh tarragon
  (optional)
freshly ground black
  pepper
350 g (12 oz) small white
  fish fillets, skinned

4 tablespoons fresh white
  breadcrumbs
SAUCE:
3 egg yolks
75 g (3 oz) butter
juice of ½ lemon
salt
freshly ground white
  pepper
slices of lemon, cut into
  triangles, to garnish

Preparation time: 25 minutes
Cooking time: about 1 hour
Oven: 180°C, 350°F, Gas Mark 4

---

1. Put the broccoli into a saucepan and cover with boiling water. Add a generous pinch of salt and cook the broccoli until it is tender, about 10 minutes. Drain thoroughly.
2. Put the broccoli into a blender or food processor with the eggs, soured cream, cheese, tarragon, and salt and pepper to taste. Purée until smooth.
3. Chop 100 g (4 oz) of the fish fillets and stir into the broccoli mixture together with the breadcrumbs.
4. Line a greased 900 ml (1½ pint) ovenproof ring mould with the remaining fish fillets, allowing the ends to hang over the rim of the mould.
5. Spoon the broccoli mixture into the mould smoothing the surface to level. Fold the overhanging fish fillets over the broccoli mixture. Cover with greased foil.
6. Stand the mould in a roasting tin and add sufficient hot water to come halfway up the sides of the mould. Bake in a preheated oven for 40–45 minutes or until firm but springy.
7. Meanwhile, make the sauce. Put the egg yolks and one-third of the butter into the top of a double saucepan, or into a heatproof bowl, over a pan of simmering water. Stir until the butter has melted. Add another third of the butter and continue stirring rapidly, until the butter melts and the sauce starts to thicken.
8. Stir in the remaining butter until melted, then add the lemon juice and salt and pepper to taste. Stir over a gentle heat for 2–3 minutes.
9. Carefully unmould the fish turban on to a serving plate. Spoon a little of the sauce over the mould and serve the remainder separately. Garnish with the lemon slices accompanied by Cucumber in cream (see next page).

CUCUMBER IN CREAM

1 large cucumber, peeled,
    halved and seeded
salt
25 g (1 oz) butter
1 garlic clove, peeled and
    crushed
1 small onion, peeled and
    finely chopped

1 teaspoon dill seed
2 tablespoons chopped
    fresh parsley
freshly ground black
    pepper
150 ml (¼ pint) soured
    cream

Preparation time: 8–10 minutes, plus draining
Cooking time: about 6 minutes

---

1. Cut the cucumber into 5 mm (¼ inch) thick slices. Put
into a colander and sprinkle generously with salt. Leave
to drain for 30 minutes, then pat dry with paper towels.
2. Heat the butter in a frying pan, add the garlic and
onion and fry gently for 3 minutes. Stir in the dill seed,
parsley, cucumber, and salt and pepper to taste. Cook,
stirring, for 2 minutes.
3. Add the soured cream and bring just to the boil. Serve
immediately.

RHUBARB CHARTREUSE

275 g (10 oz) lump or
    granulated sugar
200 ml (⅓ pint) water
juice of ½ lemon
450 g (1 lb) rhubarb, cut
    into 2.5 cm (1 inch)
    lengths

juice of 1 orange
1 tablespoon powdered
    gelatine
100 g (4 oz) mixed candied
    fruit (glacé cherries,
    angelica, candied peel,
    etc.) chopped

Preparation time: 15–20 minutes, plus chilling
Cooking time: about 16–17 minutes

---

1. Put the sugar, water and lemon juice into a saucepan.
Stir over a gentle heat until the sugar has dissolved, then
bring to the boil and boil gently for 5 minutes.
2. Add the rhubarb to the syrup and cook gently for 6–8
minutes or until the rhubarb just starts to soften. Allow to
cool.
3. Put the orange juice into a cup, sprinkle over the
gelatine and stand the cup in a pan of hot water. Stir until
the gelatine has dissolved.
4. Stir the gelatine into the rhubarb and syrup. Leave on
one side until the mixture starts to set.
5. Stir the candied fruits into the rhubarb mixture, taking
care not to break up the rhubarb. Pour the mixture into a
dampened 900 ml (1½ pint) mould. Chill until set.*
6. Carefully unmould the rhubarb chartreuse on to a
serving plate and serve it with pouring cream flavoured
with a little brandy.

POT LUCK
—FOR FOUR—

CHICKEN AND HERB HOTPOT

CABBAGE SALAD

STEAMED LEMON AND GINGER PUDDING

CHICKEN AND HERB HOTPOT

1 × 1.5 kg (3¼–3½ lb) oven-ready chicken
25 g (1 oz) butter
2 tablespoons oil
1 medium onion, peeled and thinly sliced
2 garlic cloves, peeled and crushed
300 ml (½ pint) dry cider
about 600 ml (1 pint) chicken stock
salt
freshly ground black pepper
fresh sprig of rosemary
fresh sprig of thyme
2 large bay leaves
12 small whole carrots, scraped
8 baby turnips, peeled
8 small new potatoes, scraped
SAUCE:
25 g (1 oz) butter
1½ tablespoons plain flour
3–4 tablespoons cream
1 tablespoon chopped fresh sage

Preparation time: 8 minutes
Cooking time: about 2 hours

1. Truss the chicken into a neat shape if your butcher has not already done so.* Heat the butter and oil in a large frying pan. Add the chicken and brown first on one breast and then on the other. Turn the chicken upright and brown on the underside. Transfer the chicken to a large saucepan, either one with a steamer that fits over it or position a colander over the top. (The steamer or colander is for the pudding, so if you are not serving the pudding, the hotpot may be cooked in an ordinary saucepan or flameproof casserole.)
2. Add the sliced onion and garlic to the fat remaining in the frying pan and pour over the chicken. Add the cider, chicken stock, salt and pepper to taste, and the rosemary, thyme and bay leaves tied together. Cover with the steamer top or colander and a lid. Bring to the boil and simmer steadily for 1 hour. (Place the steamed pudding in the steamer or colander at this point.)
3. Add the prepared vegetables and continue simmering for a further 45 minutes.
4. Transfer the chicken to a serving dish with a deep rim, surround with the vegetables and keep warm. Strain off 450 ml (¾ pint) of the cooking liquid and reserve.
5. Melt the butter in a saucepan and stir in the flour. Cook for 1 minute. Stir in the reserved liquid and bring to the boil, stirring until the sauce thickens. Stir in the cream and sage. Spoon the sauce over the chicken.

CABBAGE SALAD

¼ small white cabbage, finely shredded
¼ small red cabbage, finely shredded
1 small onion, peeled and finely chopped
2 tablespoons chopped walnuts
2 tablespoons raisins
finely grated rind and juice of 1 orange
5 tablespoons olive oil
salt
freshly ground black pepper
1 teaspoon caraway seeds

Preparation time: 15 minutes

This salad can be prepared up to 2 hours in advance.

1. Put the white and red cabbage into a bowl with the onion, nuts and raisins.
2. Mix the orange rind and juice with the olive oil, salt and pepper to taste, and the caraway seeds.
3. Stir the orange dressing into the prepared vegetables.*

STEAMED LEMON AND GINGER PUDDING

3 tablespoons lemon curd
1 tablespoon water
100 g (4 oz) soft margarine
100 g (4 oz) caster sugar
2 eggs
100 g (4 oz) self-raising flour
1 teaspoon baking powder
1 teaspoon ground ginger
finely grated rind of ½ lemon

Preparation time: 12 minutes
Cooking time: 1¾ hours

1. Mix the lemon curd with the water and place in the bottom of a buttered 900 ml (1½ pint) pudding basin.
2. Put all the remaining ingredients into a large mixing bowl and beat vigorously for 2–3 minutes. Spoon the mixture into the pudding basin, smoothing the top to level. Cover with a round of greased greaseproof paper, and one of foil.*
3. Stand the basin in the steamer or colander over the chicken and steam for 1¾ hours. (If not cooking with the chicken, place in a saucepan, add enough boiling water to come up to the rim of the basin, cover and steam for 1¾ hours.)
4. Unmould the cooked pudding carefully and serve hot with cream.

COLD COLLATION
FOR FOUR

FISH AND VEGETABLE TERRINE

TURKISH CHICKEN

COURGETTE SALAD

ICED COFFEE GÂTEAU

FISH AND VEGETABLE TERRINE

2 tablespoons white wine
generous pinch of saffron
   powder
225 g (8 oz) scallops
100 g (4 oz) peeled prawns
salt
freshly ground black
   pepper
1 egg, separated
300 ml (¼ pint) double
   cream

SAUCE:
½ small cucumber,
   peeled, seeded and
   grated
1 small bunch of fresh
   basil
200 ml (⅓ pint)
   mayonnaise
grated rind of ½ lemon
pinch of grated nutmeg
salt
freshly ground black
   pepper

Preparation time: 40 minutes, plus chilling
Cooking time: 50 minutes
Oven: 160°C, 325°F, Gas Mark 3

1. Warm the white wine in a small saucepan. Remove from the heat, stir in the saffron and reserve.
2. Put 175 g (6 oz) of the scallops and half the peeled prawns into a blender or food processor with salt and pepper to taste and the egg yolk. Purée until smooth, then pour into a bowl.
3. Whisk the egg white stiffly and fold lightly into the puréed mixture. Chill for 30 minutes.
4. Meanwhile, chop the remaining scallops and stir them into the saffron liquid.
5. Whip the cream until thick. Fold lightly but thoroughly into the puréed scallop mixture. Add the chopped scallops, saffron liquid, and the remaining prawns and mix together gently.
6. Pour into a small buttered 600 ml (1 pint) terrine or soufflé dish. Cover with a piece of greased foil.
7. Stand the terrine or soufflé dish in a roasting tin and add sufficient water to come halfway up the sides of the dish. Cook in a preheated oven for 50 minutes.
8. Allow the terrine to cool in the 'water bath', then chill until firm.*
9. To make the sauce, squeeze the cucumber in a clean piece of muslin or a tea towel to remove the excess moisture. Put the basil, mayonnaise, lemon rind, nutmeg, and salt and pepper to taste into the blender or food processor and purée until smooth. Stir in the cucumber.
10. Drain off any liquid that may have collected at the bottom of the terrine or soufflé dish, then turn out the terrine on to a serving dish. Serve cut into slices, accompanied by the basil and cucumber sauce.

TURKISH CHICKEN

225 g (8 oz) walnuts
3 slices of wholemeal
    bread, lightly toasted
1 teaspoon paprika pepper
3 tablespoons chicken
    stock
5 tablespoons olive or
    walnut oil
2–3 garlic cloves, peeled

juice of ½ lemon
2–3 tablespoons single
    cream (optional)
salt
1 × 1.5 kg (3 lb) chicken,
    cooked
TO GARNISH:
stoned black olives
few walnut halves

Preparation time: 30 minutes

1. To make the sauce, process the walnuts in a blender or food processor until quite fine, but not to a complete 'powder'. Reserve.
2. Break the bread into pieces and put into the blender or food processor with the paprika, stock, oil, garlic, lemon juice, cream, if using and salt to taste. Purée until smooth.
3. Stir the walnuts into the prepared sauce and thin to the desired consistency with more stock or lemon juice, or water.
4. Remove the skin from the chicken, then take the meat from the carcass and shred.
5. Fold the chicken into about two-thirds of the sauce and arrange on a serving platter. Spoon the remaining sauce over the top.* Garnish with olives and walnuts.
6. Serve with Courgette salad, and a tossed green or tomato salad.

COURGETTE SALAD

350 g (12 oz) courgettes,
    thinly sliced
4 spring onions, peeled
    and finely chopped
1 tablespoon chopped
    fresh chives
6 tablespoons olive oil
1 tablespoon white wine
    vinegar

1 garlic clove, peeled and
    crushed
salt
freshly ground black
    pepper
1 tablespoon capers

Preparation time: 10–15 minutes, plus standing

1. Mix the courgettes with the spring onions and chopped chives in a salad bowl.
2. Mix the olive oil with the wine vinegar, garlic, salt and pepper to taste, then add the capers.
3. Stir the dressing into the salad ingredients, so that the courgettes are evenly coated. Allow the salad to stand in a cool place for 1 hour to allow the flavours to mingle.*

ICED COFFEE GÂTEAU

2 egg whites
100 g (4 oz) caster sugar
2 tablespoons coffee
  liqueur
2 tablespoons instant
  coffee powder
3 tablespoons hot water

300 ml (½ pint) double
  cream
2 teaspoons icing sugar
TO DECORATE:
whipped cream
chocolate-coated coffee
  beans

Preparation time: 45 minutes, plus cooling and freezing
Cooking time: 1½ hours
Oven: 140°C, 275°F, Gas Mark 1

Chocolate-coated coffee beans can be bought from many good confectionery shops and from some Italian grocers. If you find them difficult to buy you can prepare your own by dipping medium roast coffee beans into melted plain chocolate, and leaving them to set on a sheet of lightly oiled greaseproof paper.

1. Whisk the egg whites until they hold their own shape.
2. Whisk in half the caster sugar until the mixture is stiff and glossy. Fold in the remaining caster sugar, lightly but thoroughly.
3. Using a tea-plate or sandwich tin as a guide, trace 2 circles, each 18 cm (7 inches) in diameter on a sheet of non-stick silicone or greaseproof paper. Place the paper on a baking sheet and lightly grease the greaseproof paper if using.

4. Spread half the meringue mixture to an even depth over each marked circle.
5. Bake in a preheated oven for 1½ hours, until lightly crisp but not coloured. Allow to cool.
6. Carefully remove the meringue layers from the paper.
7. Sprinkle each meringue layer with liqueur.
8. Dissolve the instant coffee in the hot water and allow to cool.
9. Whip the cream until thick, then whisk in the coffee mixture and icing sugar. Sandwich the 2 meringue layers together with the coffee-flavoured cream.
10. Wrap the assembled gâteau carefully in cling film and chill for 1 hour in the freezer.*
11. Transfer the gâteau from the freezer to the refrigerator 30 minutes before serving. Unwrap and pipe the top with whipped cream. Decorate with chocolate-coated coffee beans.

LONG
WEEKEND
FOR
FOUR

LONG WEEKEND
FOR FOUR

FRIDAY SUPPER
Carrot and ginger soup
Chicken fricassée
Green noodles with parsley butter
Wholemeal almond tart

SATURDAY BREAKFAST
Apricot and apple ring granola
Wholemeal rolls with orange butter
Salmon-topped kedgeree

SATURDAY LUNCH
Trawler soup
Cheese horns
Covent Garden salad
Tomato salad†
Wholemeal rolls†
Fresh fruits†

SPECIAL DINNER
Poached eggs in 'aspic'
Turkey surprises in Marsala sauce
Cheese soufflé courgettes
Sauté potatoes†
Raspberry meringue cheesecake

SUNDAY BREAKFAST
Fruit juice†
Cereal†
Lightly poached or boiled egg†
Toast†

SUNDAY LUNCH
Celery and walnut rémoulade
Leg of pork with red wine sauce
Roast potatoes†
Steamed vegetable medley
Pineapple condé

SUNDAY TEA
Wholemeal orange sponge cake
Chocolate drop biscuits
Nutty crunch cookies

LIGHT DINNER (SUNDAY)
Curried apple soup
Green vegetable pâté
Tomato cups
Mixed fruits in
butterscotch sauce
Shortbread biscuits†
Selection of cheeses†

MONDAY BRUNCH
Honey-glazed melon
French marmalade loaf
Toasted crumpets, with ham and cheese topping
Kipper and orange pâté
Preserves†
Oatcakes

FRIDAY SUPPER

CARROT GINGER SOUP

CHICKEN FRICASSÉE

GREEN NOODLES WITH PARSLEY BUTTER

WHOLEMEAL ALMOND TART

CARROT AND GINGER SOUP

375 g (¾ lb) carrots, peeled and sliced	1 teaspoon grated orange rind
600 ml (1 pint) chicken stock	2 tablespoons orange juice
1 piece of fresh root ginger, peeled	salt
40 g (1½ oz) butter	freshly ground black pepper
2 medium onions, peeled and sliced	TO GARNISH:
	4 tablespoons whipping cream, whipped
1 teaspoon ground ginger	4 small fresh parsley sprigs

Preparation time: 20 minutes
Cooking time: 35 minutes

1. Place the carrots, stock and ginger in a pan. Bring to the boil and simmer for 15 minutes. Discard the ginger. Remove and reserve 1 tablespoon of the carrot slices.
2. Melt the butter in a saucepan, add the onions and fry gently for 3 minutes. Stir in the ground ginger and cook for 1 minute. Stir in the orange rind and juice and add the carrots and stock. Cover the pan, bring to the boil and simmer for 10 minutes.
3. Purée the soup in a blender or food processor, or rub through a sieve. Return the purée to the pan and season to taste with salt and pepper.
4. To make the garnish, thinly slice the reserved carrot slices and stamp out shapes with aspic cutters.*
5. Reheat the soup. Pour into a heated tureen or individual bowls. Swirl on the whipped cream and garnish with the carrot shapes and parsley sprigs.

CHICKEN FRICASSÉE

4 chicken breasts, skinned
2 tablespoons plain flour
salt
freshly ground black
  pepper
50 g (2 oz) butter
16 shallots, peeled, or 3
  small onions, peeled
  and sliced
200 ml (1/3 pint) chicken
  stock

150 ml (1/4 pint) dry white
  wine
few parsley stalks
2 bay leaves
225 g (8 oz) small button
  mushrooms
1 egg yolk
150 ml (1/4 pint) double
  cream

Preparation time: 20 minutes
Cooking time: 1 hour

1. Coat the chicken breasts in the flour seasoned with salt and pepper.
2. Melt half the butter in a flameproof casserole, add the chicken and fry over a moderate heat until browned.
3. Remove the chicken pieces and keep warm. Add the shallots or onions to the casserole and fry, stirring frequently, for about 3 minutes. Stir in the stock, wine, parsley and bay leaves and return the chicken to the pot. Bring to the boil, then cover and simmer over a low heat for 40 minutes or until the chicken is cooked.
4. Melt the remaining butter in a small pan and gently fry the mushrooms, stirring occasionally, for 3 minutes.
5. Mix together the egg yolk and cream and stir it into the casserole. Heat very gently, without boiling. Stir in the mushrooms. Taste the sauce and adjust the seasoning if necessary. Discard the bay leaves. Serve hot.* Reheat for 25 minutes at 180°C, 350°F, Gas Mark 4. Serve with Green noodles with parsley butter.

GREEN NOODLES WITH PARSLEY BUTTER

2 garlic cloves, peeled and
  crushed
100 g (4 oz) unsalted
  butter, softened
1 teaspoon lemon juice
1/2 teaspoon grated lemon
  rind

3 tablespoons chopped
  fresh parsley
salt
1 tablespoon vegetable oil
275–350 g (10–12 oz)
  green ribbon noodles

Preparation time: 15 minutes
Cooking time: 20 minutes

The parsley butter can be made in advance and stored in the refrigerator for up to 2 weeks.

1. To make the parsley butter, beat the garlic into the butter. Gradually add the lemon juice, a few drops at a time, then beat in the lemon rind and parsley. Shape the butter into a roll and wrap it closely in foil.*
2. Bring a large pan of water to the boil, add salt and the oil and lower in the noodles. Stir to separate them. When the water returns to the boil, cover the pan and lower the heat so that the water is just boiling. Cook for 10 minutes or until the noodles are 'al dente' – tender but still firm to the bite. Drain in a colander and pour hot water through them. Drain thoroughly.
3. Turn the noodles into a heated serving dish. Slice the parsley butter into pats, add to the noodles and toss to coat them well. Serve at once.

WHOLEMEAL ALMOND TART

100 g (4 oz) wholemeal
  plain flour
50 g (2 oz) plain flour
salt
75 g (3 oz) hard margarine
50 g (2 oz) caster sugar
1 teaspoon lemon juice
1 egg, separated
ice cold water
Filling:
50 g (2 oz) soft margarine
50 g (2 oz) soft light
  brown sugar

2 eggs
50 g (2 oz) ground
  almonds
1 teaspoon almond
  essence
50 g (2 oz) seedless raisins
50 g (2 oz) blanched
  almonds, flaked or
  roughly chopped
25 g (1 oz) chopped mixed
  candied peel
soured or single cream, to
  serve

Preparation time: 30 minutes, plus chilling
Cooking time: 35 minutes
Oven: 180°C, 350°F, Gas Mark 4

1. Mix together the flour and salt and rub in the margarine until the mixture resembles fine crumbs. Stir in the sugar, lemon juice and egg yolk. Use just enough ice cold water to mix to a firm dough. Form the dough into a ball, cover with film or foil and chill for about 30 minutes.
2. To make the filling, beat together the margarine, sugar, eggs and remaining egg white until the mixture is light. Beat in the ground almonds and almond essence. Stir in the raisins, almonds and peel. Set the filling aside.
3. Knead the pastry lightly on a floured board. Roll it out and use to line a greased 18 cm (7 inch) flan dish. Trim the edges. Prick the bottom of the pastry case with a fork.
4. Pour in the filling and level the top. Roll out the pastry trimmings, cut them into thin strips and arrange on top of the filling in a trellis pattern.
5. Bake in a preheated oven for 30–35 minutes or until the filling is well risen and golden brown. Allow to cool.*
6. Serve cold, with soured cream or single cream.

SATURDAY BREAKFAST

APRICOT AND APPLE RING GRANOLA

SALMON-TOPPED KEDGEREE

WHOLEMEAL ROLLS WITH ORANGE BUTTER

APRICOT AND APPLE RING GRANOLA

5 tablespoons clear honey
3 tablespoons soft light
  brown sugar
350 g (12 oz) muesli cereal
  base
1 teaspoon grated lemon
  rind
1 teaspoon vanilla essence
2 tablespoons sunflower
  seeds
50 g (2 oz) whole
  hazelnuts
100 g (4 oz) dried apricots,
  quartered
100 g (4 oz) dried apple
  rings, quartered

Preparation time: 20 minutes
Cooking time: 30 minutes
Oven: 160°C, 325°F, Gas Mark 3

1. Heat the honey and brown sugar in a saucepan over a low heat until the sugar has dissolved. Stir in the cereal, lemon rind, vanilla, sunflower seeds and hazelnuts.
2. Spread the mixture on to 2 non-stick baking sheets. Bake in a preheated oven for 25 minutes, stirring occasionally.
3. Stir in the apricots and apple segments and leave to cool. When cold, store it in an airtight container.*
4. It is delicious served with chilled yogurt, buttermilk, milk or unsweetened fruit juices.

SALMON-TOPPED KEDGEREE

225 g (8 oz) long-grain rice
salt
½ teaspoon turmeric
100 g (4 oz) butter
225 g (8 oz) haddock fillet,
  cut into 2.5 cm (1 inch)
  strips
100 g (4 oz) button
  mushrooms, thinly
  sliced
freshly ground black
  pepper
pinch of cayenne pepper
2 tablespoons chopped
  fresh parsley
2 eggs, lightly beaten
2 hard-boiled eggs, sliced
100 g (4 oz) smoked
  salmon trimmings, cut
  into neat strips

Preparation time: 20 minutes
Cooking time: 20 minutes

1. Bring a large pan of water to the boil and add the rice, salt and turmeric. Stir to separate the grains, then return quickly to the boil and cover the pan. Lower the heat and cook for about 12 minutes or until the rice is just tender.
2. Drain the rice, refresh it in cold water and separate the grains by running hot water through it, then drain again.
3. Heat 25 g (1 oz) of the butter in a frying pan. Add the haddock strips and fry gently for about 6 minutes or until they are just cooked. Remove the haddock from the pan. Add 25 g (1 oz) of the remaining butter to the pan and gently fry the mushrooms for 3 minutes, stirring occasionally.
4. Mix together the rice, fish and mushrooms. Leave to cool, then store overnight in a covered container in the refrigerator.*
5. Just before serving, melt the remaining butter in a large frying pan, tip in the rice mixture and heat gently, stirring carefully to avoid breaking the fish. Season well with pepper and cayenne and stir in the parsley and beaten eggs.
6. Turn the kedgeree into a heated serving dish and garnish with the sliced hard-boiled eggs and strips of smoked salmon. Serve at once, with fingers of hot buttered toast.

WHOLEMEAL ROLLS

225 g (8 oz) wholemeal
  plain flour
225 g (8 oz) strong plain
  flour
2 teaspoons salt
25 g (1 oz) fresh yeast or
  15 g (½ oz) dried yeast
150 ml (¼ pint) lukewarm
  water

150 ml (¼ pint) milk
2 tablespoons vegetable
  oil
25 g (1 oz) butter, melted
2 tablespoons cracked
  wheat (optional)

Preparation time: 30 minutes, plus proving and thawing
Cooking time: 35 minutes
Oven: 220°C, 425°F, Gas Mark 7

1. Sift the flours and salt together and tip in the bran from the sieve.
2. Stir the yeast into the water and stand in a warm place for 15 minutes until frothy. Stir in the milk and oil.
3. Tip the yeast liquid into the flours and mix to a dough. Turn on to a lightly floured surface and knead for about 5 minutes or until smooth. Place the dough in a large, oiled polythene bag, seal the top and leave in a warm place until it doubles in size, about 45 minutes.
4. Remove the dough from the bag and knead it lightly. Divide it into 12 equal pieces and shape each one into a ball. Place the rolls on a greased baking sheet and enclose it in the plastic bag. Store overnight in the refrigerator.*
5. Remove the rolls from the bag and leave them to warm to room temperature for about 45 minutes. Brush them with the melted butter and sprinkle with the cracked wheat, if using.
6. Bake the rolls in a preheated oven for 30–35 minutes. To test if the rolls are cooked, lift one and tap the underside; it should sound hollow. Serve warm, with Orange butter (see below).
Makes 12.

ORANGE BUTTER

2 tablespoons icing sugar,
  sifted
2 tablespoons clear honey
2 teaspoons grated orange
  rind
100 g (4 oz) unsalted
  butter, softened

2 teaspoons orange juice
1 teaspoon lemon juice
1 large orange

Preparation time: 5 minutes

1. Beat the icing sugar, honey and orange rind into the butter. Gradually beat in the orange and lemon juices, a little at a time. Beat well.
2. Cut a small slice from the top of the orange and scoop out the flesh leaving firm 'walls'.
3. Pile the butter into the orange shell, wrap it in foil and store in the refrigerator for up to 3 days.*

SATURDAY LUNCH

A light lunch with little preparation. The salad is better if made a day in advance. The lunch can be extended with a tomato salad, any rolls left over from breakfast and fruit.

TRAWLER SOUP
CHEESE HORNS

COVENT GARDEN SALAD
TOMATO SALAD†
WHOLEMEAL ROLLS†

FRESH FRUITS†

TRAWLER SOUP

450 g (1 lb) fish trimmings
  (heads, tails, fins, bones)
2 bay leaves
1 onion, peeled and halved
1 carrot, peeled and sliced
2 celery sticks, sliced
few parsley stalks
900 ml (1½ pints) water
salt
freshly ground black
  pepper
450 g (1 lb) fresh haddock
  or cod fillet
25 g (1 oz) butter

1 large onion, peeled and
  sliced
1 garlic clove, peeled and
  crushed
1½ tablespoons plain
  flour
450 ml (¾ pint) milk
2 teaspoons lemon juice
4 tablespoons whipping
  cream, whipped
1 tablespoon chopped
  fresh parsley
TO GARNISH:
50 g (2 oz) potted shrimps
  or prawns
sprigs of parsley

Preparation time: 25 minutes
Cooking time: 1¼ hours

Make the fish stock day or two in advance: this is what gives the soup the extra depth of flavour.

1. Put the fish trimmings, bay leaves, onion, carrot, celery, parsley stalks and water into a saucepan and bring to the boil, skimming if necessary. Season with salt and pepper, then cover and simmer for 45 minutes. Strain, cool and chill in a covered container.
2. Pour 450 ml (¾ pint) of the fish stock into a saucepan. Add the fish and poach for 10–12 minutes or until just cooked. Strain the stock and reserve. Flake the fish.
3. Melt the butter in another saucepan, add the onion and garlic and fry over a moderate heat for 4 minutes, stirring occasionally. Stir in the flour and cook for 1 minute. Gradually add the milk, stirring, and cook until the mixture thickens. Stir in the fish stock, flaked fish, lemon juice, and salt and pepper to taste. Simmer for 5 minutes.
4. Purée the soup in a blender or food processor or rub it through a sieve. Taste and adjust the seasoning. Stir in the cream and the chopped parsley.*
5. Reheat the soup gently, then pour it into a heated tureen. Break up the block of potted shrimps and scatter them on top – the butter will melt into the soup. Alternatively, scatter with the prawns. Garnish with the parsley sprigs.

CHEESE HORNS

225 g (8 oz) full-fat soft
cheese
100 g (4 oz) cottage cheese
1 avocado, peeled, stoned
and chopped
1 garlic clove, peeled and
chopped
1 teaspoon paprika pepper
2 teaspoons lemon juice
large pinch of hot curry
powder
salt
freshly ground black
pepper

2 tablespoons finely
chopped fresh chives
2 tablespoons chopped
walnuts
8 slices of mortadella
sausage, about 225 g
(8 oz) total weight
8 twiglet sticks or cheese
straws
lettuce or endive leaves, to
serve

Preparation time: 20 minutes

1. To make the filling, beat together, or process in a blender or food processor, the cheeses, avocado, garlic, paprika, lemon juice and curry powder with salt and pepper to taste. Taste the mixture and add more seasoning if necessary. Store in a covered container.*
2. Just before assembling the cones, stir the chives and walnuts into the filling.
3. Spread the filling on to the slices of Mortadella, and wrap into a cone shape. Fill them with the remaining cheese filling, and stick a twiglet stick or cheese straw into the top of each one.
4. Arrange the cones on a plate lined with lettuce or endive leaves. Serve with Covent Garden Salad (see right) and the suggested tomato salad and generously buttered wholemeal rolls.

COVENT GARDEN SALAD

about 175 g (6 oz) firm red
cabbage, finely
shredded
2 heads of chicory, sliced
into rings
3 oranges, peeled and
segmented
6 spring onions, peeled
and sliced
75 g (3 oz) stoned dates,
chopped

DRESSING:
2 tablespoons clear honey
2 tablespoons orange juice
2 teaspoons grated orange
rind
5 tablespoons olive oil
salt
freshly ground black
pepper

Preparation time: 25 minutes

This is a salad that improves with standing, so you can make it a day in advance.

1. Toss together the cabbage, chicory, orange segments, spring onions and dates in a bowl. If you wish to make the salad in advance, mix it in a lidded container.
2. Put the honey into a small bowl and beat in the orange juice. When the honey has dissolved, beat in the orange rind and oil and season with salt and pepper to taste.
3. Pour the dressing over the salad and toss so that the fruit and vegetables are well coated. Cover and store in the refrigerator.* Allow to stand at room temperature for about 1 hour before serving.

SPECIAL DINNER

With this menu most of the hard work in preparing the 3 courses can be done the day before. On the actual day, there's less than 30 minutes' preparation and finishing to do.

POACHED EGGS IN 'ASPIC'

TURKEY SURPRISES IN MARSALA SAUCE

CHEESE SOUFFLÉ COURGETTES SAUTÉ POTATOES†

RASPBERRY MERINGUE CHEESECAKE

POACHED EGGS IN 'ASPIC'

4 eggs, (sizes 1, 2)	5 tablespoons medium
1 tablespoon water	sherry
2 teaspoons powdered	4 tablespoons single cream
gelatine	TO GARNISH:
1 × 275 g (10 oz) can	1 canned pimento, drained
condensed consommé	few parsley sprigs

Preparation time: 15 minutes, plus setting
Cooking time: 10 minutes

1. Lightly poach the eggs for 3 minutes or until the whites are set but the yolks are still runny. Plunge the eggs at once into cold water to prevent further cooking.
2. Put the water into a cup sprinkle on the gelatine and stand in a pan of hot water. Stir until the gelatine dissolves.
3. Heat the consommé until it melts, then stir in the gelatine and remove the pan from the heat. Stir in the sherry.
4. Spoon about 3 tablespoons of the consommé mixture into each of 4 large ramekin dishes. Chill for at least 30

minutes or until set.
5. Put 1 tablespoon of cream into each dish. Drain the eggs, pat them dry with paper towels and trim. Place an egg in each dish and spoon on enough consommé mixture just to cover them. Chill for a further 20 minutes.
6. Using aspic or petit fours cutters, cut decorative shapes from the pimento and arrange them on the eggs. Add sprigs of parsley to complete the decoration. Spoon on a thin layer of consommé mixture to 'set' the garnish. Cover the dishes with foil and chill before serving.*
7. Serve with thin brown bread and butter.

CHEESE SOUFFLÉ COURGETTES

4 medium courgettes,	salt
halved lengthways	freshly ground black
25 g (1 oz) butter	pepper
2 tablespoons plain flour	pinch of grated nutmeg
150 ml (¼ pint) milk	6 tablespoons fresh grated
2 eggs, separated	Parmesan cheese

Preparation time: 20 minutes, plus cooling
Cooking time: 35 minutes
Oven: 180°C, 350°F, Gas Mark 4

1. Using a teaspoon or vegetable baller, scoop out the flesh from each courgette half without piercing the 'walls'. Set the 'shells' aside. Steam the courgette flesh over boiling water for 5–6 minutes or until it is tender. Mash it to form a purée.
2. Melt the butter in a saucepan, stir in the flour and cook gently for 30 seconds. Gradually add the milk, stirring constantly. Bring to the boil, stirring until the sauce thickens, then simmer for 3 minutes.
3. Remove the pan from the heat. Beat in the egg yolks one at a time, then the courgette purée. Season to taste with salt, pepper and nutmeg and cool.
4. Whisk the egg whites until stiff, then fold them into the sauce with 4 tablespoons of the cheese.
5. Arrange the courgette shells, hollow sides upwards, in a greased baking dish. Fill the shells with the cheese mixture. Sprinkle the remaining cheese on top. This dish may be prepared 2–3 hours in advance, covered with foil and stored in the refrigerator.*
6. Bake in a preheated oven for 20 minutes or until the cheese filling is well risen and golden brown. Serve hot with Turkey surprises in Marsala sauce (page 102).

TURKEY SURPRISES IN MARSALA SAUCE

4 slices of turkey breast, about 100 g (4 oz) each	salt
75 g (3 oz) butter	freshly ground black pepper
4 lamb's kidneys, skinned, cored and chopped	1 tablespoon plain flour
75 g (3 oz) mushrooms, chopped	150 ml (¼ pint) chicken stock
2 tablespoons fresh white breadcrumbs	8 tablespoons Marsala
1 tablespoon chopped fresh parsley	4 tablespoons double cream
1 teaspoon dried sage	fresh sage or watercress sprigs, to garnish
2 tablespoons chicken stock	

Preparation time: 35 minutes, plus cooling
Cooking time: 30 minutes

Here's a perfect dish for entertaining – it looks impressive, can be prepared well in advance and needs very little last-minute attention.

1. Place the slices of turkey between 2 sheets of greaseproof paper on a board and flatten them by beating with a rolling pin. Cut each slice in half crossways.
2. To make the filling, melt half the butter in a frying pan, add the kidneys and mushrooms and fry over a moderate heat, stirring frequently, for 5–6 minutes or until the kidney is just cooked. Remove from the heat and stir in the breadcrumbs, herbs and chicken stock. Season to taste with salt and pepper and cool.
3. Divide the filling between the turkey slices and roll up like a Swiss roll. Secure the rolls with string. If preparing the day before, pack the rolls in a container and chill.*
4. Melt the remaining butter in a frying pan, add the turkey rolls and fry over a moderate heat for about 6 minutes, turning them so that they brown evenly.
5. Remove the rolls from the pan. Sprinkle the flour into the pan and stir to take up all the pan juices. Pour on the stock and Marsala and stir until the sauce thickens. Season to taste with salt and pepper. Return the turkey rolls to the pan, lower the heat and simmer gently for 10 minutes.
6. Just before serving remove the strings from the turkey and stir in the cream. Arrange the turkey rolls in a heated serving dish, pour on the sauce and garnish with sage or watercress.
7. Serve with Cheese soufflé courgettes (page 101) and sauté potatoes.

RASPBERRY MERINGUE CHEESECAKE

175 g (6 oz) digestive biscuits, finely crushed	1 teaspoon vanilla essence
50 g (2 oz) butter, melted	75 g (3 oz) caster sugar
½ teaspoon ground cinnamon	1 egg
	2 egg yolks
FILLING:	FRUIT TOPPING:
225 g (8 oz) low-fat soft cheese	350 g (12 oz) fresh raspberries or frozen raspberries, thawed
150 ml (¼ pint) soured cream	5 tablespoons redcurrant jelly
1 teaspoon grated lemon rind	MERINGUE TOPPING:
1 tablespoon lemon juice	2 egg whites
	100 g (4 oz) caster sugar

Preparation time: 45 minutes, plus cooling and chilling
Cooking time: 1 hour 10 minutes
Oven: 150°C, 300°F, Gas Mark 2;
*   180°C, 350°F, Gas Mark 4*

The cheesecake can be made up to 2 days in advance and stored in the refrigerator before adding the fruit and meringue topping.

1. Mix the biscuits with the melted butter and cinnamon. Press on to the bottom of a 23 cm (9 inch) flan dish. Leave the biscuit base in the refrigerator to set while you make the filling.
2. Beat together the cheese and soured cream, then beat in the lemon rind, lemon juice, vanilla and sugar. Beat in the whole egg and egg yolks, and continue beating until the mixture is smooth.
3. Pour the filling into the flan dish. Bake in a preheated oven for 1 hour or until the filling is set. Remove the cheesecake from the oven and leave to cool.*
4. To make the fruit topping, arrange the raspberries in a single layer on the filling. Melt the jelly in a small saucepan and spoon it over the fruit. Allow the jelly to cool and set, then cover the cake with foil and chill it in the refrigerator for at least 6 hours.
5. To make the meringue topping, whisk the egg whites until stiff. Whisk in half the sugar and continue whisking until the mixture is stiff and glossy. Fold in the remaining sugar with a metal spoon. Spread the meringue carefully over the fruit so that it is completely covered – otherwise the jelly will melt. Level the top of the meringue.
6. Cook in a preheated oven at the higher temperature for 10 minutes or until the meringue is golden brown. Serve immediately.

SUNDAY LUNCH

You can prepare much of this meal in advance – the salad; all the vegetables for steaming; their bacon topping; and the pudding. The slow cooking of the meat also leaves you free to do other things.

CELERY AND WALNUT RÉMOULADE

LEG OF PORK WITH RED WINE SAUCE

ROAST POTATOES†
STEAMED VEGETABLE MEDLEY

PINEAPPLE CONDÉ

CELERY AND WALNUT RÉMOULADE

1–2 tender, young celery
  hearts, thinly sliced
2 tablespoons finely
  chopped celery leaves
50 g (2 oz) walnuts,
  chopped
SAUCE:
1 hard-boiled egg yolk
1 egg yolk
1 tablespoon cider vinegar
1 tablespoon Dijon
  mustard

4 tablespoons olive oil
salt
freshly ground black
  pepper
2 tablespoons double
  cream
lettuce leaves, to serve
TO GARNISH:
8 walnut halves
2 hard-boiled eggs, sliced
pinch of paprika pepper

Preparation time: 20 minutes

1. Toss together the sliced celery, celery leaves and chopped walnuts.
2. To make the sauce, mash the hard-boiled egg yolk in a bowl and beat in the raw egg yolk. Gradually add the vinegar, a few drops at a time, stirring continuously. When all the vinegar has been incorporated, stir in the mustard. Pour on the oil, drop by drop at first and then in a thin stream, stirring vigorously all the time. Season to taste with salt and pepper, and beat in the cream.*
3. Just before serving, line a dish with lettuce leaves. Toss the vegetables in the sauce and pile the salad in the dish. Garnish with the walnut halves and egg slices, and sprinkle the egg with a little paprika to add colour.

STEAMED VEGETABLE MEDLEY

450 g (1 lb) carrots, peeled
  and cut into matchstick
  strips
350 g (12 oz) white
  turnips, peeled and cut
  into 1 cm (½ inch)
  cubes
225 g (8 oz) shallots or
  baby onions, peeled
salt

BACON TOPPING:
50 g (2 oz) butter
1 medium onion, peeled
  and chopped
2 streaky bacon rashers,
  rind removed, cut into
  1 cm (½ inch) squares
6 tablespoons fresh white
  breadcrumbs
1 tablespoon chopped
  fresh parsley

Preparation time: 45 minutes
Cooking time: 25 minutes

3 tablespoons of the carrots can be reserved after being cooked and included in the Tomato cups recipe (page 110) from the Light Dinner menu.

1. Place the vegetables in the top of a steamer, a folding steaming fan or a colander that fits over a large saucepan. Sprinkle the vegetables with salt and cover the pan. Steam over fast-boiling water for 12–15 minutes or until the vegetables are just tender.
2. Meanwhile, melt half the butter in a small frying pan, add the onion and bacon and fry over a moderate heat for 4–5 minutes, stirring occasionally. Stir in the breadcrumbs and cook for a further 2–3 minutes or until they are golden brown. Stir in the parsley. (The topping can be made in advance and reheated.)
3. Toss the vegetables in the remaining butter and turn them into a heated serving dish. Scatter over the bacon topping and serve hot to accompany Leg of pork with red wine sauce (see next page).

LEG OF PORK WITH RED WINE SAUCE

1 × 1.75 kg (4 lb) piece leg of pork
3 tablespoons plain flour
salt
freshly ground black pepper
SAUCE:
50 g (2 oz) raisins
200 ml (⅓ pint) red wine
1 tablespoon plain flour

1 tablespoon redcurrant jelly
TO GARNISH:
40 g (1½ oz) butter
3 dessert apples, cored and sliced into rings
1 teaspoon dried sage
1 teaspoon crushed dried rosemary

Preparation time: 25 minutes
Cooking time: 2¾ hours
Oven: 180°C, 350°F, Gas Mark 4

1. With a sharp knife, score the rind of the pork in criss-crossing lines to make diamond shapes. Rub the rind all over with the flour and season with salt and pepper.
2. Place the pork in a roasting tin and cook in a preheated oven for 2½ hours, turning the meat once.
3. Meanwhile, soak the raisins in the wine.
4. When the meat is cooked, transfer it to a heated carving dish and keep warm. Pour off the fat and juices from the roasting tin, leaving about 2 tablespoons in the pan. Stir in the flour, then add the raisins and wine in which they were soaked together with the redcurrant jelly, stirring constantly. Season to taste with salt and pepper. Bring to the boil and simmer for 3–4 minutes, stirring constantly. Remove from the heat and keep hot.
5. Melt the butter in a frying pan, add the apple rings and fry gently, turning them frequently, for 3 minutes. Sprinkle on the sage and rosemary and continue frying for 2–3 minutes or until the apples are evenly brown.
6. Garnish the pork with the apple rings. Serve hot, with the sauce, accompanied by roast potatoes and the Steamed vegetable medley (see previous page).

PINEAPPLE CONDÉ

50 g (2 oz) short-grain
  pudding rice
50 g (2 oz) sugar
600 ml (1 pint) milk
3 tablespoons water
1 teaspoon powdered
  gelatine

1 × 425 g (15 oz) can
  pineapple chunks
2 tablespoons kirsch
150 ml (¼ pint) whipping
  cream, whipped
8 'leaves' of candied
  angelica, to decorate

Preparation time: 20 minutes, plus cooling and setting
Cooking time: 35 minutes

1. Put the rice, sugar and milk into a saucepan and heat gently, stirring occasionally, until the sugar has dissolved. Bring to the boil and simmer, stirring occasionally, for 30 minutes or until the rice is tender and all the milk has been absorbed. Remove from the heat and allow to cool.
2. Put the water into a small bowl, sprinkle on the gelatine and stand the bowl in a pan of hot water. Stir until the gelatine has dissolved.
3. Drain the pineapple, reserving the syrup, and roughly chop about three-quarters of the chunks.
4. When the rice has cooled, stir in the kirsch, then fold in the whipped cream and the chopped pineapple. Divide the rice mixture between 4 large serving glasses and chill until set.
5. Measure 8 tablespoons of the pineapple syrup and stir in the gelatine. Leave until it is almost setting, about 20 minutes.
6. Arrange the whole pineapple chunks on top of the rice and spoon on the syrup mixture. Chill for at least 20 minutes.* Decorate each glass with angelica 'leaves'.

SUNDAY TEA

The main feature of this tea is a moist and delicious sandwich cake with a light, creamy frosting – suitable at any time of year. Both types of biscuit will store well.

WHOLEMEAL ORANGE SPONGE CAKE

NUTTY CRUNCH COOKIES

CHOCOLATE DROP BISCUITS

WHOLEMEAL ORANGE SPONGE

175 g (6 oz) self-raising
  81% wholemeal flour
1 teaspoon baking powder
175 g (6 oz) soft margarine
175 g (6 oz) demerara or
  'golden granulated'
  sugar
2 teaspoons grated orange
  rind
3 eggs
1 tablespoon orange juice

FILLING AND FROSTING:
75 g (3 oz) butter, softened
75 g (3 oz) full-fat soft
  cheese
100–150 g (4–6 oz) icing
  sugar, sifted
2 tablespoons clear honey
½ teaspoon vanilla
  essence
175 g (6 oz) apricot jam
4 slices of crystallized
  orange, to decorate

Preparation time: 20 minutes
Cooking time: 30 minutes
Oven: 160°C, 325°F, Gas Mark 3

1. Sift the flour and baking powder into a bowl and tip in the bran retained in the sieve. Add the margarine, sugar, orange rind and eggs and beat until the mixture is smooth. Stir in the orange juice, a few drops at a time.
2. Divide the mixture between 2 greased 19 cm (7½ inch) sandwich tins and level the tops.
3. Bake the sponge cake layers in a preheated oven for 25–30 minutes or until firm but springy to the touch. Stand the tins on a wire tray to cool.
4. To make the frosting, beat the butter, cheese, icing sugar, honey and vanilla essence together.
5. Spread 1 cake layer with the jam and cover it with half of the frosting. Place the other cake layer on top and spread it with the remaining frosting. Arrange the crystallized orange slices in a pattern to decorate.*

NUTTY CRUNCH COOKIES

100 g (4 oz) soft margarine
100 g (4 oz) caster sugar
5 tablespoons clear honey
1 egg, beaten
175 g (6 oz) wholemeal
   plain flour

1 teaspoon grated lemon
   rind
150 g (5 oz) chopped
   mixed nuts, e.g.
   walnuts, brazils,
   hazelnuts

Preparation time: 15 minutes
Cooking time: 15 minutes
Oven: 200°C, 400°F, Gas Mark 6

1. Beat the margarine and sugar together until light and fluffy, then gradually beat in the honey. (Dip the spoon in water and then in flour to coat it, to make it easier to measure the honey.) Beat in the egg a little at a time, adding a little flour with each addition to prevent the mixture from curdling. Beat in the remaining flour, then stir in the lemon rind and 50 g (2 oz) of the nuts.
2. Place a piece of cling film over one hand and shape the mixture into small balls then roll them in the remaining nuts. Arrange them, spaced apart, on 2 greased baking sheets.
3. Bake in a preheated oven for 12–15 minutes or until the cookies are turning crispy brown at the edges.
4. Leave the cookies to harden on the baking sheet, then transfer them to a wire tray to cool.
Store in an airtight tin.*
Makes about 28.

CHOCOLATE DROP BISCUITS

225 g (8 oz) plain flour
1 teaspoon baking powder
100 g (4 oz) caster sugar
100 g (4 oz) soft margarine

2 tablespoons golden
   syrup
2 tablespoons milk
50 g (2 oz) small plain
   chocolate drops

Preparation time: 15 minutes, plus chilling
Cooking time: 15 minutes
Oven: 190°C, 375°F, Gas Mark 5

1. Sift the flour and baking powder into a bowl and stir in the sugar. Beat in the margarine, syrup and milk to form a firm dough. Stir in the chocolate drops.
2. Knead the dough lightly until it is smooth. Shape into a long cylinder about 4 cm (1½ inches) in diameter. Slightly flatten the roll, to give an oval shape. Wrap the dough in film or foil and chill for about 1 hour.
3. Slice the dough into rounds about 5 mm (¼ inch) thick and arrange them on 2 baking sheets, spaced apart to allow them to spread.
4. Bake in a preheated oven for 12–15 minutes or until the biscuits are lightly browned.
5. Leave to cool on the baking sheets, then transfer to a wire tray until cold. Store them in an airtight tin.*
Makes about 24.

LIGHT DINNER (SUNDAY)

Apart from heating the soup, the meal is completely prepared and ready to serve, just when you feel like it. The bread, cheese and biscuits are optional extras.

CURRIED APPLE SOUP

GREEN VEGETABLE PÂTÉ

TOMATO CUPS
FRENCH BREAD†

MIXED FRUITS IN BUTTERSCOTCH SAUCE

SHORTBREAD BISCUITS†
SELECTION OF CHEESES†

CURRIED APPLE SOUP

25 g (1 oz) butter
1 medium onion, peeled and chopped
2 teaspoons mild curry powder (or to taste)
1 tablespoon plain flour
900 ml (1½ pints) chicken stock
750 g (1½ lb) cooking apples, peeled, cored and chopped

1 teaspoon lemon juice
1 tablespoon chopped fresh mint
salt
freshly ground black pepper
150 ml (¼ pint) single cream
TO GARNISH:
4 thin lemon slices
4 fresh mint sprigs

Preparation time: 15 minutes
Cooking time: 30 minutes

---

1. Melt the butter in a saucepan, add the onion and fry over a moderate heat for 3–4 minutes, stirring occasionally. Do not let the onions brown.
2. Stir in the curry powder and cook for 1 minute, then stir in the flour. Gradually pour on the stock, stirring constantly, and bring to the boil. Add the apples. Bring back to the boil, then cover and simmer for 15 minutes. Stir in the lemon juice and chopped mint.
3. Purée the soup in a blender or food processor or rub it through a sieve. Season to taste with salt and pepper. Stir in the cream.*
4. Gently reheat the soup without boiling. Taste and adjust the seasoning if necessary. Garnish each soup bowl with a slice of lemon and a sprig of mint.

GREEN VEGETABLE PÂTÉ

1 kg (2 lb) courgettes, grated
1 tablespoon coarse salt
50 g (2 oz) butter
1 small onion, peeled and grated or finely chopped
2 garlic cloves, peeled and crushed
4 eggs
300 ml (½ pint) double cream
1 tablespoon herb mustard

2 tablespoons chopped mixed fresh herbs, e.g. chervil, chives, mint, parsley
freshly ground black pepper
large pinch of cayenne pepper
225 g (8 oz) fresh spinach, rinsed and drained
TO GARNISH:
8 tablespoons shredded white cabbage
2 large carrots, peeled and grated
1 hard-boiled egg, sliced

Preparation time: 45 minutes, plus cooling and standing
Cooking time: 1¾ hours
Oven: 180°C, 350°F, Gas Mark 4

If you are short of time, you can omit the spinach, which makes a striking dark green covering for the pâté.

1. Line a well-greased 1 kg (2 lb) loaf tin with non-stick silicone paper.
2. Put the courgettes into a colander and sprinkle them with the coarse salt. Leave to drain for 30 minutes. Rinse the courgettes under cold running water, then drain again.
3. Melt the butter in a frying pan, add the onion and garlic and fry over a moderate heat for 3 minutes, stirring occasionally. Add the courgettes, stir well and cook gently for 10 minutes, stirring once or twice. Remove the pan from the heat and leave to cool.
4. Beat the eggs and cream together. Stir in the cooled vegetables, the mustard and herbs and season to taste with pepper and cayenne – it should not be too bland.
5. Pour the mixture into the prepared tin and cover the tin with foil. Stand the tin in a roasting tin and pour in about 4 cm (1½ inches) of cold water.
6. Cook in a preheated oven for 1¼ hours. Lift the pâté out of the roasting tin and cook for a further 15 minutes. Leave the pâté to cool in the tin.*
7. Strip the stalks from the spinach leaves. Place the spinach in a large saucepan of boiling salted water, cover and cook for 2 minutes. Drain the leaves, and pat them dry.
8. Turn the pâté out on to a serving dish and peel off the lining paper. Arrange the drained spinach leaves in an attractive pattern on top of the pâté. Toss the cabbage and carrots together and spread them in a ring round the pâté. Arrange the egg slices in an overlapping row along the centre of the pâté. Serve cold, cut into slices with Tomato cups (page 110).

TOMATO CUPS

8 medium tomatoes
salt
2 tablespoons mayonnaise
4 tablespoons soured
  cream
1 teaspoon horseradish
  sauce
1 teaspoon olive oil
½ teaspoon cider vinegar
3 tablespoons steamed
  sliced carrots (page
  104), chopped

2 spring onions, peeled
  and sliced
1 tablespoon finely
  chopped radishes
freshly ground black
  pepper
TO GARNISH:
1 teaspoon finely chopped
  fresh chives
1 bunch of watercress

Preparation time: 20 minutes

1. Cut a thin slice from the top of each tomato. Using a teaspoon, scoop out the seeds and most of the flesh, but take care not to pierce the 'walls'. Sprinkle inside the tomatoes with salt, then turn them upside-down to drain, while you make the filling.
2. Beat the mayonnaise, soured cream and horseradish sauce together, and stir in the oil and vinegar. Stir in the carrots, onions and radishes. Taste the filling and season it with salt and pepper, if necessary.
3. Spoon the filling into the tomato cases. Stand them in a serving dish. If preparing ahead, cover with foil and store in the refrigerator.*
4. Garnish each tomato with a pinch of chives and surround the tomatoes with watercress sprigs to serve. Pictured on previous page.

Variation: Use small amounts of lightly-cooked vegetables, such as peas, sweetcorn kernels, chopped cauliflower or green beans, and other raw vegetables.

MIXED FRUITS IN BUTTERSCOTCH SAUCE

50 g (2 oz) butter
175 g (6 oz) soft light
  brown sugar
100 g (4 oz) golden syrup
150 ml (¼ pint) whipping
  cream
½ teaspoon vanilla
  essence

450 g (1 lb) strawberries,
  hulled
2 bananas, sliced
25 g (1 oz) pistachio nuts,
  walnuts or blanched
  toasted almonds
whipped cream, to serve

Preparation time: 10 minutes
Cooking time: 10 minutes

You can use other fresh or frozen fruits for this quick but delicious dessert. Try sliced apricots or peaches, raspberries, dessert gooseberries or cherries.

1. Make the sauce first. Heat the butter, sugar and syrup gently in a small saucepan, stirring to dissolve the sugar. Bring just to simmering point and simmer for 5 minutes. Stir in the cream and vanilla essence and simmer for a further 2 minutes. Beat well, then pour the sauce into a covered container. Leave to cool, then cover and store in the refrigerator for up to 1 week.*
2. Mix the strawberries, bananas and nuts together in a serving bowl. Stir the sauce, then spoon a little over the fruit. Serve the rest of the sauce separately, with plenty of whipped cream.

MONDAY BRUNCH

HONEY-GLAZED MELON

FRENCH MARMALADE LOAF

TOASTED CRUMPETS, WITH HAM
AND CHEESE

KIPPER AND ORANGE PÂTÉ

PRESERVES†

OATCAKES

HONEY-GLAZED MELON

1 ripe honeydew melon,
   quartered and seeded
4 tablespoons clear honey
1 tablespoon lemon juice
about 225 g (8 oz)
   cherries, strawberries or
   blackberries

4 thin lemon slices, to
   decorate

Preparation time: 10 minutes, plus chilling
Cooking time: 5 minutes

---

1. Cut the melon flesh away from the skin. Cut each wedge of melon through into 1 cm (½ inch) slices, but leave them in place on the skin.
2. Melt the honey with the lemon juice in a small saucepan. Brush it over the melon flesh so that it runs down through the slices. Cover the melon and chill for at least 30 minutes.*
3. To serve, arrange a line of fruit down the centre of each melon wedge. Twist the lemon slices, spear each one with a cocktail stick and place it at one end of each slice. Pictured on next page.

FRENCH MARMALADE LOAF

1 small French loaf
50 g (2 oz) butter, softened
about 175 g (6 oz) orange
   marmalade

¼ teaspoon ground
   cinnamon
pinch of ground ginger

Preparation time: 10 minutes
Cooking time: 15 minutes
Oven: 200°C, 400°F, Gas Mark 6

---

1. Cut the French loaf into 2.5 cm (1 inch) slices, without cutting right through the base. Spread the slices on both sides with the butter.
2. Gently heat the marmalade and spices in a small pan. Stir to blend well then spread on the buttered slices.
3. Wrap the loaf in foil.* Place on a baking sheet, and heat it in a pre-heated oven for 12–15 minutes. Serve hot. Pictured on next page.

TOASTED CRUMPETS WITH HAM AND CHEESE

15 g (½ oz) fresh yeast, or
   2 teaspoons dried yeast
2 teaspoons caster sugar
600 ml (1 pint) lukewarm
   milk
450 g (1 lb) strong plain
   white bread flour
1 teaspoon salt
1 egg, beaten
50 g (2 oz) butter, melted
1 tablespoon vegetable oil
oil for frying

TOPPING:
100 g (4 oz) full-fat soft
   cheese
1 garlic clove, peeled and
   crushed
1 tablespoon chopped
   fresh marjoram, chervil
   or parsley
freshly ground black
   pepper
100 g (4 oz) cooked ham,
   sliced
50 g (2 oz) Gruyère cheese,
   grated

Preparation time: 30 minutes, plus rising
Cooking time: 10 minutes

These crumpets can be made in advance and frozen. They're also delicious with cream and jam for tea.

1. If you use fresh yeast, place it in a small bowl and mash in the sugar and 3 tablespoons of the milk to make a smooth paste. Then gradually stir in half the milk. To use dried yeast, stir the sugar into 300 ml (½ pint) of the milk and sprinkle the yeast on top. Stir the yeast liquid well and set it aside in a warm place, such as the top of a cooker, for about 20 minutes or until it becomes bubbly and frothy.
2. Sift the flour and salt into a bowl. Make a well in the middle and pour on the yeast liquid, the remaining lukewarm milk, the egg, butter and oil. Beat until the batter is light.
3. Cover the bowl and leave to rise in a warm place for 45 minutes to 1 hour or until the batter has doubled in bulk.
4. Heat a heavy frying pan over a moderate heat and brush it with a little oil. Brush oil around the inside of 7.5 cm (3 inch) metal crumpet moulds or plain pastry cutters. Place the rings on the frying pan.
5. Pour batter into the moulds or cutters to come halfway up the sides and cook for about 5 minutes or until the surface is covered with bubbles. Lift off the moulds or cutters and, using a spatula or fish slice, transfer the crumpets to a wire tray to cool.
6. Beat the cheese until softened, then beat in the garlic and herb. Season to taste with pepper.
7. Toast the crumpets on both sides until they are golden brown. Spread the holey side thickly with the cheese mixture. Top with sliced ham to cover completely and then with grated cheese. Toast the crumpets until the cheese is brown and bubbling. Serve at once. Pictured on next page.
Makes 16.

KIPPER AND ORANGE PÂTÉ

450 g (1 lb) kipper fillets
  or boneless kippers
175 g (6 oz) butter, melted
4 tablespoons orange juice
2 tablespoons grated
  orange rind

150 ml (¼ pint) whipping
  cream
freshly ground black
  pepper
40 g (1½ oz) butter
2 thin orange slices, to
  garnish

Preparation time: 15 minutes, plus chilling
Cooking time: 10 minutes

1. Cook the kippers in boiling water for about 5 minutes, then drain. Remove the skin, fins and any bones. Break the kippers into flakes.
2. Put the kippers, melted butter and orange juice into a blender and blend to a smooth purée.
3. Stir in the orange rind and cream and season with pepper. Turn the pâté into a serving dish.
4. Heat the 40 g (1½ oz) butter until it foams, then pour it through a coffee filter or piece of muslin to 'clarify' it. Pour it over the pâté, tipping the dish so that the butter forms a thin layer. Cover the dish and chill for at least 1 hour.*
5. Cut the orange slices into butterfly shapes (page 53) and use to garnish the pâté. Serve with toast.

OATCAKES

225 g (8 oz) rolled
  porridge oats
100 g (4 oz) wholemeal
  flour

½ teaspoon salt
1 teaspoon baking powder
50 g (2 oz) butter

Preparation time: 15 minutes
Cooking time: 25 minutes
Oven: 180°C, 350°F, Gas Mark 4

1. Mix the oats, flour, salt and baking powder in a bowl. Rub in the butter until the mixture resembles fine breadcrumbs, then add just enough cold water to make a firm dough.
2. Knead the dough on a lightly floured board, then roll it out to a thickness of 5 mm (¼ inch). Cut into rounds with a 5 cm (2 inch) biscuit cutter. Reroll the trimmings and cut more rounds.
3. Arrange the rounds on a greased baking sheet. Bake in a preheated oven for 20–25 minutes or until the oatcakes are golden brown. Leave them to cool a little on the sheet, then transfer to a wire tray to cool completely. Store the oatcakes in an airtight tin.*
4. Serve, buttered, with preserves.
Makes about 16.

MENUS
FOR
SIX

VEGETARIAN SPREAD
──FOR SIX──

ENDIVE SALAD

DEEP DISH VEGETABLE PIE

JACKET POTATOES WITH CHEESE
AND HERB FILLING
SPINACH OR BRAISED CABBAGE†

APRICOT SUÈDOISE

ENDIVE SALAD

DRESSING:
1 hard-boiled egg yolk
4 tablespoons olive oil
1 tablespoons cider
  vinegar
1 garlic clove, peeled and
  crushed
salt
freshly ground black
  pepper
2 green peppers, cored,
  seeded and thinly sliced

1 yellow pepper, cored,
  seeded and thinly sliced
1 red pepper, cored,
  seeded and thinly sliced
2 small onions, peeled and
  cut into rings
1 medium endive, torn
  into pieces
2 tablespoons chopped
  fresh mint
3 tablespoons unsalted
  peanuts (optional)

Preparation time: 20 minutes, plus marinating

---

1. To make the dressing, mash the egg yolk in a bowl, then gradually add the oil, stirring constantly. Stir in the vinegar, garlic, and salt and pepper to taste and mix well.
2. Mix together the pepper strips, add to the dressing and toss to coat. Cover marinate for 1 hour.*
3. Place the onions, endive and mint in a salad bowl. Just before serving, pour over the peppers and dressing and toss well. Scatter over the peanuts, if using.

DEEP DISH VEGETABLE PIE

25 g (1 oz) butter
1 teaspoon cumin seeds,
  crushed
1 teaspoon coriander
  seeds, crushed
450 g (1 lb) small carrots,
  scraped or peeled and
  quartered lengthways
225 g (8 oz) small
  potatoes, peeled or
  scraped and diced
1 medium cauliflower, cut
  into florets
225 g (8 oz) small white
  turnips, peeled and
  diced
225 g (8 oz) courgettes,
  thickly sliced
225 g (8 oz) shelled broad
  beans
225 g (8 oz) young French
  beans, topped and tailed
300 ml (½ pint) water
salt
SAUCE:
40 g (1½ oz) butter

1 medium onion, peeled
  and chopped
2 garlic cloves, peeled and
  crushed
1 tablespoon medium
  curry powder
1½ tablespoons plain
  wholemeal flour
300 ml (½ pint) single
  cream
salt
freshly ground black
  pepper
2 tablespoons chopped
  fresh parsley
PASTRY:
225 g (8 oz) plain
  wholemeal flour
2 teaspoons baking
  powder
salt
75 g (3 oz) white vegetable
  fat
50 g (2 oz) soft margarine
2 tablespoons cold water
beaten egg, to glaze

Preparation time: 35 minutes
Cooking time: 1 hour
Oven: 200°C, 400°F, Gas Mark 6

---

1. Heat the butter in a large pan and fry the seeds until they begin to pop. Add the vegetables and fry until lightly browned. Stir in the water and salt. Bring to the boil, then cover and simmer until the vegetables are just tender. Drain the vegetables, reserving the cooking liquid.
2. To make the sauce, melt the butter in a saucepan, add the onion and garlic and fry over a moderate heat for 3 minutes, stirring occasionally. Stir in the curry powder and cook for 1 minute. Stir in the flour and cook for a further 1 minute. Add 120 ml (4 fl oz) of the vegetable cooking water and stir. Add the cream and stir until the sauce thickens. Season to taste with salt and pepper. Stir the vegetables and parsley into the sauce and mix well.
3. Place a pie funnel in the centre of a 2 litre (3½ pint) deep pie dish. Spoon the vegetables and sauce into the dish and leave to cool.
4. To make the pastry, sift the flour, baking powder and salt into a bowl and stir in the bran from the sieve. Rub in the fats until the mixture resembles crumbs. Stir in the water and mix to a smooth dough.
5. Roll out the dough on a lightly floured board. Cut a strip of dough to fit the rim of the dish. Dampen the rim and press on the pastry strip. Cover the dish with the remaining dough and press to the strip on the rim. Trim the edges and flute them. Brush the pastry with beaten egg. Re-roll the pastry trimmings and cut out leaf shapes. Arrange them on the pie and brush them with beaten egg.
6. Stand the dish on a baking sheet. Bake in a preheated oven for 20–25 minutes or until the top is golden brown. Serve hot* with jacket potatoes (page 116) and a vegetable.

JACKET POTATOES WITH CHEESE AND HERB FILLING

6 medium potatoes, scrubbed
oil for brushing
150 ml (¼ pint) soured cream
75 g (3 oz) Brie, chopped
freshly ground black pepper
2 tablespoons chopped chives or spring onion
1 tablespoon chopped fresh parsley

Preparation time: 15 minutes
Cooking time: 50 minutes
Oven: 200°C, 400°F, Gas Mark 6

1. Prick the potatoes all over and brush the skins with oil.
2. Bake them in a preheated oven for 45 minutes or until they are tender.
3. Place the soured cream and Brie in a blender and purée. Season to taste with pepper and stir in the herbs.
4. When the potatoes are cooked, cut a thin slice from one long side and scoop out the 'flesh' into a bowl, being careful not to break the skins. Beat in the cheese and herb mixture. Taste and add more seasoning if necessary. Spoon the mixture back into the potato shells.
5. Replace the potato 'lids' and return them to the oven to reheat for 5 minutes. Pictured on previous page. Serve with Deep dish vegetable pie (page 114).

APRICOT SUÈDOISE

225 g (8 oz) dried apricots, soaked overnight and drained
600 ml (1 pint) water
thinly pared strip of orange rind
75 g (3 oz) sugar
150 ml (¼ pint) unsweetened orange juice
25 g (1 oz) powdered gelatine
MERINGUES: (optional)
2 egg whites
100 g (4 oz) soft light brown sugar
whipped cream, to serve

Preparation time: 30 minutes, plus overnight soaking and setting
Cooking time: 2½ hours
Oven: 120°C, 250°F, Gas Mark ½

This delicious dessert is quite rich when eaten as part of the complete menu. For this reason the crisp brown sugar meringues are optional. The crunchy meringues complement the rich fruity flavour of the Suèdoise.

1. Put the apricots and water into a saucepan with the orange rind. Bring to the boil, then cover the pan and simmer for 40 minutes or until the apricots are tender. Discard the orange rind.
2. Purée the apricots and liquid in a blender or rub them through a sieve. Return the purée to the pan. Add the sugar and stir over a low heat until it has dissolved. Simmer for 10 minutes.
3. Put the orange juice into a small heatproof bowl, sprinkle over the gelatine and stand the bowl in a pan of hot water. Stir to dissolve the gelatine. Stir the gelatine mixture into the apricot purée.
4. Rinse a 900 ml (1½ pint) decorative mould with cold water. Pour in the apricot mixture and set aside to cool. Chill for at least 2 hours or until set.
5. To make the meringues, if liked, whisk the egg whites until they are stiff. Gradually beat in the sugar and continue beating until the mixture is stiff again.
6. Line a baking sheet with 2 layers of lightly greased greaseproof paper or with non-stick silicone paper. Use a teaspoon to put blobs of the meringue mixture on to the paper.
7. Bake the meringues in a preheated oven for 1½ hours or until they are crisp and dry. Peel the meringues from the paper and cool them on a wire tray.
8. Turn out the apricot mould and top it with the meringues. Serve with whipped cream.*

SPECIAL DINNER
—FOR SIX—

VINE-LEAF PARCELS

PHEASANT WITH GRAPE SAUCE

BRAISED FENNEL
SAUTE POTATOES†

BLACKCURRANT MERINGUE
BASKET

VINE-LEAF PARCELS

2 × 225 g (8 oz) canned or
   bottled vine leaves,
   drained
salt
½ teaspoon ground
   turmeric
175 g (6 oz) long-grain rice
2 tablespoons vegetable
   oil
1 small onion, peeled and
   finely chopped
100 g (4 oz) dried apricots,
   finely chopped

50 g (2 oz) sultanas
pinch of ground cinnamon
pinch of ground allspice
1 tablespoon chopped
   fresh mint
½ teaspoon sugar
1 teaspoon lemon juice
300 ml (½ pint)
   unsweetened orange
   juice
150 ml (¼ pint) water

Preparation time: 45 minutes, plus cooling and chilling
Cooking time: 1 hour

1. Unroll the vine leaves carefully and put them into a bowl of water to remove the preserving liquid. Pat them dry on paper towels. You will need to use about 30 leaves; reserve the remainder.
2. Bring a large saucepan of salted water to the boil and stir in the turmeric. Add the rice and simmer for 10 minutes or until the rice is just tender. Drain the rice thoroughly and turn into a bowl.
3. Heat the oil in a small frying pan. Add the onion and fry over a moderate heat for 3–4 minutes, stirring occasionally.
4. Add the onion to the rice in the bowl, with the apricots, sultanas, spices, mint, sugar and lemon juice. Mix well together.
5. Take 1 vine leaf at a time. Place it flat on the work surface and put 1 heaped teaspoon of the rice mixture in the centre. Fold the base of the leaf over the filling, then fold over first one side, then the other. Fold over the top to make a neat parcel. Continue making parcels until you have used up all the filling.
6. Line a large frying pan with leftover vine leaves. Arrange the parcels, seam sides down, in a single layer in the pan. Cover the layer with more leaves, then make a second layer of parcels and cover them with leaves.
7. Pour on the orange juice and water and cover the pan. Cook gently over a low heat for 1 hour, adding a little boiling water from time to time, if necessary.
8. To serve warm, allow the parcels to cool slightly in the pan, then arrange uncooked vine leaves on a flat serving dish and carefully transfer the parcels to the dish. Serve immediately.
9. To serve cold, allow the parcels to cool completely in the pan, then arrange on top of uncooked vine leaves on a serving dish as above. Cover and chill.*

BRAISED FENNEL

6 small bulbs of fennel
salt
2 teaspoons lemon juice
40 g (1½ oz) butter
200 ml (7 fl oz) chicken
  stock

freshly ground black
  pepper
2 tablespoons chopped
  fresh parsley

Preparation time: 10 minutes
Cooking time: 25 minutes

1. Cut off the bases of the fennel bulbs and pull away any stringy or discoloured outer sheaths. Cut each bulb in half lengthways.
2. Cook the fennel in a saucepan of boiling salted water, with the lemon juice, for 10 minutes. Drain.
3. Place the butter and chicken stock in the clean pan and bring to the boil. Add the fennel and season to taste with salt and pepper. Simmer for 10–15 minutes or until the fennel is just tender and most of the stock has evaporated.
4. Stir in the parsley. Serve hot.* To reheat, place the fennel in a casserole and put in to the oven heated to 180°C, 350°F, Gas Mark 4 for 10–12 minutes.

PHEASANT WITH GRAPE SAUCE

3 small pheasants, thawed
  if frozen
75 g (3 oz) butter
salt
freshly ground black
  pepper
1 small onion, peeled and
  sliced
250 ml (8 fl oz) dry white
  wine
few parsley stalks
1 bay leaf

SAUCE:
250 ml (8 fl oz) dry white
  wine
225 g (8 oz) white grapes,
  seeded
2 tablespoons plain flour
300 ml (½ pint) soured
  cream
6 small bunches of white
  grapes, to garnish

Preparation time: 15 minutes
Cooking time: 1 hour
Oven: 180°C, 350°F, Gas Mark 4

1. Wipe the pheasants inside and out with a damp cloth and dry them. Put 15 g (½ oz) of the butter inside each bird and season them with salt and pepper.
2. Melt the remaining butter in a roasting tin and brown the pheasants over a moderate heat, turning them frequently. Add the onion, wine, parsley and bay leaf and bring to the boil.
3. Cover the tin with foil and place it in a preheated oven. Roast for 35–40 minutes, turning the pheasants once or twice.
4. Remove the pheasants from the tin and split each one in half. Arrange on a heated serving dish, cover with foil and keep warm. Strain the cooking liquid into a small saucepan.
5. To make the sauce, put the wine and grapes into another saucepan, bring to the boil and simmer for 5 minutes.
6. Meanwhile, skim the fat from the top of the cooking liquid and mix it with the flour to make a paste. Bring the cooking liquid to the boil, stir in the paste and stir until the mixture boils and thickens.
7. Add the wine and grapes. Stir in the soured cream and heat through without boiling. Taste and add more seasoning if necessary.
8. Pour a little of the sauce over the pheasants and serve the rest separately. Garnish the dish with the bunches of grapes.
9. Serve with Braised fennel (see previous page) and Sauté potatoes.

BLACKCURRANT MERINGUE BASKET

3 egg whites
175 g (6 oz) caster sugar
2 tablespoons icing sugar,
  sifted
FILLING:
450 g (1 lb) blackcurrants

50–75 g (2–3 oz)
  granulated sugar
2 tablespoons cassis
  (blackcurrant liqueur)
1 tablespoon cornflour
2 tablespoons water
whipped cream, to serve

Preparation time: 25 minutes, plus cooling
Cooking time: 2 hours
Oven: 120°C, 250°F, Gas Mark ½

1. Whisk the egg whites until stiff. Add half the caster sugar and whisk again until the mixture is stiff. Using a metal spoon, fold in the remaining caster sugar.
2. Line a baking sheet with 2 layers of greaseproof paper or with non-stick silicone paper. Draw an 18 cm (7 inch) circle on the paper. Lightly grease the greaseproof paper, if using.
3. Using a 1 cm (½ inch) plain nozzle, pipe a round of the meringue mixture inside the circle, then pipe a 'wall' all around the edge of the round. Dredge the meringue basket all over with the icing sugar.
4. Bake the meringue basket in a preheated oven for 2 hours or until it is firm and dry. Peel off the paper and leave the meringue basket on a wire tray to cool.
5. Put the blackcurrants into a small saucepan with the sugar (the exact amount depends on the sweetness of the fruit). Cook over a low heat until the juice runs. Increase the heat, bring to the boil and simmer until the fruit is tender. Stir in the liqueur.
6. Mix the cornflour to a smooth paste with the water. Add to the blackcurrants and bring to the boil. Boil, stirring continuously, until the fruit juice thickens and becomes clear. Remove from the heat. Cover the top with a piece of dampened greaseproof paper to prevent a skin from forming. Leave to cool.*
7. About 1 hour before serving, spoon the blackcurrant filling into the meringue basket and level the top. Serve with whipped cream.

PANCAKE DAY
FOR SIX

SPINACH PANCAKES WITH HAM
AND MUSHROOMS
or
HERB PANCAKES WITH CHICKEN
FILLING

MIXED SALAD†

BUCKWHEAT BLINIS WITH ZINGY
ORANGE SNOW AND ORANGES IN
CARAMEL SAUCE
or
FRANGIPANE CREAM AND PEACH
SAUCE

SPINACH PANCAKES WITH HAM AND MUSHROOMS

75 g (3 oz) plain flour
1 teaspoon salt
2 eggs
200 ml (7 fl oz) milk
75 g (3 oz) butter, melted
225 g (8 oz) frozen
    spinach, thawed and
    liquidized
pinch of freshly grated
    nutmeg
oil for frying
25 g (1 oz) Parmesan
    cheese, grated
FILLING:
40 g (1½ oz) butter

1 small onion, peeled and
    finely chopped
100 g (4 oz) mushrooms,
    chopped
1 tablespoon plain flour
300 ml (½ pint) single
    cream
100 g (4 oz) cooked ham,
    fat removed, finely
    chopped
1 tablespoon chopped
    fresh parsley
freshly ground black
    pepper

Preparation time: 30 minutes, plus standing
Cooking time: 1 hour 20 minutes
Oven: 180°C, 350°F, Gas Mark 4

1. Sift the flour and salt into a bowl. Beat in the eggs. Gradually beat in the milk and 25 g (1 oz) of the melted butter. Stir in the spinach purée and nutmeg. Cover the bowl and leave the batter to stand for at least 1 hour.
2. To make the filling, melt the butter in a small saucepan. Add the onion and mushrooms and fry over a moderate heat for 3 minutes, stirring occasionally. Stir in the flour and cook for 1 minute, then gradually pour on the cream, stirring constantly. Bring to the boil, stirring and simmer for 2 minutes. Stir in the ham, parsley and pepper to taste and remove from the heat.
3. Make the pancakes as described in steps 3 and 4 of Herb pancakes (see right).
4. Divide the filling between the pancakes, spreading it in a line along the centre. Roll up the pancakes. Arrange them in a greased baking dish and brush them with the remaining melted butter. Sprinkle them with the cheese.*
5. Reheat the pancakes, uncovered, in a preheated oven for 15 minutes. Serve hot with a mixed salad.

HERB PANCAKES WITH CHICKEN FILLING

100 g (4 oz) plain flour
1 teaspoon salt
1 egg
1 egg yolk
275 ml (9 fl oz) milk
75 g (3 oz) butter, melted
2 tablespoons chopped
    fresh parsley
2 tablespoons chopped
    fresh tarragon
oil for frying
FILLING:
225 g (8 oz) low-fat
    cottage cheese

225 g (8 oz) full-fat soft
    cheese
2 eggs, beaten
225 g (8 oz) cooked
    chicken meat, finely
    chopped
1 tablespoon chopped
    fresh parsley
salt
freshly ground black
    pepper
pinch of cayenne pepper
25 g (1 oz) Parmesan
    cheese, grated

Preparation time: 30 minutes, plus 1 hour standing
Cooking time: 1¼ hours
Oven: 180°C, 350°F, Gas Mark 4

1. Sift the flour and salt into a bowl. Beat in the egg and egg yolk. Gradually beat in the milk and then 25 g (1 oz) of the melted butter. Cover the bowl and leave the batter to stand for at least 1 hour.
2. To make the filling, beat together the cottage cheese, soft cheese and eggs. Stir in the chicken and parsley and season well with salt, pepper and cayenne. Set aside.
3. Stir the parsley and tarragon into the batter. Heat a 12.5 cm (5 inch) pancake or frying pan and lightly brush the bottom with oil. Pour in about 2 tablespoons of the batter and tilt the pan so that the batter covers the bottom evenly. Cook over a moderate heat for about 3 minutes or until bubbles appear on the surface of the pancake. Flip or turn it over and cook the other side for 2–3 minutes or until golden brown. If possible, use 2 pans to halve the cooking time.
4. As each pancake is cooked, stack it on a plate, cover with foil and keep warm while you cook the remaining pancakes in the same way.
5. Divide the filling between the pancakes, spreading it in a line along the centre. Roll up the pancakes. Arrange them in a greased baking dish and brush them with the remaining melted butter. Sprinkle them with the cheese.*
6. Reheat the pancakes, uncovered, in a preheated oven for 15 minutes. Serve hot with a mixed salad.
Makes about 12.

Variations:
PLAIN PANCAKES Omit the parsley and tarragon from the batter.
FIBRE-FULL PANCAKES Substitute plain wholemeal flour for the plain flour – the result is surprisingly light, 'nutty' and delicious.

BUCKWHEAT BLINIS

225 g (8 oz) plain flour
pinch of salt
2 teaspoons dried yeast
600 ml (1 pint) lukewarm
   milk
1 teaspoon caster sugar
225 g (8 oz) buckwheat
   flour, sifted

2 eggs (sizes 1, 2),
   separated
40 g (1½ oz) butter,
   melted
oil for frying

Preparation time: 20 minutes, plus standing
Cooking time: 50 minutes

Stand all mixing utensils in a warm place before using. You can make the Blinis in advance and keep them warm.

1. Sift the plain flour and salt into a large bowl. Put the yeast into a cup and stir in 3 tablespoons of the milk and the sugar. Stir until the yeast has dissolved, then pour the mixture into the flour and stir well. Pour on half of the remaining milk, beating all the time, and beat until the batter is smooth. Cover the bowl and leave it in a warm place for 30 minutes or until the batter is light and frothy and has doubled in bulk.
2. Beat the buckwheat flour into the batter alternately with the remaining milk. Beat in the egg yolks one at a time, then the melted butter. Whisk the egg whites until stiff and fold them into the batter. Cover the bowl and leave it in a warm place for a further 30 minutes or until the batter has doubled in bulk again.
3. Heat two 12.5 cm (5 inch) heavy frying pans and brush the bottoms lightly with oil.
4. Pour about 3 tablespoons of the batter into each pan and tilt the pans so that the batter covers the bottoms evenly. Cook over a moderate heat for about 3 minutes or until bubbles appear on the surface of the pancakes. Flip the pancakes over and cook the other sides for 2–3 minutes or until golden brown.
5. Pile the cooked pancakes on a heated plate, cover them with foil and keep hot over a pan of simmering water while you cook the remaining pancakes in the same way.* Spoon Zingy orange snow on top (see below). Makes about 14.

ZINGY ORANGE SNOW

225 g (8 oz) full-fat soft
   cheese
25 g (1 oz) caster sugar
grated rind of 1 small
   orange
grated rind of 1 small
   lemon

2 tablespoons orange
   liqueur
1 teaspoon lemon juice
150 ml (¼ pint) double
   cream, whipped
1 orange, peeled and
   segmented, to decorate

Preparation time: 15 minutes, plus chilling

---

1. Cream together the soft cheese and sugar. When the mixture is well blended, beat in the orange and lemon rinds. Stir in the liqueur and lemon juice a little at a time. Beat the mixture until it is smooth. Gently fold in the whipped cream.
2. Pile the mixture into a serving dish, cover and chill.*
3. Arrange the orange segments on top before serving.

PEACH SAUCE

1 tablespoon lemon juice
200 ml (7 fl oz) plus 1
   tablespoon water
100 g (4 oz) sugar
750 g (1½ lb) peaches,
   peeled, stoned and
   sliced

3 teaspoons arrowroot
3 drops of almond essence
4 tablespoons brandy

Preparation time: 15 minutes
Cooking time: 20 minutes

---

1. Put the lemon juice, 200 ml (7 fl oz) of the water and the sugar into a saucepan and stir over a low heat until the sugar has dissolved. Crack a few of the peach stones and add the kernels to the syrup. Bring the syrup to the boil and boil for 5 minutes. Remove the peach kernels.
2. Add the peaches to the syrup and simmer for 5–10 minutes or until they are tender.
3. Mix the arrowroot to a paste with the remaining water. Add to the peach mixture and stir until the sauce thickens and becomes transparent. Stir in the almond essence and brandy and bring to the boil.* Serve hot or cold with Frangipane cream (see next page).

FRANGIPANE CREAM

2 egg yolks
50 g (2 oz) caster sugar
40 g (1½ oz) plain flour
300 ml (½ pint) boiling
  milk.
50 g (2 oz) ground
  almonds

¼ teaspoon almond
  essence
4 tablespoons blanched
  almonds, toasted

Preparation time: 15 minutes, plus chilling
Cooking time: 20 minutes

---

1. In a heatproof bowl or the top of a double boiler, stir together the egg yolks, sugar and flour. Gradually pour on the milk, stirring all the time.
2. Put the bowl or pan over a pan of simmering water and stir over a moderate heat until the custard thickens, about 10–15 minutes.
3. Remove from the heat and stir in the ground almonds and almond essence. Allow to cool. Cover the surface with a piece of dampened greaseproof paper to prevent a skin forming, and chill for at least 30 minutes.*
4. Just before serving, stir in the toasted almonds and spoon into individual serving dishes. Decorate with chocolate curls (page 50). Serve accompanied by Peach sauce (see previous page).

ORANGES IN CARAMEL SAUCE

6 large oranges
300 ml (½ pint) water
225 g (8 oz) sugar

2 tablespoons orange
  liqueur

Preparation time: 20 minutes, plus chilling
Cooking time: 20 minutes

---

1. Thinly pare the rind from 2 of the oranges, using a vegetable peeler or sharp knife. Pare away any white pith on the inside. Cut the rind into matchstick strips.
2. Place the water in a saucepan and bring to the boil. Add the strips of rind and boil for 5 minutes. Drain, reserving the liquid. Refresh the rind in cold water, then drain again. Set aside.
3. Measure 150 ml (¼ pint) of the liquid into a small saucepan, add the sugar and stir over a low heat until it has dissolved. Bring to the boil and boil for 5 minutes. Stir the orange rind strips and liqueur into the syrup and bring back to the boil. Boil for a further 5 minutes. Set aside to cool.
4. Peel all the oranges, removing every trace of white pith. Slice them very thinly, discarding the pips. Pour over the syrup and chill.*

SUMMER LUNCH
FOR SIX

COLD CHERRY SOUP

QUENELLES WITH PRAWN SAUCE

LEAF SPINACH WITH ALMONDS
FLUFFY RICE†

SEMOLINA SPONGE GÂTEAU

COLD CHERRY SOUP

225 g (8 oz) caster sugar
1 cinnamon stick
900 ml (1½ pints) plus 2
   tablespoons water
500 g (1 lb 2 oz) fresh
   morello cherries,
   stoned, or canned
   cherries, drained

175 ml (6 fl oz) dry red
   wine
1 tablespoon arrowroot
4 tablespoons soured
   cream, to serve
   (optional)

Preparation time: 20 minutes, plus chilling
Cooking time: 45 minutes

1. Put the sugar, cinnamon and 900 ml (1½ pints) of the water into a saucepan and stir over a low heat until the sugar has dissolved. Bring to the boil and boil gently for 5 minutes.
2. Chop the cherries if preferred and add to the pan. Return the syrup to the boil and simmer for 30 minutes. (If using canned cherries, simmer for only 10 minutes.)

3. Remove the cinnamon, stir in the wine.

4. Mix the arrowroot to a paste with the remaining water and stir in a little of the syrup. Add the arrowroot mixture to the pan. Bring to the boil, stirring constantly, and simmer for 2–3 minutes or until clear and thickened.

5. Allow the soup to cool, then chill in a covered container in the refrigerator.*

6. To serve, swirl the soured cream on top if liked.

LEAF SPINACH WITH ALMONDS

1 kg (2¼ lb) fresh spinach
salt
65 g (2½ oz) butter

6 tablespoons flaked almonds
freshly ground black pepper

Preparation time: 10 minutes
Cooking time: 15 minutes

When fresh spinach is not in season, use 1 kg (2 lb) green broccoli spears instead.

1. Strip off the tough stalks from the spinach. Rinse it thoroughly and drain.

2. Put the spinach into a large saucepan of boiling salted water, stir well and cover the pan. Cook over a moderate heat for 10 minutes or until the leaves are tender but have not completely collapsed.

3. Meanwhile, melt 25 g (1 oz) of the butter in a small frying pan. Add the flaked almonds and fry over a moderate heat for 5 minutes, stirring to brown them evenly.

4. Drain the spinach well, pressing out all excess moisture.

5. Melt the remaining butter in the saucepan and stir in the spinach. Season well with salt and pepper and stir until the spinach is heated through.

6. Garnish with the almonds and serve hot.

QUENELLES WITH PRAWN SAUCE

250 ml (8 fl oz) milk
75 g (3 oz) butter
100 g (4 oz) plain flour,
    sifted, plus extra for
    coating
salt
450 g (1 lb) lemon sole
    fillets, skinned
1 teaspoon grated lemon
    rind
6 eggs
freshly ground white
    pepper
½ teaspoon ground
    coriander

200 ml (7 fl oz) double
    cream, whipped
SAUCE:
350 g (12 oz) prawns
1 bay leaf
1 small onion, peeled and
    sliced
few parsley stalks
1.2 litres (2 pints) water
25 g (1 oz) butter
25 g (1 oz) plain flour
150 ml (¼ pint) single
    cream
TO GARNISH:
sprigs of watercress
paprika pepper

Preparation time: 45 minutes, plus overnight chilling
Cooking time: 35 minutes

1. Put the milk and butter into a saucepan and bring to the boil. Remove from the heat. Add the flour all at once with ½ teaspoon salt, and beat to a smooth paste. This should form a ball and be glossy. Leave the paste until cold.
2. Mince the fish twice through the finest blade of the mincer, or process it in a food processor. Put the fish into a bowl. Separate 3 of the eggs. Beat the 3 egg whites into the fish, then add the cooled flour paste. Cover the bowl and chill for 15 minutes.
3. Add the 3 egg yolks and beat until the mixture is smooth. Beat in the 3 whole eggs and season to taste with salt, pepper and coriander. Beat in the double cream and continue beating until the mixture is smooth again.
4. Using 2 tablespoons, divide the mixture into 12 large egg shapes. Roll them in flour twice to coat them.
5. Arrange the quenelles on a floured baking sheet, lightly cover them and chill overnight.
6. Peel the prawns and put all the shells and trimmings into a saucepan. Add the bay leaf, onion, parsley and water. Cover the pan, bring to the boil and simmer for 45 minutes. Remove from the heat and strain the stock, discarding the shells and flavourings. Reserve the peeled prawns.*
7. Put the prawn stock into a shallow saucepan. Bring to simmering point.
8. Lower the quenelles into the stock, return to simmering point and cover the pan. Cook over a very low heat for 20 minutes. Carefully lift out the quenelles with a slotted spoon and keep them warm on a serving dish. Reserve the stock.
9. To make the sauce, melt the butter in a small saucepan, stir in the flour and cook for 1 minute. Gradually stir in 200 ml (7 fl oz) of the reserved prawn stock. Bring to the boil, stirring, and simmer for 3 minutes. Stir in the single cream, and season to taste with salt and pepper. Add the reserved prawns and heat through without boiling.
10. Pour the sauce over the quenelles. Garnish the dish with the watercress sprigs and sprinkle with paprika.
11. Serve with Leaf spinach with almonds (page 125) and fluffy rice.

SEMOLINA SPONGE GÂTEAU

3 eggs, separated
100 g (4 oz) caster sugar
grated rind of ½ lemon
1 tablespoon lemon juice
50 g (2 oz) ground
    semolina
25 g (1 oz) ground
    almonds
CREAM:
grated rind of ½ lemon

3 tablespoons icing sugar,
    sifted
300 ml (½ pint) whipping
    cream, whipped
3 tablespoons whisky
175 g (6 oz) lemon curd
thin slices of lemon, to
    decorate

Preparation time: 15 minutes, plus cooling
Cooking time: 30 minutes
Oven: 180°C, 350°F, Gas Mark 4

1. Beat together the egg yolks and sugar until they are thick and light in colour. (If not using an electric mixer, do this in a heatproof bowl over a pan of simmering water.) Beat in the lemon rind, lemon juice, semolina and ground almonds.
2. Stiffly whisk the egg whites and fold them into the mixture.
3. Turn the mixture into a greased and floured 20 cm (8 inch) sandwich tin. Bake in a preheated oven for 30 minutes.
4. Allow the cake to cool for a few minutes in the tin, then turn it out on to a wire tray to cool completely.
5. Stir the lemon rind and sugar into the cream, then gradually stir in the whisky, a little at a time.
6. With a sharp knife, split the cake into 2 layers. Spread the bottom layer with the lemon curd and then with half the cream. Replace the top layer of the cake and spread it with the remaining cream. Draw a fork across the cream in parallel lines, then draw it across at right angles to decorate the top. Cut the lemon slices in half and arrange them on the top in 'butterfly' shapes* (page 53).

THEATRE SUPPER
FOR SIX

In this menu for an after-theatre supper, the lamb cutlets are all ready, the salad is tossed, the tarts are made. You just have to heat the soup and garnish the salad.

DOMINIC'S MUSHROOM SOUP

LAMB CUTLETS PIMENTO

DUNMOW SALAD
HOT HERBY FRENCH BREAD†

LINZER CREAM TARTS WITH RASPBERRY SAUCE

DOMINIC'S MUSHROOM SOUP

50 g (2 oz) butter
350 g (12 oz) dark mushrooms, finely chopped
1 onion, peeled and sliced
300 ml (½ pint) chicken stock
25 g (1 oz) plain flour
600 ml (1 pint) milk
6 tablespoons medium sherry

salt
freshly ground black pepper
6 tablespoons double cream
TO GARNISH:
50 g (2 oz) button mushrooms, thinly sliced
1 tablespoon chopped fresh parsley

Preparation time: 10 minutes
Cooking time: 30 minutes

1. Melt 25 g (1 oz) of the butter in a saucepan. Add the mushrooms and onion and fry over a moderately low heat for 5 minutes. Stir in the stock and bring to the boil, then cover the pan and simmer for 20 minutes.
2. Sieve the mushroom mixture, or purée in a blender or food processor. Set aside.
3. Melt the remaining butter in the saucepan, stir in the flour and cook for 1 minute. Pour on the milk slowly, stirring all the time. Bring to the boil, stirring, then simmer for 3 minutes.
4. Stir in the mushroom purée and sherry, and season to taste with salt and pepper. Bring to the boil again, then stir in the cream and heat through without boiling.*
5. Ladle the soup into individual bowls. Float the sliced mushrooms on top and sprinkle them with the parsley.

LAMB CUTLETS PIMENTO

2 best ends of neck of
  lamb, 6 cutlets each
salt
freshly ground black
  pepper
1 tablespoon paprika
  pepper
SAUCE:
1 × 225 g (8 oz) can
  pimentos, drained

1 tablespoon tomato
  purée
2 tomatoes, skinned and
  chopped
3 egg yolks
1 teaspoon lemon juice
300 ml (½ pint) olive oil
salt
freshly ground black
  pepper

Preparation time: 25 minutes, plus cooling
Cooking time: 50 minutes
Oven: 160°C, 325°F, Gas Mark 3

1. Trim the racks of lamb, exposing 2.5 cm (1 inch) of each bone at the tops of the cutlets. Trim away any excess fat then pull off the skin from the meat. Season the meat with salt, pepper and the paprika and place it in a roasting tin, fat side down.
2. Roast the meat in a preheated oven for 40 minutes, turning the meat once.
3. Remove the meat from the tin and place it on a wire tray to cool. When it is cold, cut it into individual cutlets.
4. To make the sauce, put the pimentos, tomato purée and tomatoes into a small saucepan. Bring to the boil and boil for 5 minutes. Purée in a blender or food processor, or press through a sieve. Leave to cool.
5. Put the egg yolks in a bowl and beat in the lemon juice. Gradually beat in the oil, beginning by adding it a few drops at a time and then in a slow, steady stream. Season to taste with salt and pepper.
6. Stir the pimento purée into the mayonnaise. Taste and adjust the seasoning. It should be spicy.
7. To serve, put a small cutlet frill on the end of each cutlet. Arrange the cutlets in a wheel pattern on a serving dish. Place the sauce in a bowl in the centre.* Serve with Dunmow salad (see below) and Hot herby French bread.

DUNMOW SALAD

40 g (1½ oz) butter
4 garlic cloves, peeled and
  crushed
4 large slices of white
  bread, 1 cm (½ inch)
  thick, crusts removed,
  cubed
6 back bacon rashers, rind
  removed, diced
1 small lettuce, separated
  into leaves
1 bunch of watercress,
  stalks removed
2 heads of chicory,
  trimmed and sliced

DRESSING:
4 tablespoons olive oil
1 tablespoon cider vinegar
½ teaspoon mustard
  powder
pinch of sugar
2 teaspoons buttermilk or
  plain unsweetened
  yoghurt
salt
freshly ground black
  pepper

Preparation time: 15 minutes, plus cooling
Cooking time: 10 minutes

1. Melt the butter in a frying pan. Add the garlic and fry over a moderate heat for 1 minute. Add the bread cubes and fry, stirring frequently, until golden brown on all sides. Remove the croûtons with a slotted spoon and drain on paper towels. Set aside to cool.
2. Fry the bacon dice in the pan, adding a little more butter if necessary. When the bacon is crisp, drain on paper towels and leave to cool.
3. Place the lettuce, watercress sprigs and chicory in a salad bowl and toss to mix.
4. Mix together all the ingredients for the dressing with salt and pepper to taste.*
5. Just before serving, pour the dressing over the salad and toss to coat the greens thoroughly. Scatter the croûtons and bacon over the salad and serve with hot herby French bread.

LINZER CREAM TARTS WITH RASPBERRY SAUCE

275 g (10 oz) plain flour
175 g (6 oz) unsalted
  butter
100 g (4 oz) caster sugar
2 egg yolks
FILLING:
25 g (1 oz) butter
300 ml (½ pint) single
  cream
25 g (1 oz) plain flour

50 g (2 oz) caster sugar
2 egg yolks, beaten
1 teaspoon vanilla essence
sifted icing sugar, to
  dredge
SAUCE:
450 g (1 lb) raspberries
75 g (3 oz) sugar
1 teaspoon lemon juice

Preparation time: 30 minutes, plus chilling
Cooking time: 20 minutes
Oven: 200°C, 400°F, Gas Mark 6

1. To make the pastry, sift the flour into a bowl and rub in the butter until the mixture resembles crumbs. Stir in the sugar, then the egg yolks and mix to a smooth dough. Knead lightly, then cover the dough and chill for 30 minutes.
2. To make the custard filling, melt the butter with 175 ml (6 fl oz) of the cream in a small heavy saucepan. Stir together the flour, sugar and remaining cream and add to the pan. Beat well until smooth. Pour a little of the mixture on to the egg yolks and stir well, then pour into the pan. Stir over a very low heat for 5 minutes or until the custard thickens. Stir in the vanilla essence. Remove the pan from the heat and allow the filling to cool.
3. Roll out the dough on a floured surface and cut into 24 rounds using a 6.5 cm (2½ inch) cutter. Line 12 greased tartlet tins with half the dough rounds and prick them well with a fork.
4. Divide the filling between the 12 pastry cases. Dampen the pastry rims and press on the remaining dough rounds to make lids.
5. Bake the tarts in a preheated oven for 10 minutes or until they are lightly browned. Transfer them to a wire tray. Dredge the tops with icing sugar and leave to cool.
6. For the sauce, put the raspberries, sugar and lemon juice into a blender and process for a few seconds. Sieve the raspberry purée to remove the pips. Taste and add more sugar if necessary.*
7. Serve the tarts cold, with the sauce.
Makes 12.

WINTER TEA
—— FOR SIX ——

WATERCRESS SPREAD SANDWICHES

CHERRY SHORTBREAD
LEMONY MELTING MOMENTS
STICKY DATE AND ORANGE CAKE
SUGAR-CRUSTED SCONE FINGERS

WATERCRESS SPREAD SANDWICHES

1 small wholemeal loaf	2 bunches of watercress,
50 g (2 oz) butter, softened	stalks removed
100 g (4 oz) full-fat soft	freshly ground black
cheese	pepper
2 hard-boiled egg yolks	pinch of cayenne pepper

Preparation time: 15 minutes, plus chilling

1. Thinly slice the bread.
2. Beat together the butter and cream cheese, then beat in the egg yolks. Reserve some sprigs of watercress for garnishing, and finely chop the remainder. Beat the chopped watercress into the cheese mixture and season to taste with pepper and cayenne.
3. Spread half the bread slices with the filling and top with the remaining bread slices. Stamp out 6 cm (2½ inch) rounds, or star or 'club' shapes, using cutters.
4. Arrange the sandwiches on a plate and garnish them with the reserved watercress sprigs. Cover the plate with cling film or foil and chill.*

CHERRY SHORTBREAD

225 g (8 oz) plain flour	225 g (8 oz) butter, at
100 g (4 oz) icing sugar	room temperature
plus extra to dredge	175 g (6 oz) glacé cherries,
100 g (4 oz) cornflour	rinsed, drained and
	chopped

Preparation time: 15 minutes
Cooking time: 40–50 minutes
Oven: 160°C, 325°F, Gas Mark 3

1. Sift together the flour, icing sugar and cornflour. Beat the butter until it is soft, then gradually beat in the flour mixture. Stir in the chopped cherries and mix to a firm dough. Knead the dough in the bowl until it is smooth.
2. Press the dough into a greased and floured 28 × 18 cm (11 × 7 inch) baking tin and smooth the top. Prick the shortbread all over with a fork.
3. Bake in a preheated oven for 40–50 minutes.
4. Cut the shortbread into fingers and dredge with icing sugar. Leave in the tin to cool.*
Makes about 20.

LEMONY MELTING MOMENTS

100 g (4 oz) butter	150 g (5 oz) self-raising
75 g (3 oz) caster sugar	flour
1 egg yolk	4 tablespoons bran flakes,
grated rind of 1 lemon	crushed

Preparation time: 15 minutes
Cooking time: 20 minutes
Oven: 190°C, 375°F, Gas Mark 5

1. Cream together the butter and sugar until light and fluffy. Beat in the egg yolk. Stir in the lemon rind, and gradually add the flour, beating all the time.
2. Divide the mixture into 16 pieces and shape them into balls.
3. Roll the balls in the crushed bran flakes. Place them well apart as they will spread, on 2 greased baking sheets.
4. Bake in a preheated oven for 15–20 minutes. Transfer to a wire tray to cool.* When cold, store the biscuits in an airtight tin.
Makes 16.

STICKY DATE AND ORANGE CAKE

225 g (8 oz) wholemeal	175 ml (6 fl oz) vegetable
flour	oil
pinch of salt	2 eggs
2 teaspoons baking	175 g (6 oz) dates, stoned
powder	and finely chopped
75 g (3 oz) soft light	TOPPING:
brown sugar	40 g (1½ oz) plain flour
6 tablespoons clear honey	25 g (1 oz) butter
grated rind of 1 orange	40 g (1½ oz) demerara
6 tablespoons	sugar
concentrated orange	
juice	

Preparation time: 20 minutes
Cooking time: 1¼ hours
Oven: 160°C, 325°F, Gas Mark 3

1. Sift together the flour, salt and baking powder. Tip any bran retained in the sieve back into the flour. Mix together the sugar, honey, orange rind, orange juice and oil and beat in the eggs. Gradually beat in the flour mixture, and stir in the dates.
2. Turn the mixture into a greased and lined 18 cm (7 inch) round cake tin and level the top.
3. For the topping, rub the flour and butter together until crumbly and stir in the sugar. Sprinkle on the cake.
4. Bake in a preheated oven for 1¼ hours or until the cake is well risen and firm.
5. Leave the cake to cool a little in the tin, then transfer to a wire tray to cool completely. To store, wrap the cake in foil and place in an airtight tin for up to 1 week.*
Makes 1 × 18 cm (7 inch) round cake.

SUGAR-CRUSTED SCONE FINGERS

225 g (8 oz) self-raising
  flour
1½ teaspoons ground
  ginger
50 g (2 oz) caster sugar

50 g (2 oz) butter
1 egg
about 6 tablespoons milk,
  plus extra to glaze

Preparation time: 15 minutes
Cooking time: 15 minutes
Oven: 220°C, 425°F, Gas Mark 7

1. Sift the flour, 1 teaspoon of the ground ginger and half of the sugar into a bowl. Rub in the butter until the mixture resembles fine breadcrumbs. Mix in the egg and just enough milk to give a soft, pliable dough. Knead the dough in the bowl until it is smooth.

2. Press the dough into a greased and floured 18 cm (7 inch) round sandwich tin and smooth the top. Brush the top with milk. Mix together the remaining ground ginger and sugar and sprinkle over the top of the scone. Mark it into 8 wedges.

3. Bake in a preheated oven for 10–15 minutes or until the scone is well risen and firm. Leave to cool in the tin for a few minutes.* The scone is best served warm, split and spread generously with butter and ginger marmalade. Alternatively, leave it to cool completely and store it for up to a day in an airtight tin.

Makes 1 × 18 cm (7 inch) round.

BARBECUE
——FOR SIX——

*Should the weather prevent a barbecue, cook the
Crispy nut pork and the Four-in-one kebabs
under the grill – serving them in relays. Heat the
Spiced Mango sauce on a hotplate, the Pitta
bread in the oven and bake or grill
the Marzipan apples.*

CRISPY NUT PORK
FOUR-IN-ONE KEBABS IN HOT
PITTA BREAD
SPICED MANGO SAUCE

SUNRAY SALAD

MARZIPAN APPLES

CRISPY NUT PORK

6 pork spare rib chops,
  about 1.25 kg (2½ lb)
  total weight
50 g (2 oz) butter, melted
100 g (4 oz) button
  mushrooms, thinly
  sliced
COATING:
3 tablespoons French
  mustard

1 teaspoon mustard
  powder
40 g (1½ oz) butter,
  softened
salt
freshly ground black
  pepper
50 g (2 oz) walnuts,
  chopped

Preparation time: 10 minutes
Cooking time: 30 minutes

1. Cut out six 25 cm (10 inch) squares of foil. Trim the
excess fat from the chops and dry the chops with paper
towels.
2. Mix together the French mustard, mustard powder,
softened butter and salt and pepper to taste to make a
paste. Spread on to both sides of the chops.
3. Spread the chopped nuts on a piece of greaseproof
paper and press the chops into them, to coat both sides.*
Brush them with half the melted butter.
4. Place the chops over a preheated barbecue, or under a
preheated grill, and cook for 4 minutes on each side.
5. Remove the chops from the heat with tongs. Place
them on the foil squares and brush them with the
remaining melted butter. Divide the mushrooms between
them, then wrap the foil tightly around the chops.
Continue cooking for about 10 minutes, turning the
parcels once. Serve hot, in the foil with Spiced mango
sauce.

FOUR-IN-ONE KEBABS IN HOT PITTA BREAD

450 g (1 lb) lean boneless
  leg of lamb, cut into
  2.5 cm (1 inch) cubes
6 lamb's kidneys,
  quartered and cored
6 streaky bacon rashers,
  rind removed, halved
12 prunes, soaked for at
  least 30 minutes,
  drained and stoned
12 bay leaves

BASTING SAUCE:
3 tablespoons olive oil
1 tablespoon red wine
  vinegar
grated rind of ½ orange
1 tablespoon orange juice
salt
freshly ground black
  pepper
6 pieces of pitta bread, to
  serve

Preparation time: 15 minutes, plus soaking
Cooking time: 15 minutes

1. Divide the lamb, kidney and bacon into 6 portions.
Roll up the bacon pieces.
2. Thread the lamb, kidney, rolled bacon, prunes and
bay leaves on to 6 oiled kebab skewers.
3. Mix together the sauce ingredients, with salt and
pepper to taste. Brush the kebabs with half the sauce.*
4. Cook them over a preheated barbecue, or under a
preheated medium grill, for about 15 minutes. Turn the
skewers frequently and brush with the remaining sauce.
5. While the kebabs are cooking, heat the pitta bread on
the side of the barbecue or in the oven. Split the bread and
spread a little Spiced mango sauce (see below) over the
kebabs, then push them into the bread. Serve hot.

SPICED MANGO SAUCE

2 tablespoons vegetable
  oil
1 onion, peeled and finely
  chopped
1 garlic clove, peeled and
  crushed
1 teaspoon chilli powder
pinch of ground allspice
1 tablespoon tomato
  purée

6 tablespoons chicken
  stock
6 tablespoons mango
  chutney, finely chopped
salt
freshly ground black
  pepper

Preparation time: 5 minutes
Cooking time: 10 minutes

1. Heat the oil in a small saucepan. Add the onion and
garlic and fry over a moderate heat for 3–4 minutes,
stirring occasionally, until just beginning to brown. Stir in
the chilli powder and allspice and cook for 1 minute.
2. Stir in the tomato purée and chicken stock and
continue stirring until well blended. Stir in the chutney
and bring to the boil.
3. Taste the sauce and season well with salt and pepper.*
Serve hot with the chops or kebabs.

SUNRAY SALAD

450 g (1 lb) young carrots,
   scraped and cut into
   matchstick strips
salt
1 small firm white
   cabbage, cored and
   shredded
1 × 225 g (8 oz) can
   sweetcorn kernels,
   drained
DRESSING:
1 small onion, peeled and
   finely chopped

1 tablespoon orange juice
1 tablespoon lemon juice
3 tablespoons olive oil
pinch of sugar
salt
freshly ground black
   pepper
2 tablespoons chopped
   fresh coriander or
   chervil
few lettuce leaves

Preparation time: 15 minutes, plus cooling
Cooking time: 5 minutes

1. Cook the carrot strips in boiling salted water for 3 minutes, then drain and allow to cool. Place them in a bowl with the cabbage and sweetcorn.
2. Mix together all the ingredients for the dressing.*
3. Line a serving dish with the lettuce leaves. Just before serving, pour the dressing over the carrot mixture and toss to mix well. Spoon the salad on to a bed of lettuce. Pictured on previous page.

MARZIPAN APPLES

6 large cooking apples,
   cored
175 g (6 oz) marzipan
2 tablespoons chopped
   blanched almonds

40 g (1½ oz) butter, cut
   into small pieces
2 tablespoons demerara
   sugar
pinch of ground mixed
   spice

Preparation time: 10 minutes
Cooking time: 25 minutes on a barbeque
            40 minutes under a grill

1. Cut out 6 pieces of foil about 25 cm (10 inches) square and grease them. With a sharp knife, cut a slit around the circumference of each apple.
2. Mix together the marzipan and chopped almonds and shape into a block. Using the apple corer, cut out 6 cylinders of the paste.
3. Place an apple on each square of foil. Push a cylinder of marzipan into the cavity in each apple. Chop the remaining marzipan and scatter it over the apples. Dot them with the butter. Mix together the sugar and spice and sprinkle over the apples. Wrap the foil around the apples and double-fold the edges to seal them completely.*
4. Cook the apple parcels over a preheated barbecue for 20–25 minutes or under a preheated medium grill for about 40 minutes, turning them over ocasionally until they are soft but still hold their shape. If liked, serve with scoops of ice cream or whipped cream.

MENUS
FOR
EIGHT *to* TEN

SPECIAL OCCASION
—FOR EIGHT—

*The meal begins with a Mediterranean selection
of vegetables served cold and ends with a
spectacular greengage flan – and both courses
are cooked well ahead.*

RATATOUILLE WITH GARLIC CHEESE

ROAST SADDLE OF LAMB WITH ARTICHOKE CASES

BROCCOLI WITH ORANGE HOLLANDAISE SAUCE ROAST POTATOES†

GREENGAGE BORDALOUE TART

RATATOUILLE WITH GARLIC CHEESE

2 medium aubergines, cut
  into 1 cm (½ inch)
  cubes
salt
6 tablespoons vegetable
  oil
1 medium onion, peeled
  and sliced
3 garlic cloves, peeled and
  crushed
2 red peppers, cored,
  seeded and sliced
1 green pepper, cored,
  seeded and sliced
350 g (12 oz) courgettes,
  sliced
225 g (8 oz) tomatoes,
  skinned and chopped
100 g (4 oz) button
  mushrooms, sliced

1 × 50 g (2 oz) can tomato
  purée
300 ml (½ pint) hot
  chicken stock
freshly ground black
  pepper
1 tablespoon chopped
  fresh mint
2 tablespoons chopped
  fresh parsley
CHEESE:
350 g (12 oz) full-fat soft
  cheese
3 garlic cloves, peeled and
  crushed
3 tablespoons chopped
  mixed fresh herbs

Preparation time: 30 minutes, plus standing and chilling
Cooking time: 35 minutes

1. Put the aubergine cubes into a colander and sprinkle with salt. Leave them to drain for 30 minutes. Rinse off the salt and dry the aubergine cubes on paper towels.
2. Heat the oil in a large saucepan. Add the onion and garlic and fry over a moderate heat for 2 minutes, stirring once or twice. Add the aubergine cubes and stir-fry for a further 2 minutes. Add the peppers and courgettes, stir well and fry for 3 minutes. Add the tomatoes and mushrooms and cook for 2 minutes.
3. Mix together the tomato purée and hot stock and pour over the vegetables. Season to taste with salt and pepper.
4. Bring to the boil, then cover the pan and simmer for 15–20 minutes or until the vegetables are only just tender – they should not 'collapse' and lose their shape.
5. Meanwhile, beat the soft cheese well, then beat in the garlic and herbs. Season to taste with salt and pepper. Chill until needed.
6. Stir the herbs into the ratatouille. Taste and add more seasoning if necessary. Allow to cool, then chill.*
7. Serve cold accompanied by the chilled cheese.

ROAST SADDLE OF LAMB WITH ARTICHOKE CASES

*1 small saddle of lamb,
    about 3 kg (7 lb)*
salt
*freshly ground black
    pepper*
*2 garlic cloves, peeled and
    thinly sliced*
75 g (3 oz) butter, softened
4 sprigs of fresh rosemary
*150 ml (¼ pint) beef or
    chicken stock*

*300 ml (½ pint) dry red
    wine*
1 tablespoon plain flour
TO GARNISH:
*1 × 450 g (1 lb) can globe
    artichoke bottoms*
75 g (3 oz) frozen peas
2 tablespoons apple jelly
sprigs of fresh rosemary

Preparation time: 25 minutes
Cooking time: 2 hours
Oven: 200°C, 400°F, Gas Mark 6

---

1. Season the lamb with salt and pepper. Make vertical slits all over the lamb at intervals and stick in the garlic slices. Rub the meat with 50 g (2 oz) of the butter and place the rosemary sprigs on top.*
2. Place the meat on a wire tray in a roasting tin and pour in the stock. Roast in a preheated oven for 1¼ hours, basting the lamb frequently with the stock in the tin. Add the wine and continue roasting for 15–30 minutes or until the lamb is cooked to your liking. Test it by piercing with a sharp knife – it is most tender when the juices that run out are still a little pink.
3. Remove the meat from the tin, discard the rosemary and place it on a heated serving dish. Cover with foil and keep warm.
4. Mix the remaining butter and the flour to a paste. Skim the fat from the top of the cooking liquid in the tin and stir in the paste. Cook over a moderate heat, stirring constantly, for 3–4 minutes or until the sauce thickens.
5. Heat the artichoke bottoms in the liquor from the can. Meanwhile, cook the peas in boiling salted water according to the directions on the packet. Drain the peas and mix with the apple jelly. Drain the artichoke bottoms and fill with the peas.
6. Garnish the meat with fresh rosemary sprigs and arrange the artichoke cases around it. Serve hot with roast potatoes and Broccoli with orange hollandaise sauce (see next page).

BROCCOLI WITH ORANGE HOLLANDAISE SAUCE

1 kg (2 lb) broccoli, cut into florets
salt
SAUCE:
4 tablespoons white wine vinegar
2 tablespoons water
12 black peppercorns
4 egg yolks

225 g (8 oz) unsalted butter, cut into small pieces
grated rind of 1 orange
4 tablespoons orange juice
salt
freshly ground white pepper

Preparation time: 15 minutes
Cooking time: 30 minutes

---

1. Sprinkle the broccoli florets with salt and steam over boiling water for 10–12 minutes or until just tender.
2. Meanwhile make the sauce. Put the vinegar, water and peppercorns into a small saucepan and bring to the boil. Boil briskly until reduced by half.
3. Strain into the top of a double boiler or a heatproof bowl placed over a pan of simmering (not boiling) water. Over a low heat, beat in the egg yolks one by one, then beat in the butter, a few pieces at a time. When all the butter has been incorporated and the sauce is thick enough to coat the back of a spoon (after 10–15 minutes) beat in the orange rind and juice. Season the sauce to taste with salt and pepper and add a pinch of sugar if needed.
4. If the sauce is not to be served at once, cover the surface with a piece of dampened greaseproof paper and leave over barely simmering water.*
5. To serve, arrange the broccoli in a serving dish, season it well with pepper and spoon on a little sauce to garnish. Serve the rest of the sauce separately.

GREENGAGE BORDALOUE TART

300 g (11 oz) plain flour
200 g (7 oz) butter
100 g (4 oz) icing sugar, sifted
1 egg
FILLING:
350 g (12 oz) full-fat soft cheese
2 eggs
15 g (½ oz) cornflour
grated rind of ½ lemon
1 tablespoon lemon juice
50 g (2 oz) caster sugar

25 g (1 oz) ground almonds
1.25 kg (2½ lb) greengages, quartered and stoned
40 g (1½ oz) demerara sugar
SAUCE:
750 g (1½ lb) greengages, stoned and chopped
4 tablespoons water
75 g (3 oz) sugar
4 tablespoons brandy

Preparation time: 40 minutes, plus chilling
Cooking time: 50 minutes
Oven: 200°C, 400°F, Gas Mark 6

When greengages are not in season use yellow or red plums instead.

1. To make the pastry, sift the flour into a bowl. Rub in the butter until the mixture resembles fine breadcrumbs. Stir in the sugar. Add the egg and mix to a dough. Knead the dough lightly in the bowl. Cover it with cling film or foil and chill for at least 1 hour.
2. Meanwhile, make the filling. Beat the cheese until softened and beat in the eggs, one at a time. Beat in the cornflour, then the lemon rind, lemon juice, sugar and ground almonds.
3. Roll out the dough on a lightly floured board and use to line a greased 25 cm (10 inch) flan tin or flan ring placed on a greased baking sheet. Trim the edges and prick the bottom all over with a fork.
4. Spread the filling in the pastry case and level the top.
5. Arrange the greengage segments in overlapping rings, skin side down on the filling. (The effect resembles a water lily.) Sprinkle the fruit with the demerara sugar.
6. Bake in a preheated oven for 30–35 minutes. Cover the top with foil towards the end of the cooking time if it is browning too much. Leave to cool on a wire tray.
7. To make the sauce, place the greengages and water in a saucepan and cook for about 15 minutes or until they are soft. Rub through a sieve and return the purée to the pan. Add the sugar and stir over a low heat until it has dissolved. Bring to the boil and simmer for 5 minutes. Stir in the brandy and leave to cool.* Serve the sauce with the cold tart.

COOK-AHEAD DINNER
——FOR EIGHT——

Use this menu to entertain with confidence, knowing that the pâté, chicken casserole – even the rice dish to go with it – and the dessert are all deliciously ready.

HUNTER'S PÂTÉ

RED-SPICED CHICKEN CASSEROLE

STEAMED COURGETTES AND CAULIFLOWER FLORETS†
GOLDEN SWEETCORN AND RICE

ORANGE POSSET

HUNTER'S PÂTÉ

350 g (12 oz) streaky bacon rashers, rind removed
450 g (1 lb) boneless rabbit
450 g (1 lb) belly of pork, skin and any bones removed
225 g (8 oz) pig's liver
225 g (8 oz) garlic sausage, skinned
2 large onions, peeled

1 tablespoon chopped fresh sage, or 2 teaspoons dried sage
225 g (8 oz) pork sausage meat
6 tablespoons sherry
salt
freshly ground black pepper
2–3 bay leaves
cucumber slices, to garnish

Preparation time: 25 minutes
Cooking time: 3 hours
Oven: 160°C, 325°F, Gas Mark 3

---

1. Gently fry the bacon rashers in a frying pan for 4–5 minutes. Drain on paper towels.
2. Mince the rabbit, pork, liver, garlic sausage, onions and fresh sage. Mix in the dried sage, if using, the sausage meat and sherry, and season to taste with salt and pepper.
3. Arrange the bay leaves in a greased 1 kg (2 lb) loaf or 18 cm (7 inch) deep cake tin. Line the tin with some of the bacon rashers. Spoon in the rabbit mixture, level the top and cover with the remaining bacon rashers. Cover with foil and place the tin in a roasting tin. Pour about 4 cm (1½ inches) of water into the roasting tin.
4. Cook in a preheated oven for 3 hours. Cool in the tin.*
5. Turn out the pâté on to a serving dish garnished with cucumber slices. Serve, cut into slices, with melba toast or toasted brown bread cut into fingers.

RED-SPICED CHICKEN CASSEROLE

8 chicken breasts
2 tablespoons lemon juice
salt
freshly ground black
   pepper
75 g (3 oz) butter
2 tablespoons vegetable
   oil
2 large onions, peeled and
   thinly sliced
2 garlic cloves, peeled and
   finely chopped
1 red pepper, cored,
   seeded and sliced
1 green pepper, cored,
   seeded and sliced

2 tablespoons tomato
   purée
½ teaspoon cayenne
   pepper
1 tablespoon French
   mustard
2 tablespoons
   Worcestershire sauce
4 tablespoons red wine
   vinegar
50 g (2 oz) soft dark
   brown sugar
4 tablespoons chicken
   stock or water

Preparation time: 20 minutes
Cooking time: 1¼ hours
Oven: 200°C, 400°F, Gas Mark 6;
   180°C, 350°F, Gas Mark 4

1. Rub the chicken breasts all over with the lemon juice and season with salt and pepper.
2. Melt 50 g (2 oz) of the butter in a roasting tin. Add the chicken breasts and turn to coat with the butter. Cook in a preheated oven for 30 minutes, turning them frequently to brown on all sides.
3. Meanwhile melt the remaining butter with the oil in a frying pan. Add the onions, garlic, red and green peppers and fry over a moderate heat for 5 minutes, stirring once or twice.
4. Mix together the remaining ingredients and add them to the vegetables in the pan. Bring to the boil, stirring well.
5. Pour off the fat in the roasting tin and pour the vegetable mixture over the chicken breasts. Cover with foil, reduce the oven heat and cook for a further 35–40 minutes or until the chicken is tender. Taste the sauce and add more seasoning if necessary.*
6. Serve with steamed courgettes and cauliflower florets, accompanied by Golden sweetcorn and rice. To reheat, place in the oven heated to 180°C, 350°F, Gas Mark 4 for 40–45 minutes.

GOLDEN SWEETCORN AND RICE

4 cobs of sweetcorn, husk
   and silk removed
salt
400 g (14 oz) long-grain
   rice
50 g (2 oz) butter
1 medium onion, peeled
   and finely chopped

1 teaspoon ground
   coriander
2 tablespoons chopped
   fresh parsley
freshly ground black
   pepper

Preparation time: 20 minutes
Cooking time: 35 minutes

1. Cook the corn-on-the-cob in a large pan of boiling salted water for 5–8 minutes or until it is tender. Drain. When the sweetcorn is cool enough to handle, strip off the kernels, cutting them away from the cob with a sharp knife. Set aside.
2. Cook the rice in a large pan of boiling salted water for 10–12 minutes, or until it is just tender. Drain the rice in a colander and rinse it under cold running water to refresh and separate the grains. Drain well.
3. Mix together the sweetcorn kernels and rice. When cool, chill them in a covered container.*
4. Melt the butter in a large saucepan, add the onion and fry over a moderate heat, stirring occasionally, for 5 minutes. Stir in the coriander, then the sweetcorn and rice. Lower the heat, cover the pan and heat through for 4–5 minutes, stirring frequently. Stir in the parsley and season well with pepper. Serve hot.

ORANGE POSSET

600 ml (1 pint) double
   cream
1 tablespoon grated
   orange rind
1 teaspoon grated lemon
   rind
150 ml (¼ pint) dry white
   wine
4 tablespoons orange juice
1 tablespoon lemon juice

100 g (4 oz) icing sugar,
   sifted
3 egg whites
2 tablespoons caster sugar
TO DECORATE:
150 ml (¼ pint) whipping
   cream, whipped
   (optional)
25 g (1 oz) ratafia biscuits,
   crumbled
1 orange, sliced

Preparation time: 20 minutes, plus chilling

1. Whip the cream until stiff, and stir in the orange and lemon rinds. Very gradually pour on the wine, beating it in well before adding more. Gradually beat in the orange and lemon juices – if you add too much, too quickly, the cream could curdle. Beat in the icing sugar.
2. Whisk the egg whites until stiff, then gradually beat in the caster sugar until the mixture is stiff again.
3. Fold the meringue mixture into the cream mixture. Pile the mixture into a serving dish and chill for 4 hours.*
4. To decorate, pipe rosettes of whipped cream on the posset. Just before serving decorate with the crumbled ratafia biscuits and orange slices.

SUMMER SPREAD
FOR EIGHT

BROAD BEAN SOUP WITH PRAWNS

BOEUF À LA MODE
EN GELÉE

TOMATOES AND MUSHROOMS
WITH SWEET PEPPER DRESSING
GREEN SALAD†

STRAWBERRY
ALMOND TARTS

BROAD BEAN SOUP WITH PRAWNS

50 g (2 oz) butter
2 onions, peeled and sliced
1 garlic clove, peeled and crushed
1.25 kg (3 lb) fresh broad beans, shelled, or 750 g (1½ lb) frozen broad beans, thawed
1.6 litres (2¾ pints) chicken stock
1 thinly pared strip of orange rind
4 tablespoons chopped fresh summer savory or parsley

salt
freshly ground black pepper
300 ml (½ pint) single cream
TO GARNISH:
25 g (1 oz) butter
4 spring onions, peeled and thinly sliced into rings
225 g (8 oz) cooked peeled prawns
3 tablespoons chopped fresh parsley

Preparation time: 30 minutes
Cooking time: 45 minutes

---

1. Melt the butter in a large saucepan. Add the onions and garlic and fry over a moderate heat for 3–4 minutes, stirring occasionally. Add the broad beans, stir to coat them with the butter and cook gently for a further 3–4 minutes.
2. Pour on the stock. Add the orange rind and 2 tablespoons of the savory or parsley, and season to taste with salt and pepper. Bring to the boil, then cover and simmer for 20 minutes.
3. Discard the orange rind. Purée the soup in a blender or rub it through a sieve. Return the purée to the pan and add the remaining savory or parsley and the cream. Taste and adjust the seasoning.* Bring just to the boil, stirring frequently.
4. To prepare the garnish, melt the butter in a small frying pan, add the spring onions and fry over a moderate heat for 4 minutes, stirring occasionally. Add the prawns and stir-fry for 2 minutes. Sprinkle the chopped parsley on a piece of greaseproof paper. Tip the prawn mixture on to the parsley and toss to coat.
5. Turn the soup into a heated serving dish, add the prawn garnish and serve at once. This soup can be served with fresh granary bread cut into wedges.

BOEUF À LA MODE EN GELÉE

450 ml (¾ pint) red wine
5 tablespoons vegetable oil
1 onion, peeled and sliced
2 garlic cloves, peeled and halved
few parsley sprigs
few fresh thyme sprigs
2 bay leaves
6 juniper berries, lightly crushed
6 allspice berries, lightly crushed
12 black peppercorns
1 × 2 kg (4¾ lb) joint topside of beef, rolled
4 tablespoons vegetable oil

350 g (12 oz) carrots, peeled and sliced
350 g (12 oz) onions, peeled and sliced
150 ml (¼ pint) brandy, warmed
4 pig's trotters, chopped
1 bouquet garni
900 ml (1½ pints) beef stock
salt
freshly ground black pepper
1 large honeydew melon, chilled, peeled, seeded and cubed
1 bunch of watercress, to garnish

Preparation time: 1 hour, plus marinating and setting
Cooking time: 5 hours
Oven: 150°C, 300°F, Gas Mark 2

---

1. Mix together the wine, oil, onion, garlic, herbs, berries and peppercorns in a large bowl. Place the meat in the marinade and baste well. Cover the bowl and leave to marinate in the refrigerator for about 12 hours. Turn the meat occasionally.
2. Drain the meat, reserving the marinade, and dry with paper towels. Strain the marinade.
3. Heat the oil in a large flameproof casserole. Add the carrots and onions and fry over a moderately high heat, stirring occasionally, for 5–6 minutes or until browned. Add the meat and cook, turning it so that it browns and seals on all sides. Pour on the warm brandy and set alight carefully. Add the pig's trotters, bouquet garni, stock, strained marinade, and salt and pepper to taste. Bring to the boil.
4. Cover the casserole and cook in a preheated oven for 4–4¼ hours, turning the meat occasionally.
5. Transfer the meat to a wire tray to cool. Strain the stock, cover and chill for about 5 hours or until it has set to a firm jelly. Wrap the meat closely in foil and put it in the refrigerator.
6. To serve, carve the meat in thick slices and arrange them around the outside of a platter. Melt about 8 tablespoons of the jellied stock, leave until it is almost setting and spoon it over the meat. Leave it to set and glaze the meat.
7. Chop the remaining jelly into cubes and mix with the melon cubes. Pile into the centre of the platter. Garnish with sprigs of watercress.* Serve accompanied by Tomatoes and mushrooms with sweet pepper dressing (pictured on the next page) and a green salad of lettuce, cucumber, spring onions, green pepper and chicory.

TOMATOES AND MUSHROOMS WITH SWEET PEPPER DRESSING

*1 × 200 g (7 oz) can
  pimentos, drained*
7 tablespoons olive oil
*3 tablespoons red wine
  vinegar*
1 teaspoon dry mustard
1 teaspoon salt
1 teaspoon caster sugar
*2 tablespoons chopped
  fresh coriander or
  parsley*

*8 large button
  mushrooms, stalks
  removed*
*8 small button
  mushrooms, stalks
  removed*
*8 large, slightly under-ripe
  tomatoes*
1 small lettuce

Preparation time: 20 minutes, plus marinating

1. To make the dressing, halve the pimentos and place with the oil, vinegar, mustard, salt and sugar in a blender and liquidize. Stir in the coriander or parsley. Pour into a bowl.

2. Add the mushrooms to the dressing, toss to coat and leave to marinate for at least 1 hour.

3. Using a small, sharp knife cut each tomato through from the top 4 times, so that it opens into 8 wedges. Do not cut right through to the bottom.

4. Drain the mushrooms, reserving the dressing, and place a large and a small mushroom cap in the centre of each tomato. Thinly slice the remaining pimento and arrange the slices in a criss-cross pattern on the mushrooms.

5. Cover a serving dish with lettuce leaves and arrange the tomatoes on top.* Just before serving, spoon on the reserved pepper dressing.

FRESH STRAWBERRY ALMOND TARTS

225 g (8 oz) butter
100 g (4 oz) caster sugar
2 egg yolks
350 g (12 oz) plain flour, sifted
100 g (4 oz) ground almonds
FILLING:
225 g (8 oz) full-fat soft cheese

1 tablespoon caster sugar
1 teaspoon grated lemon rind
750 g (1½ lb) strawberries
5 tablespoons redcurrant jelly, melted
4 tablespoons blanched almonds, toasted

Preparation time: 30 minutes, plus chilling
Cooking time: 20 minutes
Oven: 190°C, 375°F, Gas Mark 5

---

1. Cream together the butter and sugar until light and fluffy. Beat in the egg yolks. Gradually stir in the flour and ground almonds, and knead to a smooth dough. Cover with cling film or foil and chill for 1 hour.
2. Divide the dough into 8 or 16 pieces. Roll out each one into a round and use to line 8 greased 11 cm (4½ inch) individual tartlet or Yorkshire pudding tins, or 16 smaller tartlet tins. Prick the surface of the pastry cases all over with a fork, then line each one with a round of foil and fill with baking beans.
3. Bake the pastry cases 'blind' in a preheated oven for 15 minutes. Remove the foil and beans and return the pastry cases to the oven to bake for 3–4 minutes longer or until they are golden brown. Cool them in the tins on a wire tray.
4. To make the filling, beat together the cheese, sugar and lemon rind. Spread a little of the cheese mixture in each pastry case.
5. Reserve 8 or 16 of the best strawberries. Hull and slice the remainder. Arrange the strawberry slices in rings in the pastry cases. Spoon the redcurrant jelly over the strawberries and leave to set.*
6. Just before serving, top with the reserved strawberries and scatter over the toasted almonds.

ELEGANT LUNCH
—FOR TEN—

The salad starter and ice cream dessert can be prepared in advance, as can the Cumberland sauce which accompanies the delicious rack of lamb. The meal is elegant in both its simplicity and its presentation.

SALAD OF AVOCADO AND KIWI FRUITS

RACK OF LAMB IN PASTRY

CUMBERLAND SAUCE
POTATOES GLAZED IN LEMON BUTTER
YOUNG GREEN BEANS†

BRANDY SNAP CUPS WITH GINGER ICE CREAM

SALAD OF AVOCADO AND KIWI FRUITS

10 tablespoons olive oil	freshly ground black pepper
1 teaspoon grated grapefruit rind	4 avocados, peeled, stoned and thinly sliced
5 tablespoons grapefruit juice	1 small lettuce (optional)
2 tablespoons dry vermouth	10 kiwi fruits, peeled and thinly sliced
2 tablespoons clear honey	2 bunches of watercress
1 teaspoon caster sugar	5 tablespoons chopped fresh mint
salt	

Preparation time: 30 minutes

Cool green fruits, a bitter-sweet dressing and careful presentation make this a stylish first course.

1. To make the dressing, combine the oil, grapefruit rind and juice, vermouth, honey and sugar, and salt and pepper to taste, in a liquidizer. Blend thoroughly. Taste the dressing and add more sugar or seasoning if necessary.
2. Toss the avocado slices in the dressing to prevent discoloration, then remove them with a slotted spoon. Reserve the dressing.
3. Arrange lettuce-leaves, if using, on 10 individual plates. Arrange a fan shape of avocado slices and a circle of overlapping kiwi fruit slices on top of each. Garnish the plates with watercress sprigs.*
4. Just before serving, stir the mint into the dressing and spoon it over the salad.

RACK OF LAMB IN PASTRY

2 joints of best end of neck of lamb, 5 large chops in each	6 lamb's kidneys, skinned, cored and finely chopped
salt	175 g (6 oz) mushrooms, finely chopped
freshly ground black pepper	25 g (1 oz) pine nuts (optional)
50 g (2 oz) butter	2 tablespoons chopped fresh parsley
1 tablespoon vegetable oil	2 tablespoons red wine
FILLING:	450 g (1 lb) frozen puff pastry, thawed
25 g (1 oz) butter	beaten egg, to glaze
1 medium onion, peeled and finely chopped	TO GARNISH:
2 garlic cloves, peeled and crushed	1 orange, cut into wedges sprigs of parsley

Preparation time: 50 minutes, plus cooling
Cooking time: 1 hour
Oven: 190°C, 375°F, Gas Mark 5;
230°C, 450°F, Gas Mark 8;
200°C, 400°F, Gas Mark 6

1. Trim the excess fat and meat from the tip of the bones, leaving about 7.5 cm (3 inches) of bone exposed. Using a darning needle and fine twine, sew the 2 joints of lamb together to make a continuous rack – or ask the butcher to do this for you. Season the meat with salt and pepper.
2. Melt the butter with the oil in a roasting tin. Put the lamb in the tin and roast in a preheated oven for 10 minutes. Remove the lamb from the tin and allow to cool.
3. To make the filling, melt the butter in a frying pan. Add the onion and garlic and fry over a moderate heat for 3–4 minutes, stirring occasionally. Add the kidneys and stir-fry for 2–3 minutes. Add the mushrooms and pine nuts, if using. Stir well and cook for 5 minutes. Stir in the parsley and wine, season to taste with salt and pepper and bring to the boil. Boil for 2–3 minutes or until the wine has evaporated. Allow the mixture to cool completely.
4. Spread the kidney filling over both sides of the meat and press it on well against the meat to form a thick coating.
5. Roll out the pastry dough on a floured board until it is about 36 × 30 cm (14 × 12 inches). Place the rack of lamb on its side on the dough and push the bones through the dough. Press the dough close to the meat. Bring round the dough edges and join them to form a neat seal at the ends and under the chops. Trim the ends. Reroll the trimmings and cut out decorative leaf shapes. Brush the dough with beaten egg, arrange the leaves in a pattern and brush them with egg.
6. Stand the lamb on a baking sheet. Increase the oven temperature and cook for 10 minutes, then reduce the temperature and cook for a further 15 minutes or until the pastry is well browned. Serve hot garnished with the orange wedges and parsley, and the Cumberland sauce (page 148).
7. Green beans and Potatoes glazed in lemon butter (page 148) make suitable vegetable accompaniments.

CUMBERLAND SAUCE

2 oranges
2 lemons
450 g (1 lb) redcurrant
   jelly

150 ml (¼ pint) port
4 teaspoons arrowroot
1 tablespoon water

Preparation time: 20 minutes
Cooking time: 20 minutes

Make the sauce the day before it is needed, so that the flavours mellow.

1. Thinly pare the rind from the oranges and lemons. Cut the rind into thin matchstick strips. Blanch them in boiling water for 5 minutes. Drain, refresh in cold water and drain again. Squeeze 4 tablespoons of juice from an orange and 2 tablespoons of juice from a lemon.
2. Melt the redcurrant jelly in a saucepan and add the fruit juices. Bring to the boil and simmer for 5 minutes. Stir in the port. Mix the arrowroot to a smooth paste with the water and stir into the pan. Bring to the boil again, stirring. Add the orange and lemon rind strips and remove the pan from the heat. Leave to cool.*

POTATOES GLAZED IN LEMON BUTTER

1.5 kg (3 lb) small
   potatoes, peeled or
   scraped
salt
75 g (3 oz) butter
1 large onion, peeled and
   finely chopped

1 tablespoon grated lemon
   rind
3 tablespoons lemon juice
freshly ground black
   pepper
1 tablespoon chopped
   fresh parsley, to garnish

Preparation time: 15 minutes
Cooking time: 1 hour
Oven: 190°C, 370°F, Gas Mark 5

1. Cook the potatoes in boiling salted water for 3 minutes, then drain them.
2. Melt the butter in a flameproof dish. Add the onion and fry over a moderate heat for 3 minutes, stirring occasionally. Stir in the lemon rind and juice, add the potatoes and season well with salt and pepper. Stir to coat the potatoes with the lemon mixture.*
3. Transfer the dish to a preheated oven and bake for 50 minutes or until the potatoes are crisp and golden brown. Serve hot, garnished with the parsley.

BRANDY SNAP CUPS WITH GINGER ICE CREAM

75 g (3 oz) sugar
75 g (3 oz) butter
75 g (3 oz) golden syrup
75 g (3 oz) plain flour,
    sifted
¼ teaspoon ground ginger
1 tablespoon brandy
ICE CREAM:
300 ml (½ pint) single
    cream
300 ml (½ pint) double
    cream
175 g (6 oz) caster sugar

175 g (6 oz) ginger snap
    biscuits, finely crushed
4 tablespoons ginger syrup
175 g (6 oz) preserved
    ginger, drained and
    finely chopped
SAUCE:
6 tablespoons clear honey
2 tablespoons brandy
4 tablespoons ginger syrup
4 tablespoons water
75 g (3 oz) raisins

Preparation time: 40 minutes, plus freezing
Cooking time: 25 minutes
Oven: 190°C, 375°F, Gas Mark 5

1. Melt the sugar, butter and syrup in a small saucepan and remove from the heat. Stir in the flour and ground ginger and then the brandy.
2. Put about 16 teaspoons of the mixture, well spaced apart, on 2 greased baking sheets. Bake in a preheated oven for 5–7 minutes or until golden brown.
3. Cool the biscuits slightly. As soon as you can handle them, lift each one from the baking sheet and drape it over a large orange, pressing the brandy snap gently into a rounded cup shape. Leave the brandy snaps to cool on a wire tray. They can be stored in an airtight tin.
4. To make the ice cream, whip together the single and double creams and the sugar until thick. Turn into chilled metal ice-cube trays, cover with foil and freeze for 1 hour.
5. Turn the mixture into a chilled bowl and beat well. Beat in the crushed biscuits and ginger syrup, then stir in the chopped ginger. Cover and freeze again for 1 hour.
6. Beat well again to break down ice crystals, then cover and freeze for at least a further 2 hours.
7. To make the sauce, put the honey, brandy, ginger syrup, water and raisins into a small saucepan. Bring to the boil and simmer for 5 minutes. Remove from the heat and allow to cool.*
8. Transfer the ice cream to the refrigerator 1 hour before serving to allow to soften. Just before serving, place scoops of the ice cream in the brandy snap cups. Serve the sauce separately.

MOVEABLE FEAST
—FOR TEN—

There's a tasty hot soup in case it's chilly and a feast of cold dishes to choose from!

TOMATO AND COURGETTE SOUP

TURKEY SAUSAGES WITH
MUSTARD
MAYONNAISE DIP
SPICED PORK AND VEAL PIE

CHICORY AND FRUIT SALAD

APPLE AND BANANA KOLAC

TOMATO AND COURGETTE SOUP

50 g (2 oz) butter
2 medium onions, peeled and chopped
2 garlic cloves, peeled and crushed
750 g (1½ lb) courgettes, sliced
750 g (1½ lb) tomatoes, skinned and sliced
4 tablespoons tomato purée
2 tablespoons chopped fresh basil, or 1 teaspoon dried basil

1 tablespoon chopped fresh parsley
grated rind of ½ orange
2 tablespoons orange juice
1.5 litres (2½ pints) chicken stock
salt
freshly ground black pepper
2 teaspoons caster sugar
300 ml (½ pint) soured cream
2 tablespoons sunflower seeds, to garnish

Preparation time: 20 minutes
Cooking time: 30 minutes

1. Melt the butter in a large saucepan. Add the onions and garlic and fry over a moderate heat for 3–4 minutes, stirring occasionally. Add the courgettes, stir well and cook for 5 minutes. With a slotted spoon, remove half the courgettes and set them aside.
2. Add the tomatoes to the pan with the tomato purée, herbs and orange rind and juice. Bring to the boil and simmer for 10 minutes.
3. Purée the contents of the pan in a blender, or rub it through a sieve.
4. Return the purée and the reserved courgettes to the pan and pour on the stock. Season to taste with salt and pepper and add the sugar. Bring to the boil, then cover and simmer for 10 minutes.
5. Stir in the soured cream and bring just to the boil. Taste and adjust the seasoning.
6. Pour the soup into heated vacuum flasks.* Scatter with the sunflower seeds to serve.

TURKEY SAUSAGES

2 metres (6 ft) pig's or
　sheep's intestine, for
　casing (see method)
1 kg (2¼ lb) turkey meat
450 g (1 lb) hard pork fat
225 g (8 oz) lean bonelesss
　pork
1 teaspoon salt

½ teaspoon freshly
　ground black pepper
½ teaspoon grated
　nutmeg
¼ teaspoon ground mace
2 teaspoons dried oregano
¼ teaspoon saltpetre

Preparation time: 1½ hours, plus soaking and drying
Cooking time: 15 minutes

Find a butcher who makes his own sausages and ask him to sell you some of the natural skin casing.

1. Soak the skin in warm water for 1 hour before using.
2. Mince the meat and fat, either coarsely or finely, as you wish. Stir in the remaining ingredients.
3. Fry 2 teaspoons of the mixture and taste it. Adjust the seasonings if necessary.
4. Drain the skin. Tie one end to the nozzle of a large funnel, or to the sausage-making attachment of an electric mixer if you have one. Tie the other end of the skin closed with cotton thread. Push the meat mixture through the funnel and into the skin, then gradually work the mixture along the skin, squeezing it with your fingers.
5. Hang up the sausage in an airy place for 24 hours.
6. To separate the mixture into sausages, work it along the skin to leave a gap at 10 cm (4 inch) intervals. Twist the skin firmly then cut it.
7. Fry the sausages for about 15 minutes in the usual way, turning them to brown evenly. Allow to cool.*
8. Serve with Mustard mayonnaise dip (see below) and plentry of crisp spring onions. Pictured on page 151. Makes about 20.

MUSTARD MAYONNAISE DIP

2 egg yolks
1 tablespoon Dijon
　mustard
salt
freshly ground black
　pepper

1 teaspoon lemon juice
300 ml (½ pint) olive oil
1 tablespoon boiling water
2 spring onions, finely
　chopped, to garnish

Preparation time: 10 minutes

1. Be sure that all the ingredients are at room temperature. Stir together the egg yolks, mustard and salt and pepper to taste. Stir in the lemon juice. Beat the mixture until well blended.
2. Pour on the oil drop by drop, beating all the time. As the sauce thickens, pour the oil in a thin, steady stream, still beating constantly.
3. Beat in the boiling water. Taste and adjust the seasoning. Cover and chill until needed.*
4. Sprinkle with the chopped spring onions just before serving. Pictured on page 151.

SPICED PORK AND VEAL PIE

40 g (1½ oz) butter
1 medium onion, peeled
　and chopped
1 garlic clove, peeled and
　crushed
½ teaspoon ground
　coriander
½ teaspoon ground
　allspice
750 g (1½ lb) lean
　boneless pork, diced
350 g (12 oz) boneless
　veal, diced
450 ml (¾ pint) chicken
　stock

1 pig's trotter, halved
2 bay leaves
few parsley sprigs
salt
freshly ground black
　pepper
450 g (1 lb) shortcrust
　pastry
100 g (4 oz) raisins
1 tablespoon chopped
　fresh oregano or dried
　oregano
beaten egg, to glaze

Preparation time: 30 minutes, plus cooling
Cooking time: 2 hours
Oven: 200°C, 400°F, Gas Mark 6

1. Melt the butter in a saucepan. Add the onion and garlic and fry over a moderate heat for 3–4 minutes, stirring occasionally. Increase the heat and add the spices and meat. Cook for 5 minutes, stirring to seal the meat on all sides.
2. Pour on the stock and add the pig's trotter, bay leaves, parsley and salt and pepper to taste. Bring to the boil and simmer for 45 minutes.
3. Remove the meat with a slotted spoon and set aside to cool. Discard the bay leaves and parsley. Simmer the stock for about 20 minutes or until it has reduced to about 200 ml (⅓ pint). Taste the stock and adjust the seasoning. Discard the pig's trotter.
4. Divide the dough into 2 portions, one slightly larger than the other. Roll out the larger portion and use to line a greased 25 cm (10 inch) pie plate. Prick the bottom with a fork.
5. Mix the meat with the raisins and oregano and spread it over the bottom of the pastry case. Dampen the pastry rim. Roll out the remaining dough and place on top. Pinch together and seal the edges. Brush the top with beaten egg. Reroll the pastry trimmings and cut them into decorative shapes. Put the decorations in place and brush them with egg. Cut a hole in the centre of the lid.
6. Bake in a preheated oven for 35–40 minutes or until the pastry is golden brown.
7. Allow the pie to cool. Pour in the stock through the hole in the lid and leave it to set.* Serve the pie cold, cut into slices with Chicory and fruit salad (page 154).

CHICORY AND FRUIT SALAD

5 heads of chicory, thinly
  sliced into rings
2 celery hearts, thinly
  sliced into rings
4 oranges, peeled and
  segmented
225 g (8 oz) seedless white
  grapes
225 g (8 oz) black grapes,
  halved and seeded
100 g (4 oz) button
  mushrooms, thinly
  sliced

2 bunches of watercress
DRESSING:
9 tablespoons olive oil
3 tablespoons orange juice
1 tablespoon lemon juice
1 teaspoon caster sugar
2 spring onions, peeled
  and thinly sliced
salt
freshly ground black
  pepper

Preparation time: 35 minutes

1. Toss together the chicory, celery, oranges, grapes and mushrooms. Separate the watercress into sprigs. Set the watercress aside in a covered container.
2. Mix together all the ingredients for the dressing, with salt and pepper to taste.
3. About 1 hour before serving, pour the dressing on to the salad and toss to mix well.*
4. Transport the salad in a covered container. Toss in the watercress just before serving.

APPLE AND BANANA KOLAC

225 g (8 oz) plain
  wholewheat flour
2 teaspoons baking
  powder
½ teaspoon salt
100 g (4 oz) butter
50 g (2 oz) soft light
  brown sugar
1 egg, beaten
whipped cream, to serve
FILLING:
350 g (12 oz) cottage
  cheese

1 teaspoon grated lemon
  rind
3 bananas, peeled and
  mashed
50 g (2 oz) sultanas
3 dessert apples, cored and
  thinly sliced
50 g (2 oz) soft light
  brown sugar
½ teaspoon ground
  cinnamon
40 g (1½ oz) butter,
  melted

Preparation time: 25 minutes
Cooking time: 40 minutes
Oven: 190°C, 375°F, Gas Mark 5

1. Sift the flour, baking powder and salt into a bowl and tip in the bran from the sieve. Rub in the butter until the mixture resembles fine breadcrumbs, then stir in the sugar. Mix to a stiff dough with the egg and knead lightly.
2. Roll out the dough on a floured board and use to line a greased 28 × 18 cm (11 × 7 inch) tin. Trim the edges and prick the dough with a fork.
3. Mix together the cottage cheese and lemon rind and spread over the bottom of the pastry case. Mix together the banana and sultanas and spread over the cheese. Arrange the apple slices in rows over the banana. Stir the sugar and cinnamon together and sprinkle on the apples. Dribble the melted butter all over the top.
4. Bake in a preheated oven for 35–40 minutes or until the top is golden and crunchy. Leave to cool in the tin.* Serve with whipped cream.

CELEBRATION
MENUS

CHRISTMAS FARE
FOR SIX

CHRISTMAS EVE SUPPER
Tuna fish moussaka
Winter salad
Cheese and fruit†

CHRISTMAS DAY BREAKFAST
Cinnamon toast Hot poppy seed rolls
with honey butter

CHRISTMAS LUNCH/DINNER
Asparagus mousse
Roast turkey with sausage and sage stuffing
Roast potatoes Ginger orange carrots Sprouts
with almonds
Christmas pudding with Brandy butter
Chocolate nests with truffle eggs

TRADITIONAL TEA
Pâté and watercress rolled sandwiches
Chestnut log Christmas cake Mince pies

BOXING DAY
Boxing Day soup Turkey espagnole
Mincemeat brûlée

CHRISTMAS EVE SUPPER

TUNA FISH MOUSSAKA

WINTER SALAD

CHEESE AND FRUIT†

TUNA FISH MOUSSAKA

oil
2 medium aubergines,
  thinly sliced
25 g (1 oz) butter
1 medium onion, peeled
  and finely chopped
1 garlic clove, peeled and
  crushed
2 tablespoons plain flour
300 ml (½ pint) milk
150 ml (¼ pint) chicken
  stock
100 g (4 oz) button
  mushrooms, sliced

2 × 200 g (7 oz) cans tuna
  fish, drained and flaked
grated rind of ½ lemon
salt
freshly ground black
  pepper
50 g (2 oz) Parmesan
  cheese, grated
TOPPING:
300 ml (½ pint) plain
  unsweetened yogurt
2 eggs
100 g (4 oz) Cheddar
  cheese, grated
sprigs of parsley, to
  garnish

Preparation time: 25 minutes
Cooking time: 50–55 minutes
Oven: 190°C, 375°F, Gas Mark 5

You can prepare this dish as far as the asterisk. Cover it with foil and chill overnight in the refrigerator. Finish the top of the dish and bake it in the oven when it is needed.

1. Brush 2 baking sheets with oil. Arrange the aubergine slices in single layers on the baking sheets and brush the aubergines with oil.
2. Bake in a preheated oven for about 15 minutes or until the aubergines start to colour and soften.
3. Meanwhile, melt the butter in a saucepan, add the onion and fry gently for 5 minutes. Add the garlic and cook for a further minute.
4. Stir the flour into the butter and onion and cook for 1 minute. Gradually stir in the milk and chicken stock. Bring to the boil, stirring, and simmer until thickened.
5. Add the mushrooms to the prepared sauce and simmer for 2 minutes. Stir in the tuna, lemon rind, salt and pepper to taste, and the grated Parmesan cheese.
6. Put half the tuna sauce into a greased ovenproof dish and top with half the aubergine slices. Add the remaining tuna sauce and a top layer of the remaining aubergine slices.*
7. Beat the yogurt with the eggs and half the grated Cheddar cheese. Spread evenly over the top layer of aubergine slices, and sprinkle with the remaining Cheddar cheese.
8. Bake in the oven for 35–40 minutes or until piping hot and the top is golden brown. Serve hot and garnish with sprigs of parsley.

WINTER SALAD

275 g (10 oz) red cabbage,
  cored and finely
  shredded
3 large carrots, peeled and
  grated
4 celery sticks, finely
  chopped
4 spring onions, finely
  chopped
50 g (2 oz) sultanas

150 ml (¼ pint) olive oil
juice of 1 orange
salt
freshly ground black
  pepper
1 bunch of watercress,
  divided into sprigs
  (optional)
2 tablespoons chopped
  walnuts

Preparation time: 20 minutes

1. Put the cabbage, carrots, celery, spring onions and sultanas in a large bowl.
2. Mix the olive oil with the orange juice, and season to taste with salt and pepper.
3. Stir the dressing into the prepared salad ingredients.* (Keep covered in a cool place until needed.)
4. Stir the sprigs of watercress if liked, and nuts into the salad just before serving.

CHRISTMAS DAY BREAKFAST

CINNAMON TOAST

HOT POPPY SEED ROLLS WITH HONEY BUTTER

CINNAMON TOAST

75 g (3 oz) butter	6 slices of bread
2 teaspoons ground cinnamon	3 tablespoons demerara sugar

Preparation time: 8–10 minutes
Cooking time: about 2 minutes

1. Cream the butter until softened, then beat in the cinnamon.
2. Spread the cinnamon butter fairly generously over each slice of bread, making sure that it reaches right to the crusts.
3. Sprinkle the buttered surfaces with demerara sugar and place on a baking sheet.
4. Place under a preheated moderately hot grill until the toast is golden and crisp.
5. Cut into triangles and serve hot.

HOT POPPY SEED ROLLS WITH HONEY BUTTER

100 g (4 oz) butter	¼ teaspoon salt
grated rind and juice of ½ lemon	50 g (2 oz) butter
3 tablespoons honey	2 tablespoons finely chopped walnuts
ROLLS:	poppy seeds
225 g (8 oz) plain flour	6 tablespoons milk
1½ teaspoons baking powder	beaten egg, to glaze

Preparation time: 25 minutes
Cooking time: 10–12 minutes
Oven: 230°C, 450°F, Gas Mark 8

1. First make the honey butter. Cream the butter until softened, then beat in the lemon rind and juice and the honey until light and fluffy. Cover and chill until needed.
2. Sift the flour, baking powder and salt into a bowl. Rub in the butter until the mixture resembles coarse crumbs.
3. Add the walnuts and 1 tablespoon of the poppy seeds. Stir in the milk to give a soft dough.
4. Form the dough into 8 even-sized balls. Place them on a greased baking sheet and flatten them slightly.
5. Brush the tops with beaten egg and sprinkle with poppy seeds.
6. Bake in a preheated oven for 10–12 minutes.* (The rolls can be made a day or two in advance and then warmed through in the oven, wrapped in foil, when needed.)
7. Serve hot with the chilled honey butter.
Makes 8.

CHRISTMAS LUNCH/DINNER

ASPARAGUS MOUSSE

ROAST TURKEY WITH SAUSAGE AND SAGE STUFFING

ROAST POTATOES
GINGER ORANGE CARROTS
SPROUTS WITH ALMONDS

CHRISTMAS PUDDING WITH BRANDY BUTTER
CHOCOLATE NESTS WITH TRUFFLE EGGS

ASPARAGUS MOUSSE

1 × 275 g (10 oz) can asparagus tips
3 hard-boiled eggs, chopped
salt
freshly ground black pepper
2 tablespoons dry sherry

15 g (½ oz) powdered gelatine
300 ml (½ pint) double cream
TO GARNISH:
lemon twists
parsley sprigs

Preparation time: 20–25 minutes, plus chilling

1. Put the canned asparagus tips and their juice into a blender or food processor with the shelled hard-boiled eggs and salt and pepper to taste. Blend until smooth.
2. Put the sherry into a small bowl and sprinkle over the gelatine. Stand in a pan of hot water and stir until the gelatine has dissolved.
3. Stir the dissolved gelatine into the asparagus mixture.
4. Whip the cream until it holds soft peaks. Fold lightly into the asparagus mixture. Divide into 6 heart-shaped moulds lined with oiled greaseproof paper, or ramekin dishes. Chill until set.*
5. Garnish with lemon twists and parsley sprigs, and serve with triangles of brown bread and butter.

ROAST TURKEY WITH SAUSAGE AND SAGE STUFFING

1 × 5.5 kg (12 lb) oven-ready turkey
1 small onion, peeled and stuck with 4 cloves
1 bay leaf
75 g (3 oz) butter, softened
watercress, to garnish
STUFFING:
40 g (1½ oz) butter
1 medium onion, peeled and finely chopped
1 garlic clove, peeled and crushed

100 g (4 oz) pork sausage meat
75 g (3 oz) fresh breadcrumbs
grated rind and juice of ½ lemon
1 tablespoon chopped fresh sage
1 egg, beaten
salt
freshly ground black pepper

Preparation time: 30 minutes, plus standing
Cooking time: 4 hours 20 minutes
Oven: 180°C, 350°F, Gas Mark 4

If you are using a frozen bird, make sure that it has thawed out completely before stuffing it – allow about 28 hours at room temperature for this size of turkey. The turkey will serve 6 with plenty left over for eating cold or to use in other dishes.

1. Remove the giblets from the turkey. Put them into a saucepan with the onion, bay leaf and enough water to cover the giblets. Bring to the boil, then cover and simmer gently for 1 hour. (If making the giblet stock, which will be used for the gravy, the day before, strain and store, covered, in the refrigerator.)
2. Meanwhile, to make the stuffing, melt the butter in a frying pan, add the onion and fry gently until lightly golden and softened.
3. Put the onion into a bowl and add the garlic, sausage meat, breadcrumbs, lemon rind and juice and sage. Mix well, adding sufficient beaten egg to bind. Season to taste with salt and pepper.*
4. Wipe the turkey inside and out with paper towels.
5. Push the prepared stuffing into the neck end of the bird, then secure the flap of neck skin under the bird with a skewer. (If you have any leftover stuffing, it can be cooked in a separate dish in the oven with the turkey for 30 minutes.)
6. Put the turkey into a large roasting tin. Rub all over with the softened butter, and season with salt and pepper.
7. Roast in a preheated oven for 3¼ hours. As soon as the skin of the bird is nicely browned, cover it with foil to prevent the turkey from going too dark. Baste from time to time with the pan juices to keep the bird moist.
8. Remove the turkey from the oven and allow to stand, covered with foil, for 10–15 minutes before carving (this allows the turkey flesh to 'set' slightly and makes carving easier, and more economical).
9. Serve the turkey garnished with watercress and accompanied by gravy (made from the strained giblet stock and turkey pan juices), cranberry jelly, Roast potatoes, Ginger orange carrots, and Sprouts with almonds.

ROAST POTATOES
Arrange peeled and par-boiled medium potatoes around the turkey for the last 1½ hours cooking time.

GINGER ORANGE CARROTS

1 kg (2 lb) carrots, peeled and thinly sliced
50 g (2 oz) butter
½ teaspoon ground ginger
salt
freshly ground black pepper

300 ml (½ pint) orange juice
2 tablespoons chopped fresh parsley

Preparation time: 3–4 minutes
Cooking time: 15–20 minutes

1. Layer the sliced carrots in a large shallow saucepan with small knobs of butter, a sprinkling of ground ginger, and salt and pepper to taste.
2. Pour over the orange juice. Cover the pan and cook gently for 15–20 minutes or until the carrots are just tender.
3. Sprinkle with chopped parsley and serve hot.

SPROUTS WITH ALMONDS

1 kg (2 lb) Brussels sprouts
salt
50 g (2 oz) butter
3 tablespoons flaked almonds

freshly ground black pepper

Preparation time: 4–5 minutes
Cooking time: 16–18 minutes

1. Trim the sprouts and make a small cross in the base of each one.*
2. Cook the prepared sprouts in a saucepan of boiling salted water until just tender, 12–14 minutes. Drain well.
3. Melt the butter in a clean saucepan, add the almonds and toss over the heat until golden.
4. Add the cooked sprouts to the pan and mix gently with the browned almonds and butter. Season to taste with salt and pepper. Serve hot.

CHRISTMAS PUDDING

100 g (4 oz) currants	1 dessert apple, cored and
100 g (4 oz) raisins	grated
100 g (4 oz) sultanas	½ teaspoon mixed spice
100 g (4 oz) chopped	1 teaspoon ground
mixed candied peel	cinnamon
75 g (3 oz) nuts, chopped	100 g (4 oz) dark soft
50 g (2 oz) ground	brown sugar
almonds	grated rind of 1 lemon
100 g (4 oz) black treacle	grated rind of ½ orange
100 g (4 oz) fresh	2 eggs
wholemeal	4 tablespoons brandy
breadcrumbs	4 tablespoons port
100 g (4 oz) shredded suet	extra brandy, for flaming
1 medium carrot, peeled	
and grated	

Preparation time: 15 minutes
Cooking time: 8 hours in advance, plus 2 hours on the
day

Christmas pudding should be made at least 3 months before Christmas, to give the pudding time to mature. If you have a microwave oven, you can reheat a pudding of this size in 4 minutes, set on full power. (If you are going to reheat your pudding by this method, remember *not* to insert silver coins or charms.)

1. Place the dried fruit, peel, nuts, treacle, breadcrumbs, suet, carrot, apple, spices, sugar and fruit rinds in a large bowl and mix together.
2. Beat the eggs with the brandy and port and stir into the other ingredients. Mix together thoroughly. Add any silver coins or charms.
3. Spoon the pudding mixture into a greased 1.2 litre (2 pint) pudding basin. Cover with a double layer of greased greaseproof paper pleated down the centre, then tie a pudding cloth or double thickness of pleated foil over the top of the basin.
4. Steam the pudding for 8 hours, checking the level of water from time to time.
5. Remove from the pan of water and allow the pudding to become quite cold.
6. Remove the pudding cloth or foil and paper, and cover the pudding with a fresh piece of greased grease-proof paper. Overwrap in foil and store in a cool place until required.*
7. On the day, steam the pudding for a further 2 hours. Turn it out on to a warmed plate.
8. Warm a little brandy in a spoon or ladle, pour immediately over the hot pudding and carefully set alight.
9. Take the pudding to the table 'flaming', and serve with Brandy butter.

BRANDY BUTTER

75 g (3 oz) butter, unsalted	50 g (2 oz) soft brown
100 g (4 oz) icing sugar,	sugar
sifted	2 tablespoons brandy

Preparation time: 10 minutes

If you are making the brandy butter in advance, cover it well with cling film, and keep in a cool place.

1. Cream the butter until soft and light in texture.
2. Gradually beat in the icing sugar and brown sugar alternately with the brandy.* Serve chilled, if preferred.

CHOCOLATE NEST WITH TRUFFLE EGGS

50 g (2 oz) plain chocolate	TRUFFLE EGGS:
1½ tablespoons chocolate	225 g (8 oz) white
spread	chocolate
2 teaspoons oil	2 tablespoons double
225 g (8 oz) marzipan,	cream
softened	75 g (3 oz) butter
cocoa powder	rum essence
	edible food colourings of
	your choice

Preparation time: 1 hour 20 minutes, plus chilling

The nest and truffle eggs can be made up to 2 days in advance. Wrap well and keep in a cool place.

1. To make the nest, break the plain chocolate into pieces and put it into a heatproof bowl with the chocolate spread. Stand the bowl over a pan of hot water and stir until the chocolate has melted and is smooth. Remove from the heat.
2. Stir the oil into the melted chocolate. Add the marzipan and work together until the marzipan paste is an even chocolate colour.
3. Knead the marzipan paste lightly on a work surface dusted with cocoa powder.
4. Roll out the paste until it is 5 mm (¼ inch) thick. Cut into long thin strips like noodles, about 5 mm (¼ inch) wide.
5. Intertwine the chocolate marzipan strips to form a nest shape on a flat serving platter, pressing the strips gently together. Wrap in cling film until needed.
6. To make the truffle eggs, break the white chocolate into small pieces and put into a heatproof bowl with the cream.
7. Stand the bowl over a pan of hot water and stir until the white chocolate has melted and is smooth.
8. Remove the bowl from the heat and beat in the butter in small pieces. Add rum essence to taste.
9. Chill until the mixture is firm enough to mould, then divide the mixture into 3 portions. Tint one portion pink, and one green, leaving the remaining portion plain. Shape into about 20 small egg shapes.
10. 'Speckle' the truffle eggs with cocoa powder.
11. Fill the nest with the prepared truffle eggs.*

TRADITIONAL CHRISTMAS TEA

PÂTÉ AND WATERCRESS ROLLED
SANDWICHES
CHESTNUT LOG
CHRISTMAS CAKE
MINCE PIES

PÂTÉ AND WATERCRESS ROLLED SANDWICHES

12 slices of brown bread, crusts removed	salt
softened butter, for spreading	freshly ground black pepper
175 g (6 oz) smooth pâté	sprigs of watercress, to garnish
4 tablespoons chopped watercress	

Preparation time: 20–25 minutes

1. Flatten each slice of bread with a rolling pin: this makes the rolling up of the filled sandwich much easier.
2. Spread each slice with butter and then with pâté.
3. Sprinkle chopped watercress over the pâté and season to taste with salt and pepper.
4. Roll up 'Swiss roll fashion', securing each sandwich with a cocktail stick.
5. Wrap in cling film, watching the points on the sticks.*
6. Just before serving, remove the sticks from the sandwiches and garnish with sprigs of watercress.
Makes 12.

CHRISTMAS CAKE

225 g (8 oz) butter	100 g (4 oz) blanched almonds, chopped
225 g (8 oz) dark soft brown sugar	8 tablespoons brandy
2 tablespoons black treacle	TO DECORATE:
225 g (8 oz) plain flour	750 g (1½ lb) marzipan
1 teaspoon baking powder	4 tablespoons apricot jam, melted and sieved
1 teaspoon mixed spice	1.25 kg (2½ lb) icing sugar
½ teaspoon ground ginger	4 egg whites
½ teaspoon salt	2 teaspoons lemon juice
5 eggs, beaten	green food colouring
225 g (8 oz) currants	red food colouring
225 g (8 oz) sultanas	small red ribbon bows
225 g (8 oz) raisins	red ribbon, 5 cm (2 inches) wide
100 g (4 oz) glacé cherries, chopped	
100 g (4 oz) chopped mixed candied peel	

Preparation time: 25 minutes, plus maturing, marzipanning, drying and icing
Cooking time: 3½–4 hours
Oven: 140°C, 275°F, Gas Mark 1

A Christmas cake needs time to mature, so do make it well in advance, preferably 3 to 4 months before Christmas. Put the marzipan on the cake about 2 weeks in advance, and ice the cake a week before Christmas.

1. Line a 20 cm (8 inch) round deep cake tin with a double thickness of greased, greaseproof paper.
2. Cream the butter until softened, then beat in the brown sugar until soft, light and fluffy. Beat in the treacle.
3. Sift together the flour, baking powder, spices and salt. Gradually beat the eggs into the butter mixture, adding a little of the dry ingredients to prevent the creamed mixture from curdling.
4. Fold in the remaining dry ingredients then stir in the fruit, peel, nuts and half the brandy.
5. Spread the cake mixture evenly in the prepared cake tin. Make a slight depression in the centre. Bake in a preheated oven for 3½–4 hours or until a fine skewer inserted in the centre of the cake comes out clean. Cool in the tin for 10 minutes, then turn out on to a wire tray to cool completely.
6. Remove the lining paper from the cake. Pierce the bottom of the cake at regular intervals and sprinkle over the remaining brandy.
7. Wrap the cake tightly in 2 layers of cling film, and then in a layer of foil. Store in a cool, dry place until you are ready to marzipan the cake.
8. Roll out about 275 g (10 oz) of the marzipan to a round the same diameter as the top of the cake. Spread the top of the cake with a thin layer of sieved apricot jam and fix the round of marzipan in place. Smooth the marzipan gently with a rolling pin.
9. Roll out about 350 g (12 oz) of the marzipan into a strip long enough to go around the sides of the cake and about the same depth. Brush the sides of the cake with sieved apricot jam and fix the strip of marzipan in position. Trim then dry for 2 days.
10. Roll out the remaining marzipan 5 mm (¼ inch) thick, and cut out a bell shape.
11. To ice the cake, sift just under 1 kg (2 lb) of the icing sugar. Whisk the egg whites lightly, just enough to break them up, and beat in about 8 tablespoons of the sifted icing sugar. Gradually beat in the remaining sifted icing sugar and the lemon juice.
12. Place the cake on a cake board. Spread the prepared icing evenly over the top and sides of the cake, spreading it smooth with a spatula. Cover the remaining icing.
13. Once the icing on the cake has set, add a little extra sifted icing sugar to the remaining icing to give a fairly stiff piping consistency. Divide into 2 portions and tint one half green and the other red.
14. Fit a small piping bag with a medium writing nozzle and fill with some of the green icing. Pipe bands on the bell. Fill a clean piping bag with the red icing and pipe a fine line around the outer edge.
15. Pipe clusters of small red dots around the top edge of the cake. Fix the bell in the centre and decorate with a small bow. Tie the red ribbon around the side of the cake.

CHESTNUT LOG

3 eggs
75 g (3 oz) caster sugar
50 g (2 oz) plain flour
35 g (1½ oz) cocoa
    powder
1 tablespoon warm water
CHESTNUT FILLING:
1 × 250 g (8¾ oz) can
    chestnut spread
1 tablespoon brandy
CHOCOLATE BUTTER
    CREAM:
100 g (4 oz) butter,
    softened

225 g (8 oz) icing sugar,
    sifted
50 g (2 oz) plain chocolate,
    melted
1 tablespoon brandy
TO DECORATE:
icing sugar, sifted
6 marrons glacés, halved
small sprigs of artificial
    holly

Preparation time: 55 minutes, plus cooling
Cooking time: 8–10 minutes
Oven: 200°C, 400°F, Gas Mark 6

---

1. Line a 23 × 30 cm (9 × 12 inch) Swiss roll tin with greased greaseproof paper.
2. Whisk the eggs and sugar together in a heatproof bowl over a pan of hot water, or using an electric mixer, until thick, pale and creamy; the mixture should fall off the whisk in ribbons that will hold their own shape.
3. Sift together the flour and cocoa powder. Fold half into the egg mixture lightly but thoroughly.
4. Add the remaining flour and cocoa and fold in lightly, together with the warm water.
5. Pour the sponge mixture into the prepared Swiss roll tin. Spread evenly with a spatula.
6. Bake in a preheated oven for 8–10 minutes or until pale golden and springy to the touch.
7. Meanwhile, rinse a clean tea towel in hot water, wring out well and place flat on the work surface. Top with a sheet of greaseproof paper dusted with caster sugar.
8. Turn the cooked Swiss roll out on to the sugared greaseproof paper. Quickly and carefully peel the lining paper from the sponge.

9. Cover with a sheet of oiled greaseproof paper, and roll up securely but not too tightly, wrapping the complete roll in the damp tea towel. Leave to cool completely.
10. Mix the chestnut spread with the brandy.
11. Carefully unroll the Swiss roll, removing all the paper. Spread with the chestnut filling and re-roll.
12. To make the butter cream, beat the butter with the icing sugar, melted chocolate and brandy.
13. Completely coat the Swiss roll with the chocolate butter cream. Using a large pronged fork, score the surface of the buttercream so that it looks like a log.
14. Dust with icing sugar to resemble snow, and decorate with marrons glacés and sprigs of holly.* Store in an airtight tin for up to 4 days. Pictured on page 165.

MINCE PIES

275 g (10 oz) puff pastry
beaten egg
225 g (8 oz) mincemeat

3 tablespoons flaked
    almonds

Preparation time: 20–25 minutes
Cooking time: 25 minutes
Oven: 200°C, 400°F, Gas Mark 6

---

1. Roll out the puff pastry quite thinly and cut out 12 rounds 7.5 cm (3 inches) in diameter, and 12 rounds 5 cm (2 inches) in diameter.
2. Line 12 patty tins with the larger pastry rounds and brush the edges with beaten egg.
3. Put a teaspoonful of mincemeat into each pastry case. Lay a smaller pastry round over the top of the mincemeat and press down gently with the rim of an egg cup – this helps to seal the 2 pastry surfaces together.
4. Brush the top of each pie with beaten egg and sprinkle with nuts.
5. Bake in a preheated oven for about 25 minutes or until puffed and golden.* Pictured on page 165.
6. Serve warm, with Brandy butter (page 163) if liked. Makes 12.

BOXING DAY

BOXING DAY SOUP

TURKEY ESPAGNOLE

MINCEMEAT BRÛLÉE

BOXING DAY SOUP

turkey carcass
1 medium onion, peeled
  and stuck with 4 cloves
1 bay leaf
1 small bunch of parsley
  stalks
40 g (1½ oz) butter
4 sticks celery, chopped
1 medium onion, peeled
  and chopped

225 g (8 oz) cooked
  vegetables, left over
  from Christmas Day
  e.g. (Brussels sprouts,
  carrots)
150 ml (¼ pint) double
  cream
salt
freshly ground black
  pepper

Preparation time: 8 minutes
Cooking time: 2½ hours

If you have any stuffing left over, mix it with a little beaten egg and form it into small balls, about the size of a grape. Drop the stuffing balls into the blended soup and simmer gently for a further 5 minutes. Avoid boiling otherwise the stuffing is inclined to break up.

1. Put the carcass, clove-studded onion, bay leaf and parsley stalks into a large saucepan – if the turkey carcass is too large for any pan that you have, cut it into sections with poultry shears.
2. Add sufficient cold water to cover the carcass well. Bring to the boil, skimming off any scum that rises to the surface, and simmer gently for 2 hours. Strain the stock and reserve.
3. Melt the butter in another saucepan, add the celery and chopped onion and fry gently for 4 minutes.
4. Add the cooked vegetables and 1.2 litres (2 pints) of the strained turkey stock. Simmer gently for 20 minutes.
5. Purée the soup in a blender or food processor until smooth. Transfer the soup to a clean saucepan and stir in 85 ml (3 fl oz) of the cream.* Add salt and pepper to taste and heat through gently. Swirl in the remaining cream just before serving.

TURKEY ESPAGNOLE

25 g (1 oz) butter
1 tablespoon oil
1 medium onion, peeled
 and chopped
1 garlic clove, peeled and
 crushed
40 g (1½ oz) plain flour
300 ml (½ pint) chicken
 stock
300 ml (½ pint) red wine

2 tablespoons tomato
 purée
6 tomatoes, skinned,
 seeded and chopped
1 teaspoon caster sugar
salt
freshly ground black
 pepper
2 green peppers, cored,
 seeded and cut into strips

350 g (12 oz) cooked,
 skinless, boneless turkey
 meat, broken into bite-
 size pieces
boiled rice or saffron
 risotto (see page 84), to
 serve

TOPPING:
3 tablespoons oil
2 tablespoons fresh
 breadcrumbs
finely grated rind of 1
 lemon
2 tablespoons chopped
 fresh parsley

Preparation time: 15 minutes
Cooking time: 30–35 minutes

1. Heat the butter and oil in a deep frying pan. Add the onion and fry gently for 5 minutes. Add the garlic, then stir in the flour and cook for 1 minute.
2. Gradually stir in the stock and wine and bring to the boil.
3. Stir in the tomato purée, chopped tomatoes, sugar, salt and pepper to taste, and the strips of green pepper.
4. Simmer the sauce gently for 10–15 minutes or until the pepper is just tender.
5. Add the pieces of turkey and simmer gently for a further 5 minutes.
6. Meanwhile prepare the topping. Heat the oil in a frying pan, add the breadcrumbs and fry gently until crisp and golden.
7. Mix the breadcrumbs with the lemon rind and parsley.
8. Transfer the turkey and sauce to a heated serving dish. Sprinkle over the breadcrumb topping, and serve with rice and a crisp green salad.

MINCEMEAT BRÛLÉE

225 g (8 oz) mincemeat
5 egg yolks
25 g (1 oz) caster sugar
600 ml (1 pint) single
 cream

2 tablespoons brandy
50–75 g (2–3 oz)
 demerara sugar

Preparation time: 25–30 minutes, plus chilling
Cooking time: about 50 minutes
Oven: 160°C, 325°F, Gas Mark 3

1. Grease a shallow ovenproof dish, about 900 ml (1½ pint) capacity. Spread the mincemeat evenly over the bottom of the dish.
2. Beat the egg yolks with the caster sugar.
3. Heat the cream to blood heat, without boiling. Remove the cream from the heat and stir in the brandy.
4. Beat the warmed cream gradually into the egg yolk mixture and pour into the prepared dish.
5. Stand the dish in a baking tin and add sufficient hot water (not boiling) to the tin to come halfway up the sides of the dish.
6. Bake in a preheated oven for 45 minutes or until set.
7. Allow to cool slightly, then sprinkle the top of the 'custard' with a generous layer of demerara sugar – about 5 mm (¼ inch) thick.
8. Put under a preheated grill and cook until the sugar turns to a golden brown caramel.
9. Cool and chill for 3 hours before serving. This gives the delicious caramel topping a chance to soften slightly before eating.*

YOUNG CHILDREN'S PARTY
FOR TEN

PIZZA FACES

BANANA AND STRAWBERRY
SANDWICHES

RAINBOW CAKE

ICE CREAM BITES

PIZZA FACES

1 large or 2 medium tomatoes, halved	freshly ground black pepper
5 baps, halved	4 tablespoons finely chopped fresh parsley
softened butter	
225 g (8 oz) mild cheese, grated	5 small gherkins, halved crossways
4 tablespoons mayonnaise	20 slices of stuffed olive
salt	

Preparation time: 10–15 minutes
Cooking time: 3–4 minutes

You can use crumpets as a base for the cheese topping in place of baps.

1. Scoop the centre seeds from the tomato halves, leaving just a thin layer of flesh under the tomato skin (use this centre tomato for a soup or sauce). Cut 10 half moon shapes from the tomato skin, to use as 'mouths'.
2. Lightly toast the halved baps on the cut surface. Spread lightly with butter.
3. Mix the grated cheese with the mayonnaise, and season to taste with a little salt and pepper.
4. Spread the cheese mixture evenly over each half bap.
5. Place the baps under a preheated moderately hot grill until bubbling and lightly golden.
6. Sprinkle the parsley round the top edge of the baps to represent hair. Garnish each half toasted bap with a tomato 'mouth', a gherkin 'nose' and two olive 'eyes'.

BANANA AND STRAWBERRY SANDWICHES

2 large ripe bananas, thinly sliced	butter, softened
juice of 1 lemon	3 tablespoons strawberry jam
caster sugar	
6 large slices of wholemeal bread	

Preparation time: 15–20 minutes

1. Toss the banana slices in the lemon juice and sprinkle with a little caster sugar to taste.
2. Spread one side of each slice of bread with softened butter.
3. Spread half the slices with strawberry jam and top with a layer of banana slices.
4. Sandwich together with the remaining slices of bread.
5. Cut off the crusts and cut each round of sandwiches either into triangles, or into small shapes using biscuit cutters.* Remember to wrap sandwiches carefully and tightly when preparing them in advance.
Makes 3 rounds, i.e. 12 small sandwiches.

RAINBOW CAKE

250 g (9 oz) butter,
  softened or soft
  margarine
250 g (9 oz) caster sugar
4 eggs, beaten
250 g (9 oz) plain flour
1 tablespoon baking
  powder
4 tablespoons milk
raspberry jam

BUTTER CREAM:
150 g (5 oz) butter
275 g (10 oz) icing sugar,
  sifted
½ teaspoon vanilla
  essence
1 egg yolk
red food colouring
225 g (8 oz) assorted
  coloured sweets, to
  decorate

Preparation time: about 1 hour 10 minutes
Cooking time: 25–30 minutes
Oven: 190°C, 375°F, Gas Mark 5

If the cake is for a birthday, fix small coloured candles and holders on the top.

1. To make the cake, cream the butter and sugar together until light and fluffy.
2. Beat in the eggs gradually, a spoonful at a time, until all the eggs have been incorporated.
3. Sift the flour with the baking powder, and fold into the creamed mixture, together with the milk, to give a soft dropping consistency.
4. Divide the mixture between 2 greased and bottom-lined 25 cm (10 inch) sandwich tins, and smooth the tops.
5. Bake in a preheated oven for 25–30 minutes or until well risen and golden.
6. Allow the cakes to cool in their tins for about 5 minutes, then turn out on to wire trays to cool completely. (If you are not using the cakes immediately, store them in airtight tins.)
7. To make the butter cream, cream the butter until softened, then gradually beat in the icing sugar. Beat in the vanilla essence, egg yolk, and sufficient food colouring to tint the butter cream a pretty pink colour. (The prepared butter cream can be kept in the refrigerator for 3–4 days, but soften at room temperature before using.)*
8. Cut each cake in half across the centre, to give 4 even half-circles of cake.

9. Sandwich the shaped pieces of cake together with raspberry jam and a little of the prepared butter cream, to give a half-circle shaped cake.
10. Turn the cake on to its flat cut surface, and stand on a cake board or rectangular plate.
11. Coat the cake all over with the remaining butter cream.
12. Stud both sides of the cake with curved rows of sweets, sticking to just one colour for each row, e.g. an orange row, then a red row, a green row, a yellow row, a mauve row and a blue row, to give a rainbow effect.

ICE CREAM BITES

10 heaped tablespoons or
  scoops of 'soft scoop'
  strawberry or chocolate
  ice cream

20 chocolate-covered
  digestive biscuits

Preparation time: 3 minutes, plus freezing

This recipe is based on an American idea for serving ice cream at a party. If you are worried about children's fingers getting unduly messy, use plain digestive biscuits rather than chocolate-covered ones.

1. Spread a tablespoon or scoop of ice cream on the plain side of 10 of the biscuits – work quickly so that the ice cream does not melt.
2. Sandwich together with the remaining biscuits, so that the plain sides touch the ice cream.
3. 'Open-freeze' for 1 hour, then wrap each ice cream and biscuit sandwich in freezer film and return to the freezer until needed.*
4. Allow the bites to soften for 3–4 minutes at room temperature before serving.

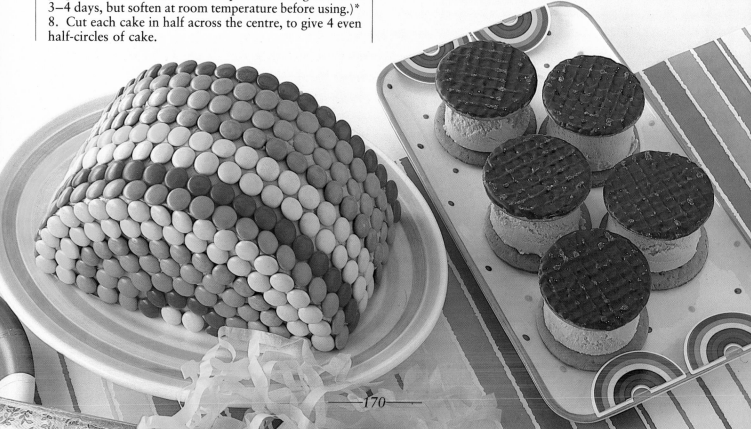

CELEBRATION DINNER
——FOR TWELVE——

This menu offers an unusual but simple first course and a choice of 2 desserts – all made well in advance – so you can concentrate on the main course: the roast goose.

TOMATO AND BASIL ICE

ROAST GOOSE WITH RAISIN AND NUT STUFFING

BRUSSELS SPROUTS WITH ONION HOOPS
ROAST POTATOES†

CHOCOLATE RUM GÂTEAU
APRICOT CHARLOTTE RUSSE

TOMATO AND BASIL ICE

750 g (1½ lb) tomatoes, skinned	2 garlic cloves, peeled and crushed
2 tablespoons tomato purée	1 tablespoon lemon juice
5 tablespoons chopped fresh basil or mint	salt
300 ml (½ pint) soured cream	freshly ground black pepper
300 ml (½ pint) mayonnaise	TO GARNISH:
	12 small fresh mint sprigs
	1 egg white, lightly beaten
	2 tablespoons caster sugar

Preparation time: 30 minutes, plus freezing

1. Purée the tomatoes, tomato purée and basil or mint in a blender or food processor. Turn the mixture into a bowl.
2. Stir in the soured cream, mayonnaise, garlic and lemon juice, and season well with salt and pepper. Beat the mixture until it is smooth.
3. Turn the mixture into chilled metal trays, cover and chill in the freezer, or the freezing compartment of a refrigerator at the lowest setting, for 1 hour.
4. Turn the mixture into a chilled bowl and beat it well. Cover and continue freezing for 2 hours.
5. To make the garnish, dip the mint sprigs first into the egg white and then into the sugar. Toss them to coat completely. Spread them out on a piece of foil or greaseproof paper and leave to dry in a warm place for about 2 hours.
6. Transfer the tomato ice to the main compartment of the refrigerator 1 hour before serving.* Serve in scoops in chilled individual glasses or small bowls, garnished with a sprig of frosted mint.

ROAST GOOSE WITH RAISIN AND NUT STUFFING

2 × 3.5–4 kg (8–9 lb) geese, oven-ready with giblets

STOCK:
2 medium onions, peeled and sliced
2 large carrots, peeled and sliced
4 celery sticks, sliced
4 bay leaves
few parsley stalks
1 bouquet garni
12 black peppercorns
1.2 litres (2 pints) water
salt

STUFFING:
225 g (8 oz) seedless raisins
150 ml (¼ pint) port or full-bodied red wine
75 g (3 oz) butter
2 medium onions, peeled and finely chopped
6 streaky bacon rashers, rind removed, diced
225 g (8 oz) pork sausage meat
150 g (5 oz) fresh breadcrumbs
100 g (4 oz) walnuts, chopped

3 tablespoons chopped fresh parsley
2 teaspoons dried marjoram
2 teaspoons ground coriander
2 eggs, beaten
salt
freshly ground black pepper
120 ml (4 fl oz) brandy
8 tablespoons fresh breadcrumbs
2 tablespoons finely chopped walnuts
2 tablespoons grated orange rind

TO GARNISH:
4 tablespoons demerara sugar
2 teaspoons ground coriander
large pinch of grated nutmeg
3 large cooking apples, peeled and cut into thin rings
2 tablespoons plain flour

Preparation time: 1½ hours, plus soaking
Cooking time: 3¼–3½ hours
Oven: 200°C, 400°F, Gas Mark 6;
    160°C, 325°F, Gas Mark 3

The secret of cooking a goose to perfection is to start it at a high temperature, pouring off the fat as it is released, and then reducing the oven heat. That way the bird is not too fatty, and not too dry. You can make the giblet stock and the stuffing 1–2 days in advance and store in covered containers in the refrigerator.

1. To make the stock, put the goose giblets (except the livers which will be used in the stuffing) into a saucepan with the vegetables, herbs, peppercorns and water. Season with salt, cover the pan, bring to the boil and simmer for 1½–2 hours.
2. Meanwhile, make the stuffing. Soak the raisins in the port or wine for at least 2 hours, or overnight. Melt the butter in a frying pan, add the onions and bacon and fry over a moderate heat for 5–6 minutes, stirring occasionally. Using a slotted spoon, transfer the onions and bacon to a bowl. Fry the sausage meat in the pan, stirring with a wooden spoon until it is evenly browned. Transfer the sausage meat to the bowl, and discard the fat in the pan. Stir in the breadcrumbs, chopped goose livers, soaked raisins, walnuts, herbs and coriander. Add the beaten eggs and season well with salt and pepper.

3. Wipe the geese inside and out with a damp cloth and dry. Pull out any remaining feather tips and cut off any loose pieces of fat.
4. Pack the stuffing into the birds. Using a trussing needle or large darning needle and thread, sew up the birds to enclose the stuffing completely. Prick the geese all over many times with a needle.
5. Place the geese on their sides (so they are supporting each other) in the largest roasting tin that will fit into the oven. Roast in a preheated oven for 30 minutes, turning the geese round after about 15 minutes.
6. Remove the tin from the oven and reduce the temperature. Pour off all the fat from the tin. Turn the geese over in the tin, breasts side up again and continue cooking them for a further 2¼–2½ hours, pouring off the fat and turning the geese round once or twice, during the cooking time.
7. Strain the stock and reserve 600 ml (1 pint).
8. Heat the brandy in a small pan and carefully set light to it. Pour it over the breasts of the geese to burn off the excess fat. Stand well back while doing this as ignition is quite fierce. Mix together the breadcrumbs, walnuts and orange rind. Sprinkle the mixture over the birds and pat it on firmly.
9. To prepare the garnish, mix together the sugar, coriander and nutmeg. Dip in the apple slices to coat them on both sides. Arrange them in an overlapping row down the centre of the breast of each bird. Return the geese to the oven to roast for a further 15 minutes.
10. Transfer the geese to a heated serving platter and keep warm. Stir the flour into the juices in the tin, then add the strained stock and stir until the sauce thickens. Taste and adjust the seasoning. Serve with the geese.
11. Roast potatoes and Brussels sprouts with onion hoops (see below) go well with the geese.

BRUSSELS SPROUTS WITH ONION HOOPS

1.75 kg (4 lb) small, young Brussels sprouts, trimmed
salt
2 tablespoons lemon juice
50 g (2 oz) butter

2 tablespoons vegetable oil
3 large onions, peeled and thinly sliced into rings
freshly ground black pepper

Preparation time: 20 minutes
Cooking time: 20 minutes

---

1. Cook the Brussels sprouts in boiling salted water, with the lemon juice, for 10–12 minutes or until they are just tender.
2. Meanwhile, heat the butter and oil in a large frying pan, add the onion rings and fry over a moderately high heat for 3–4 minutes, stirring, until they are just beginning to turn brown. Remove them from the pan with a slotted spoon.
3. Drain the Brussels sprouts well and turn into a heated serving dish. Scatter the onions on top and season well with pepper.

CHOCOLATE RUM GÂTEAU

*225 g (8 oz) bitter
  chocolate*
225 g (8 oz) plain flour
*1 tablespoon baking
  powder*
*½ teaspoon bicarbonate
  of soda*
pinch of salt
100 g (4 oz) butter
75 g (3 oz) caster sugar
*3 eggs (at room
  temperature), separated*

300 ml (½ pint) milk
1 teaspoon vanilla essence
SYRUP:
100 g (4 oz) sugar
150 ml (¼ pint) water
5 tablespoons dark rum
FILLING AND DECORATION:
4 tablespoons dark rum
*300 ml (½ pint) whipping
  cream, stiffly whipped*
chocolate leaves (page 50)

Preparation time: 30 minutes, plus overnight soaking
Cooking time: 50 minutes
Oven: 180°C, 350°F, Gas Mark 4

This is a perfect dessert to make for a special occasion. It is baked the day before and left to soak overnight in rum syrup, becoming more delicious all the time. It is very quick to assemble and decorate an hour or so before serving.

1. Break up the chocolate and place in a heatproof bowl over a pan of hot water. Melt, stirring occasionally, then remove the bowl from the heat and leave to cool a little.
2. Sift together the flour, baking powder, soda and salt. Cream the butter with the sugar until light and fluffy. Gradually beat in the egg yolks one at a time, then the melted chocolate. Beat in the flour mixture and the milk alternately, then add the vanilla essence. Stiffly beat the egg whites and beat into the mixture until smooth.
3. Pour the mixture into 2 greased and floured 20 cm (8 inch) sandwich tins. Bake in a preheated oven for 30 minutes. Leave to cool slightly, then turn out on to a wire tray to cool completely.
4. To make the syrup, put the sugar and water into a small saucepan and stir over a low heat until the sugar has dissolved. Bring to the boil and boil for 5 minutes. Away from the heat stir in the rum and remove the pan from the heat.
5. Place the 2 cake layers on a piece of foil on a baking sheet. Prick all over with a skewer. Pour on the hot rum syrup, and spoon over any syrup that runs off. Cover the cakes and leave overnight.*
6. Stir the rum into the whipped cream.
7. Using 2 fish slices, carefully lift 1 cake layer on to a serving dish – the cake will be rather moist and fragile. Spread half the rum cream over it and place the second layer on top, spread more cream on the top and sides.
8. Using a large star nozzle, pipe swirls of the remaining rum cream on the top edges. Decorate with the chocolate leaves.

APRICOT CHARLOTTE RUSSE

1 tablespoon apricot jam
about 18 sponge finger
  biscuits
1 × 450 g (1 lb) can
  apricot halves
5 teaspoons powdered
  gelatine
8 egg yolks
100 g (4 oz) caster sugar
300 ml (½ pint) milk

300 ml (½ pint) double
  cream
6 tablespoons Amaretti
  liqueur
TO DECORATE:
150 ml (¼ pint) whipping
  cream, stiffly whipped
6 tablespoons blanched
  almonds, halved and
  toasted

Preparation time: 45 minutes, plus chilling
Cooking time: 20 minutes

---

1. Spread the jam in a thin line around the inside of a 20 cm (8 inch) deep round cake tin with a fixed base. Cut off one rounded end of each sponge biscuit so that it will stand level. Stand the biscuits edge to edge around the dish, sugared sides against the dish and rounded end up. Press them lightly into the jam to hold them in place.
2. Drain the apricots, reserving the syrup. Purée the fruit in a blender or food processor with 5 tablespoons of the syrup.
3. Put 3 tablespoons of the remaining syrup into a small cup, sprinkle over the gelatine and stand the cup in a pan of hot water. Stir until the gelatine has dissolved.

4. Beat together the egg yolks and caster sugar in a heatproof bowl over a pan of hot water until creamy and light in colour. Heat the milk to simmering point and strain on to the egg mixture. Stir, still over hot water, until the custard thickens enough to coat the back of a spoon. Stir the gelatine into the custard. Remove the bowl from the heat and leave to cool.
5. Stir the apricot purée into the custard. Chill the mixture until it is syrupy and just on the point of setting. Whip the double cream until thick, and fold into the apricot mixture with the liqueur.
6. Pour the mixture into the prepared dish. Chill for at least 3 hours or until set.
7. To unmould the dessert, run a knife round between the biscuits and the dish. Dip the base of the dish into hot water for 2–3 seconds. Have the serving dish ready. Invert a large plate over the mould, then turn the mould upside-down and give a sharp shake to release it. Place the serving dish over the base of the dessert. Turn it over quickly and remove the other plate.
8. Tie a ribbon around the outside of the dessert. Using a star nozzle, pipe rosettes of whipped cream on top. Stick the toasted almonds into the cream rosettes to decorate. Chill the dessert until required.*

DRINKS PARTY
–FOR TWENTY FOUR–

There is either a warm and welcoming mulled red wine or a refreshing, chilled white wine cup, together with a selection of savoury pastry dishes, which can be prepared well in advance. Points you shouldn't forget: provide small plates – disposable ones if you like – and plenty of paper napkins. And for the calorie conscious, dishes of crisp, crunchy raw vegetable sticks – celery, carrots, cucumber, green pepper and cauliflower.

ABBOT'S MULL or
ASCOT WINE CUP

SMOKED OYSTER QUICHES

CHOUX BITES

ONION PIZZA

FETA CHEESE ENVELOPES

ABBOT'S MULL

10 bottles of fruity red wine	thinly pared rind of 2 oranges
2 cinnamon sticks	450 g (1 lb) demerara sugar
12 cloves	
2 teaspoons grated nutmeg	1 bottle of medium dry sherry
4 teaspoons ground mixed spice	½ bottle of brandy

Preparation time: 20 minutes
Heating time: 45 minutes

Inexpensive red wine is the basis of this traditional mulled wine recipe. Choose a full-bodied, fruity red wine from Italy or Spain, or a French country wine or Vin de Pays.

1. Pour the red wine into a large pan such as a preserving pan, or make it in several batches in smaller saucepans. Add the spices, orange rind and sugar and heat very slowly, stirring until the sugar has dissolved. Heat for a further 15 minutes over a low heat.
2. Pour in the sherry, stir and continue heating over a low heat for 15 minutes. Taste the wine and add more sugar or spices if liked.
3. Pour in the brandy and heat slowly for a further 10 minutes. Do not boil at any stage.
4. Serve it piping hot.* Strain the wine if preferred, and ladle it into a ceramic bowl or a heatproof jug. Have a silver spoon ready to stand in each glass as you pour the wine, to protect the glass from cracking. To keep the wine hot and make serving easier, you can pour some into a large vacuum flask and transfer it into the serving bowl or jug as you need it. Alternatively, fill heatproof jugs with the hot mulled wine and stand in a large pan of simmering water.

Variation:
To make the mulled wine go a little further, or in consideration of guests who have to drive, you can add up to 1 litre (1¾ pints) water to the red wine in step 1 of the recipe.

ASCOT WINE CUP

450 g (1 lb) strawberries, hulled and halved	10 bottles of medium dry white wine, chilled
225 g (8 oz) peaches, stoned and thinly sliced	1 bottle of medium dry sparkling white wine, chilled
225 g (8 oz) small seedless white grapes	24 small fresh mint or borage sprigs, to decorate (optional)
225 g (8 oz) caster sugar	
½ bottle of kirsch or other cherry liqueur	
1 bottle of sweet white vermouth, chilled	

Preparation time: 30 minutes, plus macerating and chilling

For this delightful summer wine cup, choose a fruity, medium dry white wine such as Soave, Riesling or a crisp Hock or Mosel. If you buy the wine in 1 litre bottles, you will need 8 litres for this recipe.

1. Put the fruit into a large silver, ceramic or glass serving bowl, sprinkle on the sugar and pour on the kirsch. Leave for 30 minutes for the fruit to take up the flavour of the liqueur.
2. Pour on the vermouth and stir, taking care not to break the fruit. Pour on the white wine and stir to blend well.
3. Just before serving, pour on the sparkling wine.
4. Use a ladle to serve the wine into goblets, making sure that each one has at least 1 piece of fruit. Decorate each with a sprig of mint or borage.

SMOKED OYSTER QUICHES

500 g (1¼ lb) shortcrust
pastry
2 × 100 g (4 oz) cans
smoked oysters, drained
and chopped
4 teaspoons chopped fresh
parsley

3 eggs
450 ml (¾ pint) single
cream
freshly ground black
pepper
pinch of cayenne pepper

Preparation time: 20 minutes
Cooking time: 30 minutes
Oven: 220°C, 425°F, Gas Mark 7;
    190°C, 375°F, Gas Mark 5

---

1. Roll out the dough thinly and cut into rounds using a
6 cm (2½ inch) cutter. Line 48 greased tartlet tins with
the dough rounds and prick all over with a fork.
2. Bake the pastry cases 'blind' in a preheated oven for
10 minutes. Remove from the oven* and reduce the heat.
3. Mix together the chopped oysters and parsley and
divide the mixture between the pastry cases.
4. Beat together the eggs and cream and season to taste
with pepper and cayenne. Pour the mixture into the
pastry cases.
5. Bake the tartlets for a further 20 minutes or until the
filling is set and golden brown. Makes about 48.

CHOUX BITES

PLAIN CHOUX PASTRY:
65 g (2½ oz) plain flour
pinch of salt
150 ml (¼ pint) water
50 g (2 oz) butter
2 eggs, lightly beaten

TOMATO CHOUX PASTE:
65 g (2½ oz) plain flour
pinch of salt
150 ml (¼ pint) water
50 g (2 oz) butter
2 teaspoons tomato purée
2 eggs, lightly beaten

CHEESE FILLING:
100 g (4 oz) full-fat soft
cheese
3 tablespoons whipping
cream
2 tablespoons finely
chopped walnuts
1 tablespoon chopped
fresh mixed herbs
salt
freshly ground black
pepper

'RED CAVIAR' FILLING:
1 × 100 g (4 oz) jar red
lumpfish roe
1 teaspoon grated lemon
rind
1 teaspoon lemon juice
150 ml (¼ pint) whipping
cream, stiffly whipped
freshly ground black
pepper

Preparation time: 50 minutes, plus cooling
Cooking time: 20 minutes
Oven: 220°C, 425°F, Gas Mark 7

The plain and tomato choux pastes can be made separately. Alternatively measure the combined quantities of
flour, salt, water and butter and make as follows.

1. To make the choux pastes, sift together the flour and
salt. Melt the butter in the water then bring to the boil.
Remove from the heat and tip in the flour. Stir quickly
with a wooden spoon until the paste forms into a ball and
leaves the sides of the pan. Cool. Divide into 2 batches.
2. Beat the tomato purée into one batch.
3. Gradually beat 2 eggs into each batch of mixture until
smooth and glossy.
4. Spoon the plain choux paste into a piping bag fitted
with a large, plain nozzle. Pipe large walnut-sized blobs
of the mixture, well apart, on 2 dampened baking sheets.
5. Bake in a preheated oven for 10 minutes or until the
pastry is well risen, firm and deep brown. Slit each bun at
the side and transfer to a wire tray to cool.
6. Bake the tomato choux paste in the same way.
7. To make the 'red caviar' filling, stir the lumpfish roe,
lemon rind, juice and pepper into the whipped cream.
8. To make the cheese and walnut filling, beat the cheese
and whipping cream together. Stir in the walnuts and
herbs and season to taste with salt and pepper.*
9. Fill the puffs just before serving. Makes about 48.

ONION PIZZA

450 g (1 lb) plain flour
2 teaspoons baking
  powder
1 teaspoon salt
50 g (2 oz) butter
300 ml (½ pint) soured
  cream
TOPPING:
4 tablespoons vegetable
  oil
4 large onions, peeled and
  thinly sliced into rings
1 × 400 g (14 oz) can
  tomatoes, drained

1 teaspoon sugar
1 tablespoons dried mixed
  herbs
2 tablespoons chopped
  fresh parsley
salt
freshly ground black
  pepper
2 × 50 g (2 oz) cans
  anchovy fillets, drained
100 g (4 oz) Parmesan
  cheese, grated
4 tablespoons black olives,
  halved and stoned

Preparation time: 25 minutes
Cooking time: 1 hour
Oven: 220°C, 425°F, Gas Mark 7

1. Sift the flour, baking powder and salt into a bowl and rub in the butter until the mixture resembles fine breadcrumbs. Stir in the soured cream and mix to a firm dough. Knead the dough until smooth.
2. Roll out the dough and used to line 2 greased 28 × 18 cm (11 × 7 inch) baking tins.
3. To make the topping, heat the oil in a frying pan, add the onion rings and fry gently, stirring occasionally, for about 8 minutes. Remove from the heat.
4. Put the tomatoes into a saucepan, add the sugar and herbs and season with salt and pepper. Bring to the boil, and simmer for 10–15 minutes, mashing with a wooden spoon until the mixture forms a thick paste.
5. Spread the tomato mixture thinly over the pizza dough. Cover with the onion rings and anchovy fillets, scatter over the cheese and arrange the olives on top.
6. Bake in a preheated oven for 25–30 minutes or until the dough is well risen and the topping brown. Cut each tray of pizza into 12 slices or 24 fingers.* Serve hot. To reheat, place in the oven heated to 200°C, 400°F, Gas Mark 6, for 10 minutes. Makes 24 slices, or 48 fingers.

FETA CHEESE ENVELOPES

450 g (1 lb) frozen puff
  pastry, thawed
FILLING:
225 g (8 oz) cottage cheese
100 g (4 oz) feta or
  Wensleydale cheese,
  finely crumbled

2 tablespoons chopped
  fresh parsley
freshly ground black
  pepper
pinch of grated nutmeg
1 egg, beaten
milk, to glaze

Preparation time: 30 minutes
Cooking time: 20 minutes
Oven: 190°C, 375°F, Gas Mark 5

1. Divide the pastry into 4 equal pieces. Roll out two portions to 28 × 23 cm (11 × 9 inch) rectangles. Use to line the bottom of 2 greased Swiss roll tins.
2. To make the filling, mix together the cheeses, parsley, pepper to taste and nutmeg and bind the mixture with the egg. Beat well.
3. Place teaspoons of the cheese mixture on the pastry in rows, about 2 cm (¾ inch) apart. Brush between the rows with milk.
4. Roll out the other 2 pieces of pastry to the same size rectangles as before and place over the filling. Press them down to seal the edges and run your finger along the rows between the filling – the pastry will look like large sheets of ravioli. Cut the pastry almost through into squares along the rows and brush the top with milk.
5. Bake in a preheated oven for 20 minutes or until the pastry is well risen and golden brown.
6. Leave to cool a little in the tins, then cut the pastry into squares and serve warm. If it is more convenient, leave the pastry to cool.* Reheat in a moderate oven for about 10 minutes. Makes about 40.

FORMAL BUFFET
—FOR FORTY TO FIFTY—

Take this large undertaking in easy stages, make careful lists of what you have to buy, even the serving dishes, crockery, cutlery and glasses you will need and you will find the preparation surprisingly easy.

ORCHARD CUP or
BUCK'S FIZZ

HONEY-GLAZED HAM
CHICKEN IN TARRAGON CREAM
SAUCE
ASPARAGUS MOULD
SMOKED SALMON QUICHES

FENNEL, BEAN AND MUSHROOM
SALAD
TOMATO AND BASIL SALAD†
GREEN SALAD†
RICE SALAD†

LEMON RASPBERRY TRIFLE
BRAZIL NUT MERINGUE CAKES
SUNRAY FRUIT SALAD

ORCHARD CUP

12 bottles of medium dry
   white wine, chilled
7 bottles of still, clear
   apple juice, chilled
1 bottle of Calvados,
   chilled

450 g (1 lb) red dessert
   apples, cored and thinly
   sliced

Preparation time: 10 minutes, plus chilling

Here's a fruit cup that's really different. If it's a spring celebration and there's apple blossom in the garden, float a few blossom flowers on the wine cup, too, and arrange small branches of the blossom on the table for an unusual flower decoration. Choose a medium dry German or Italian white wine and have it well chilled. If you buy the wine in the economical 1 litre bottles, you will need 9 litres.

1. Pour the wine, apple juice and Calvados into a large silver, ceramic or glass serving bowl and stir to blend well.*
2. Just before serving, float the apple slices on the punch.
3. To serve, ladle the punch into goblets, making sure there's at least 1 slice of apple in each. Pictured on previous page.

BUCK'S FIZZ

4.5 litres (8 pints)
   unsweetened orange
   juice, chilled
1 bottle of brandy, chilled

12 bottles of non-vintage
   Champagne, or
   sparkling white wine,
   chilled

Preparation time: 5 minutes, plus chilling

You can have the orange juice and brandy in the glasses already, but open the champagne only as you need it: the popping corks are all part of the fun!

1. Mix together the orange juice and brandy. Pour it into the wine glasses to quarter-fill them.*
2. Open the Champagne as you need it. Pour it at once into the glasses so that they are three-quarters full (you must leave room for the bubbles!). Serve at once.

HONEY-GLAZED HAM

2 × 3 kg (7 lb) shank ends
   of gammon
4 bay leaves
8 cloves
8–12 black peppercorns
2 large onions, peeled and
   sliced
1.2 litres (2 pints) sweet
   cider

100 g (4 oz) soft dark
   brown sugar
GLAZE:
225 g (8 oz) clear honey
about 4 tablespoons
   whole cloves
6 tablespoons demerara
   sugar

Preparation time: 15 minutes, plus overnight soaking and
   cooling
Cooking time: 3 hours
Oven: 220°C, 425°F, Gas Mark 7

Make this the appetizing centrepiece of your party table. Buy 2 half gammons and you achieve the best of both worlds – you can have one ready carved, to speed up service, and carve the second one once guests have had time to admire it!

1. Soak the hams in cold water overnight, or bring them to the boil in a large saucepan of water, then drain. Pat the hams dry with paper towels.
2. Place each ham in a large saucepan. Divide the bayleaves, cloves, peppercorns, onions, cider and sugar between them. Pour on enough cold water to cover. Bring the water to the boil, skimming if necessary. Cover the pans and simmer for 2 hours 20 minutes, or 20 minutes to each 450 g (1 lb).
3. Remove the hams from the stock. (Reserve the stock to make soup, sauces and to cook dried pulses.) When the hams are cool enough to handle, carefully cut away the skin. Trim off some of the fat, taking care to leave a smooth, even surface.
4. Brush all over the surface of the hams with the honey. Stick the cloves into the fat to make a lattice pattern. Sprinkle the sugar over the fat.
5. Place each ham in a roasting tin and bake in a preheated oven for 30 minutes, turning the meat once.
6. Transfer the hams to a dish to cool. Wrap them in foil and chill. Remove them from the refrigerator and leave at room temperature for 4-5 hours before serving.* To carve the hams, see page 47.

CHICKEN IN TARRAGON CREAM SAUCE

4 × 2 kg (4½ lb) oven-
   ready chickens
4 large carrots, peeled and
   sliced
8 celery sticks, sliced
4 onions, peeled and sliced
few parsley stalks
few fresh French tarragon
   sprigs (if available)
4 bay leaves
1 lemon, quartered
about 12 black
   peppercorns
salt
fresh French tarragon or
   parsley sprigs, to
   garnish

SAUCE:
50 g (2 oz) butter
40 g (1½ oz) plain flour
4 egg yolks
600 ml (1 pint) single
   cream
4–5 tablespoons chopped
   fresh French tarragon,
   or 1½ tablespoons
   dried tarragon
freshly ground black
   pepper

Preparation time: 1 hour, plus overnight cooling
Cooking time: 1½ hours

1. You can cook the chickens in separate pans or together in a large preserving pan closely covered with a double layer of foil as a lid. Put the chickens in the pans and divide the vegetables, herbs, lemon, peppercorns and salt between them. Cover the pans, bring slowly to the boil and simmer for 1 hour.

2. Remove the pans from the heat and leave the chickens to cool in the stock. Remove the chickens and pat dry. Strain the stock and reserve 600 ml (1 pint) for the sauce.

3. To make the sauce, melt the butter in a saucepan, stir in the flour and cook gently for 1 minute. Gradually stir in the reserved stock and bring to the boil, stirring constantly. Simmer for 2–3 minutes.

4. Beat together the egg yolks and cream. Stir in a little of the sauce then pour the egg mixture into the remaining sauce in the pan. Add the tarragon and stir over a low heat, without boiling, for 2–4 minutes. Taste the sauce and adjust the seasoning if necessary. Pour the sauce into a bowl, cover the top with dampened greaseproof paper and leave to cool, preferably overnight.

5. Skin the chickens and cut the flesh from the bones in neat, even pieces. Arrange the chickens on serving dishes.

6. Stir the sauce and spoon it over the sliced chicken to coat. Cover the dishes loosely with foil and chill.* Garnish with sprigs of tarragon or parsley before serving.

ASPARAGUS MOULD

6 × 225 g (8 oz) packets
   frozen asparagus spears,
   thawed
225 g (8 oz) frozen peas,
   thawed
1 kg (2 lb) carrots, peeled
salt
1 litre (1¾ pints) water
2 tablespoons aspic jelly
   powder
3 tablespoons dry sherry
SAUCE:
150 ml (¼ pint) water
50 g (2 oz) powdered
   gelatine
8 egg yolks

4 eggs
3 tablespoons dry mustard
4 tablespoons sugar
300 ml (½ pint) white
   wine vinegar
4 tablespoons lemon juice
300 ml (½ pint) single
   cream
600 ml (1 pint) soured
   cream
300 ml (½ pint)
   mayonnaise
salt
freshly ground white
   pepper

Preparation time: 1 hour, plus cooling and setting
Cooking time: 30 minutes

This is a highly decorative and tempting way to serve young and colourful vegetables, set in a mould in a light soured cream and mayonnaise sauce. You can ring the changes and use other seasonal vegetables.

1. Cook the asparagus, peas and carrots separately in boiling salted water until they are just tender. Drain. Chop 450 g (1 lb) of the asparagus. Cut the carrots into small dice. Leave all the vegetables to become completely cold.
2. Heat a little of the water and dissolve the aspic jelly powder in it. Stir in the remaining water and the sherry and stand the container in iced water to speed up setting.
3. When the aspic is on the point of setting, and is like thick syrup, spoon it into four 900 ml (1½ pint) moulds. Use the back of a spoon to smooth out the jelly and fill out any decorative patterns on the moulds.
4. Press the whole spears of asparagus into the aspic layer, arranging them in a decorative 'wheel' pattern. Chill the moulds and allow the aspic to set firmly.
5. To make the sauce, place the water in a small heatproof bowl, sprinkle over the gelatine and stand the bowl in a pan of hot water. Stir until the gelatine has dissolved.
6. Beat together the egg yolks, eggs, mustard and sugar. Put the vinegar and lemon juice into a small saucepan and bring to simmering point. Pour into a heatproof bowl placed over a pan of hot water. Add the egg mixture and cook gently, stirring, for about 10 minutes or until the mixture thickens. Stir in the dissolved gelatine. Remove the bowl from the heat and leave to cool for about 20 minutes.
7. When the custard mixture is on the point of setting, stir in the cream, soured cream and mayonnaise. Taste and adjust the seasoning. Stir in the cooked vegetables, including the chopped asparagus.
8. Pour the sauce into the prepared moulds and level the tops. Chill for at least 4 hours or until set.*
9. To unmould, invert a plate over the top of each mould. Wrap the mould in a tea towel wrung out in hot water. Turn over the mould and shake it firmly. Lift off and serve.

SMOKED SALMON QUICHES

900 g (2 lb) plain flour
4 tablespoons icing sugar
½ teaspoon salt
2 teaspoons lemon juice
500 g (1¼ lb) butter
FILLING:
4 tablespoons olive oil
2 large onions, peeled and
   finely chopped
16 eggs
1.2 litres (2 pints) single
   cream

600 ml (1 pint) milk
salt
freshly ground black
   pepper
pinch of cayenne pepper
8 tablespoons grated
   Gruyère cheese
450 g (1 lb) smoked
   salmon off-cuts, reserve
   a few pieces, to garnish

Preparation time: 1 hour, plus chilling
Cooking time: 40 minutes
Oven: 230°C, 450°F, Gas Mark 8;
   180°C, 350°F, Gas Mark 4

1. Sift the flour, icing sugar and salt into a bowl. Stir in the lemon juice, and rub in the butter until the mixture is like fine breadcrumbs. Stir in just enough ice cold water to mix to a firm dough. Shape the dough into a ball, wrap in film or foil and chill for at least 1 hour.
2. Divide the dough into 4 equal pieces. Roll them out on a lightly floured board and use to line 4 greased and floured 25 cm (10 inch) flan tins. Trim the edges and prick the bottoms with a fork. Chill for 30 minutes.
3. Cover the bottoms of the pastry cases with rounds of foil and fill with baking beans. Bake the pastry 'blind' in a preheated oven for 10 minutes. Remove the pastry from the oven and remove the foil and beans. Reduce the oven temperature.
4. To make the filling, heat the oil in a frying pan, add the onions and fry over a moderate heat for 3–4 minutes, stirring frequently. Do not allow to brown. Remove from the heat.
5. Beat together the eggs, cream and milk, and season to taste with salt, pepper and cayenne.
6. Divide the onion between the 4 pastry cases, spreading it over the bottoms. Cover the onion with the slices of smoked salmon. Pour on the egg mixture and sprinkle with the grated cheese.
7. Bake for 20–25 minutes or until the filling is set and golden brown.* Ideally, make the flans on the day of the buffet and if possible reheat them just before serving. Makes four 25 cm (10 inch) quiches, 10–12 servings each. Garnish with the reserved salmon just before serving.

FENNEL AND BEAN SALAD

750 g (1½ lb) dried white
  haricot or green
  flageolet beans, soaked
  overnight and drained
5 heads of fennel, thinly
  sliced
750 g (1½ lb) button
  mushrooms, thinly
  sliced
2 red peppers, cored,
  seeded and very thinly
  sliced
DRESSING:
2 teaspoons dry mustard
2 teaspoons caster sugar

2 teaspoons salt
3 garlic cloves, peeled and
  crushed
6 tablespoons orange juice
1 tablespoon lemon juice
450 ml (¾ pint) olive oil
freshly ground black
  pepper
curly endive leaves, to
  serve
12 spring onions, peeled
  and sliced
2 small onions, peeled and
  thinly sliced into rings

Preparation time: 40 minutes, plus overnight soaking and
  marinating
Cooking time: 1¼ hours

Serve several salads with this buffet: a tomato salad
sprinkled with basil, a green salad, a rice salad and this
unusual and tasty recipe using fresh fennel and dried
beans.

1. Cook the beans in boiling water for about 1¼ hours
or until they are just tender. Drain and cool.
2. Toss together the beans, fennel, mushrooms and red
peppers.
3. Stir together the mustard, sugar, salt and garlic and
stir in the orange and lemon juices. Whisk in the olive oil
and season well with pepper. Taste and add more
seasoning if needed.
4. Pour the dressing over the mixed vegetables and stir
carefully, to avoid breaking the mushrooms. Cover and
leave to marinate at room temperature for 1–2 hours.*
5. Arrange the endive leaves to line a large serving dish.
Spoon on the salad and scatter the onions on top.

LEMON RASPBERRY TRIFLE

1 kg (2 lb) raspberries, fresh or frozen
about 225 g (8 oz) icing sugar
3 × 20 cm (8 inch) sponge cakes, or 2 × packets of trifle sponge cakes
200 ml (⅓ pint) medium sweet white wine
150 ml (¼ pint) Framboise (raspberry liqueur)
CUSTARD:
600 ml (1 pint) milk
600 ml (1 pint) single cream

2 teaspoons cornflour
75 g (3 oz) caster sugar
10 eggs
TOPPING:
1 tablespoon grated lemon rind
1.2 litres (2 pints) whipping cream, whipped
4 tablespoons medium sherry
4 lemons, thinly sliced
candied angelica

Preparation time: 50 minutes, plus cooling
Cooking time: 30 minutes

1. Put the raspberries and icing sugar into a saucepan and heat gently until the fruit juice begins to run. Stir to dissolve the sugar, then bring to the boil. Rub the fruit through a sieve to make a purée and leave to cool. Taste the purée and stir in more icing sugar if the fruit is rather sharp.
2. Bring the milk and cream to the boil in a heavy saucepan. Mix together the cornflour and sugar and gradually beat in the eggs. Pour on the boiling milk mixture, stirring constantly. Return the custard to the pan and stir over a very low heat for about 10 minutes, or until thickened. Remove from the heat and leave to cool.
3. Split each sponge cake into 2 layers and sandwich back together with the raspberry purée. Cut into fingers and arrange them to fit the bottom of two 1.75 litre (3 pint) serving bowls. Mix together the white wine and liqueur and pour it over the sponge cakes.
4. Pour the custard over the sponge cakes and level the top. Leave to cool completely.
5. Stir the lemon rind into the whipped cream and gradually stir in the sherry. Spread the cream over the custard, reserving a little for decoration. Pipe the reserved cream in rosettes around the edge of the cream topping.
6. Halve the lemon slices. Cut each half from the centre almost through to the rind and twist it. Arrange the twisted slices on the cream. Cut stalk and leaf shapes from the angelica and arrange them in place. Chill well before serving.* Makes 2 trifles, 12 servings each.

BRAZIL NUT MERINGUE CAKES

225 g (8 oz) brazil nuts, ground
12 egg whites
750 g (1½ lb) caster sugar
2 teaspoons lemon juice
225 g (8 oz) bitter chocolate

1 × 450 g (1 lb) can unsweetened chestnut purée
100 g (4 oz) caster sugar
600 ml (1 pint) double cream, thickly whipped

Preparation time: 40 minutes, plus cooling
Cooking time: 50 minutes
Oven: 180°C, 350°F, Gas Mark 4;
190°C, 375°F, Gas Mark 5

1. Spread the ground brazil nuts on 2 baking sheets and toast them in a preheated oven for 5–6 minutes, stirring them once or twice. Remove from the oven and leave to cool. Increase the oven temperature.
2. Whisk the egg whites until stiff, then add half the sugar and whisk until the mixture is glossy. Mix the toasted brazil nuts with the remaining sugar and fold into the meringue mixture. Fold in the lemon juice.
3. Spread the meringue mixture into four 25 cm (10 inch) rounds on baking sheets lined with non-stick silicone or lightly greased greaseproof paper and level the tops. Bake in the oven for 30–40 minutes or until the meringues are dry and crisp on top. Peel off the paper and leave the meringue layers to cool on wire trays.
4. To make the filling, melt the chocolate in a heatproof bowl over a pan of hot water. Beat the chestnut purée until it is soft and smooth. Beat in the melted chocolate and sugar. Fold in half the whipped cream.
5. Reserve a little of the filling to decorate. Divide the remainder between 2 of the meringue layers, spreading smoothly. Place the remaining meringue layers on top.
6. To decorate, spoon the remaining whipped cream into a piping bag fitted with a large star nozzle and pipe an edging around the top and a flower shape in the centre. Using a smaller star nozzle, pipe small rosettes of the reserved chestnut filling on top of the cream.* Assemble the meringue cakes up to about 4 hours before serving.

SUNRAY FRUIT SALAD

300 ml (½ pint) unsweetened pineapple juice, chilled
225 g (8 oz) clear honey
3 × 450 g (1 lb) cans lychees
3 large pineapples, skinned, cored and diced
450 g (1 lb) fresh or drained canned cherries, stoned
12 kiwi fruit, peeled and thinly sliced

450 g (1 lb) black grapes, seeded
450 g (1 lb) blanched almonds, halved
120 ml (4 fl oz) lemon juice
150 ml (¼ pint) sweet white wine
1 kg (2 lb) red dessert apples, thinly sliced
1 kg (2 lb) bananas, peeled and sliced
fresh borage flowers or mint sprigs, to decorate

Preparation time: 1 hour, plus overnight marinating

1. Stir together the pineapple juice and honey in a large bowl. When the honey has dissolved, tip in the cans of lychees and their syrup. Add the pineapple, cherries, kiwi fruit, grapes and almonds as they are prepared. Cover and leave in a cool place overnight.
2. Mix together the lemon juice and white wine. As close as possible to the time of serving, prepare the apples and bananas and stir them into the mixture to coat them thoroughly. Stir into the fruit salad. Chill before serving.*
3. Decorate the salad with sprigs of fresh herbs as available – borage or mint, for example.

INDEX

ACKNOWLEDGEMENTS

The publishers wish to thank the following organizations and individuals for their kind permission to reproduce the photographs in this book:

Interiors Magazine 10, 11, 24; Elizabeth Whiting and Associates 16, 18 left, 25

Special Photography:

Bryce Attwell 15, 28–30; Michael Boys 31; John Cook 36–47; James Jackson 12, 77, 78, 85, 86, 87, 94–99, 100, 101, 103, 104–107, 114–116, 131, 136–137, 138, 139, 150–151, 153, 154, 180–187; Pete Myers 18 right, 19 above, 26, 34, 48–53, 79, 80, 81, 88, 109, 110, 112, 122–123, 129, 140, 143, 144–145, 169, 170–175; Spike Powell 7; Paul Webster Half Title, 2–3, 4–5, 13, 14, 17, 19 below, 20–21, 22–23, 27, 33, 35, 57–72, 74–75, 82, 83, 90–91, 92, 117–121, 124–125, 127, 132, 134, 147, 148, 149, 157, 158, 159, 161, 162, 165, 166, 167, 168, 177, 178–179

Illustrations by:

Liz Moyes; Julie Hazlewood; Suzanne Chapman

The publishers would also like to thank the following companies for the loan of props for photography:

Selfridges, Oxford Street, London W1; Habitat, 206/222 Kings Road, London SW3; The Conran Shop, 77/79 Fulham Road, London SW3; D.H. Evans, Oxford Street, London W1; Neal Street Shops, 23 Neal Street, London WC2; NOELS; David Mellor, 4 Sloane Square, London SW1; Dickens & Jones, Regent Street, London W1; Eldridge of London; Acquisitions, 269 Camden High Street, London NW1; China from: Wedgwood, Royal Dalton, Royal Worcester, Spode, Minton, Graham & Green.